# The Radical Twenties
## Writing, Politics, and Culture

## John Lucas

*Rutgers University Press*
*New Brunswick, New Jersey*

First published in the United States 1999
by Rutgers University Press, New Brunswick, New Jersey

First published in Great Britain 1997
by Five Leaves Publications

Copyright © John Lucas 1997

Library of Congress Cataloging-in-Publication Data

Lucas, John, 1937–
    The radical twenties : writing, politics, and culture /
John Lucas.
        p. cm.
    Reprint. Originally published : Nottingham : Five Leaves
Publications, 1997.
    Includes bibliographical references and index.
    ISBN 0-8135-2681-7 (cloth : alk. paper). — ISBN 0-8135-
2682-5 (pbk : alk. paper)
        1. Great Britain—Civilization—20th century.   2. Politics
and literature—Great Britain—History—20th century.
3. English literature—20th century—History and criticism.
4. Great Britain—Politics and government—1910–1936.
5. Radicalism—Great Britain—History—20th century.
6. Nineteen twenties.   I. Title: Radical 20's.
    DA578.L77   1999
    941.082—dc21                                          98-52817
                                                          CIP

Manufactured in the United States of America

*Acknowledgements*

I am grateful to the following for information and/or suggestions.

Elaine Aston, the late Catherine Beeston, Ian Clarke, Barry and Rita Cole, Paddy Garman, Mervyn Gould, Pauline Lucas, Rennie Parker, Arnold Rattenbury, Professor Marion Shaw, Matt Simpson, Katherine Thompson, Mark Thompson, Elizabeth West.

Professor Graham Martin, who read an earlier draft of the present book, made any number of invaluable suggestions and saved me from some glaring errors. I owe him much. Whatever errors remain, are my responsibility alone.

The author wishes to acknowledge funding from the British Academy, which made possible the completion of this book.

# CONTENTS

# PREFACE

As its title implies, *The Radical Twenties* is not intended to be a comprehensive account of the decade that followed the Great War. It is, however, an attempt to shift attention away from accounts which for too long have been accepted as definitive. Alison Light begins her excellent study, *Forever England: Femininity, Literature and Conservatism Between the Wars,* by remarking that we are used to historical accounts "which make what was actually a mess of immediacy into a narrative; they give us the illusion of being *in media res*, of experiencing or knowing a culture first hand whilst actually shaping it into a form, a generality, a knowability which depends on a pre-given sense of ending." (p. 2). Most accounts of the 1920s take for granted that it came to an end with the Wall Street Crash in 1929. That event conveniently closes a decade which is held to have begun with.... But here dates don't fit quite so well. Did the 1920s spring to life with the Armistice in late 1918, or with the following year's Versailles Peace Treaty, or with the newly powerful militancy of the dockers in 1920? And what of votes for women? The truth is – or seems to be – that it is easier to decide when the 1920s ended than when it began.

But that, of course, depends on regarding the 1920s in terms of those accounts which, as I say, have for long done service as somehow defining the decade or at least telling us all we need to know about it. The 1920s is therefore "The Jazz Age" or the "Age of Bright Young Things". And we have then to notice that these labels were first affixed to the 1920s *in* the 1920s. They were provided by some of those who, living in post-war England, felt that both they and it were special. This is well put by Douglas Goldring, in his *Odd Man Out: The Autobiography of a "Propaganda Novelist,"* written and published in 1935. Goldring, about whose work there will be a good deal to say in the course of *The Radical Twenties,* is a very interesting commentator on the period. Born in the 1880s, he had been a pacifist throughout the war, and as a convinced and life-long

1

socialist, he was contemptuous of those who, in the post-war years, tried to pretend – or who managed to persuade themselves and others – that the war had changed little, that the values of pre-war England had survived the events of 1914-18. Too old to belong to the "lost generation", he was nevertheless sympathetic to much that, as he saw it, explained and even justified the generation's behaviour. In a chapter called "The Strangest Decade" he sets out his own views of social life in London during the 1920s. "Over-indulgence in sex and gin was its main surface characteristic," he says; and adds that the pace was often set by ex-officers, many of them nervous wrecks.

> The callous, unimaginative citizens, who had sent their sons to the war as cheerfully as if it was a Rugby football match, who had foamed at the mouth at the mere mention of the fact that "our gallant lads" might welcome a reasonable negotiated peace, were the most bitter in their recriminations against these festive veterans who preferred to go to bed drunk and "sleep tight" rather than lie awake screaming. The younger generation of boys and girls largely took their tone from their elders. The Universities produced an astonishing number of effeminates of the type known as "fairies", and a mannerless crowd of young hooligans, with money to burn, was turned out by the larger public schools. Brought up in a disordered world, without the salutary criticism of their fathers and elder brothers, these irresponsibles, and their female counterparts, started a "wild party" which lasted as long as their money did. Finding the gossip writers ready to paragraph their antics they called themselves "Bright Young People", popularised gate-crashing, took drugs, indulged, or pretended to indulge in unnatural vices, and drove their cars around at high speed, when under the influence of drink, in the hope, if there was a smash, that the case would be reported in the Sunday newspapers. Publicity was the drug for which they chiefly craved... (*Odd Man Out*, Chapman and Hall, 1935, pp. 266-7).

I have quoted this at some length because it provides as good an account as any of what was undoubtedly a phenomenon of the decade: the revolt of the young against an older generation whose values the young clearly and with good reason despised. These are matters which, *inter alia,* are of especial concern in the first four chapters of *The Radical Twenties,* although their influence can be felt throughout the book. But as Goldring no doubt thought he was making plain, the Bright Young People can hardly be taken to define post-war England. And anyway, theirs was by and large an ersatz version of a revolt that was being far more seriously conducted elsewhere. If their glitzy world might be thought to have come to an unforeseen end in 1929, others foresaw a very different ending, one that was not to be marked off by the closing of a decade but by a renewal of war. Not long after the war to end all wars had ceased, and especially after Versailles, many began to realise that the horrors of mass war would have to be re-lived. In this sense the 1920s came to an end in 1939, and the intervening period is then to be called, as Graves and Hodge did indeed call it, "The Long Weekend".

And what of the millions who could not be Bright Young people, yet who lived through the war and began adult life just after it and for whom the post-war years meant something very different from the Jazz Age. As his tart commentary indicates, Goldring knew how absurd it was to define the 1920s in terms of "the social life of London". Yet that is how it has so often come to be regarded. A tiny, unrepresentative part is seen as the whole. At the beginning of Chapter 40 of *Bleak House* Dickens writes that "England has been in a dreadful state for some weeks. Lord Coodle would go out, Sir Thomas Doodle wouldn't come in, and there being nobody in Great Britain (to speak of) except Coodle and Doodle, there has been no Government". Dickens is pre-eminently the novelist who finds a way of speaking for the unspeakable; even more significantly, he allows the unspeakable to speak. His England is a place of multifarious voices, lives, ways of being, which between them wonderfully challenge and expose as ignorant folly the claims of those in authority who claim to know. Like Dickens, my concern in what follows is with England, although I mention the Irish "troubles" and Civil War, and I touch on the terrific difficulties – and heroism – of the Welsh miners and the advanced political radicalism to be found in post-war Scotland. But my principal concern is to provide evidence that England in the years following the Great War cannot sensibly be accounted for as London Society writ large.

This is of the first importance. As soon as we turn from the glittering lives of the social butterflies we can see that the definitive moment for the 1920s is not the Wall Street Crash but the General Strike. Even more than the election of two minority Labour Governments, first in 1924 and then again in 1929, the calling of the strike in May, 1926, and its ignominious collapse after 10 days, made for a wholesale change in the way an increased number of people, including writers and intellectuals, thought about the society they lived in and of its, and therefore inevitably their, social and political values. I am not certain how quickly the change happened or was perceived to have taken place. For some, immediately. Others, looking back, realised that 1926 marked an occasion when something momentous had occurred. The strike itself might not have been the moment but it was undoubtedly the catalyst. That was how it seemed to T.S. Eliot, writing a retrospective and farewell to *The Criterion* in 1939; and in his autobiographical account of the inter-war years, *Downhill All the Way,* Leonard Woolf similarly thought of the moment of the General Strike as of the greatest possible significance. I am not arguing that this was how 1926 presented itself to everyone at the time. But I am certain that what before might have often been a vague dissatisfaction with current political and social arrangements, now sharpened into a considered radicalism. With this in mind, it is perfectly possible to see the terrible defeat of the strikers as beginning an historical period which culminated in the Labour victory of 1945.

To follow this through would be beyond the scope of the present book, but it does explain why in Chapter 5 I trace some of the fears and hopes that preceded 1926. And it also explains why the last chapter, which deals with writing that comes after that year, is called "Taking Sides". But I should add that I have not tried to construct *The Radical Twenties* as a linear narrative. To have done so would have required me to commit myself to clearing a way through "the mess of immediacy" which on reflection invariably turns out to mean clearing it away. Instead, I have concentrated my attention on writers who have for the most part been written out of the record, or reduced to footnotes in accounts which see the 1920s as dominated by the socialite novelist satirists, Huxley, Gerhardie and pre-eminently, Evelyn Waugh; or in which the post-war years are defined in terms of the great modernist writers taking upon themselves the task of "saving civilisation."

I could not possibly have written about the 1920s without mentioning Eliot, Joyce, Lawrence, Pound, Woolf, Wyndham Lewis, Yeats, and, of the younger generation, Evelyn Waugh, especially as Joyce and Lawrence, in particular, mattered a great deal to some of the writers with whom I am concerned. All these canonical writers were profoundly dissatisfied with the post-war years, although for most such disaffection expressed itself in terms of a reactionary rad-

4

icalism, of passionate anti-democratic sympathies which have often enough been studied and which I see no point in poring over yet again. I do, however, regret not having the space to devote chapters either to anti-imperialism or what is perhaps best characterised as green politics *avant la lettre*. And I especially regret that Lewis Grassic Gibbon's *Grey Granite*, the concluding novel of his great trilogy, *A Scots Quair*, was published in 1934. As a result, I have felt unable to discuss his treatment of the 1920s in that novel, compelling and authoritative though it is.

Against these absences there are compensations. Nobody needs to be told what genius the young Auden had, although seeing *Paid on Both Sides* in the context of post 1926 does help to identify just how radical that genius was. Edgell Rickword, on the other hand, is probably more mentioned than read; and we are still in the process of discovering that Ivor Gurney was a great poet. Hence, the attention I pay to both. As to Henry Green, Patrick Hamilton and Sylvia Townsend Warner: a major reason for writing about these novelists is that, separately and between them, they change out of recognition those features of the 1920s which for so long have been passed off as its true appearance. Not the least of their achievements is, as it is with Auden, Gurney and Rickword, to make us realise that to speak of England after 1918 is to allow those who can't be spoken of to speak for themselves. This is a radical ambition. Achieving it requires the adoption of new forms, or adaptations of old, disused ones. The assaults on Georgian poetry and on fictional realism by the writers on whom I concentrate are essential to their radicalism.

## CHAPTER ONE

# ENDINGS, BEGINNINGS

The 1920s was a notoriously self-conscious decade. And the labels which at the time were most often fixed to it – the Jazz Age, the Age of the Bright Young Things – were usually attached by those who loved the publicity they professed to despise. This was not entirely new. Popular newspapers of the 1890s had for the first time made people famous for being famous, a matter Henry James satirised in his tart story *The Papers* (1902). Both *Tit-Bits* and *The Daily Mail* specialised in what would later be called "gossip columns". The 1920s was, however, the decade when such columns came into their own. For gossip columnists like "William Hickey" labels went with "personalities" and "headlines". More surprisingly, or so it may initially seem, the same labels are still applied to the 1920s by a certain kind of social historian as though they can be relied on to give an adequate account of the decade. Yet a moment's reflection will account for this. Such labels do after all promise that anyone wanting to peer inside the boxed-up centos will be rewarded with gamey, scandalous tales aplenty. All those upending of tables, of proprieties, of taboos: all those vile bodies. It isn't difficult to market the 1920s in these or equivalent terms.

And of course the terms carry a measure of truth. The decade was in some ways and for some people a time of self-proclaimed and often joyless hedonism, its brittle pleasures to be associated with the young who saw themselves as distinctively of their moment. But that moment cannot be understood in isolation from what had gone before, any more than the 1890s can. Much, probably most, of what happened in the years that followed the Great War would have been inconceivable without the war itself or without what the war was taken to have meant, what it revealed to the young about their parents' generation or, more largely, the nation which had entered into the war with such enthusiasm. This is a matter to which Samuel Hynes gives due consideration in his *A War Imagined* (1992). To

7

take an example more or less at random, though not one that Hynes takes. In Douglas Goldring's novel, *The Merchant of Souls* (1926), the female protagonist, Betty, muses at one point over the men in her life and comes to the conclusion that they all "lived on the surface. It was no doubt a reaction after the war, this bandaging of the eyes of the soul by sensuality and sloth, by hectic excitement and pursuit of pleasure." (ch.15). There is therefore nothing either new or challenging in suggesting that people living through the 1920s were in various ways reacting to the traumas of those four years, 1914-18. It is however rather more challenging to argue that one way led unerringly to a wholesale radicalism: social, sexual, cultural, political.

The Hitchhiker's Guide to the 20th Century tells us that the superficial glitter of the 1920s was succeeded by the earnest radicalism of the 1930s. Yet the 1920s has a claim to be thought of as more radical than the decade that succeeded it. During the 1920s two Labour Governments took office. Admittedly, they were minority governments and neither lasted for long; but there was no Labour administration during the following decade, and if the evidence of the admittedly crude opinion polls of 1939 are anything to go by, Labour would have fared even worse in the then pending general election than it had in 1935. We will never of course know whether those predictions would have been proved correct. Nevertheless, the radical 1930s didn't produce a general strike; and by the end of the decade union membership was lower than it had been at its outset. The reason is obvious: more people were out of work in 1939 than in 1929. But the experience of prolonged unemployment in the 1930s seems to have produced a spirit nearer to apathy than resistance among many working-class people, and this is in sharp contrast to the radical energies of the 1920s. No doubt disappointment at MacDonald's minority administrations, which failed to advance or even protect the interests of labour, and the humiliating defeat of the 1926 strike, between them account for much that often seems close to defeatism in the decade that follows. But such defeatism is ignored by commentators who wish to see the 1930s as a political decade, and who as frequently regard the 1920s as all of a glitter: a time of profoundly superficial attractions which came to an end in 1929, with the Wall Street Crash. That was when the kissing had to stop.

Most commentators, however, note the effect of the Great War on those who survived it or who were born too late to have contributed to it and as a result of which, so one of their spokespersons Christopher Isherwood says, they felt a deep uneasiness, even guilt. The young were living in the aftermath of one of the most cataclysmic episodes in Western history. They belonged to that "lost generation" of Gertrude Stein's famous remark to the young Ernest Hemingway: they were lost for values or ideals or beliefs with which they could identify, because all of those had, it seemed, been exhausted or destroyed by the war; and lost in the sense that the immediate elders from whom they might have learnt were, many of them, dead, their bodies left on the battlefields of Western Europe. The lost generation was as lost for words as it was for worlds. New ones had to be found: new styles of architecture, a change of heart. The alternative was to dance on the grave of a wrecked civilisation.

To put matters this way may seem to do little more than parody complex issues. But parody is implicit in a good deal of writing about and sometimes of the time. When Evelyn Waugh heard that two of his friends were to be married, he confided in his diary (although I have no doubt he hoped to share the "confidence") that the news made him sad "because any sort of happiness or permanence seems so infinitely remote from any one of us"[1].

Waugh's entry is dated 1 February, 1925. On 11 November, 1918, D.H. Lawrence attended an afternoon party which the Bloomsberries had called to celebrate the armistice announced earlier that day. According to David Garnett, Lawrence "in tones of sombre joy" told his fellow guests that they were wrong to think the war was over.

> The hate and the evil are greater now than ever. Very soon war will break out again and overwhelm you.... The crowd outside thinks that Germany is crushed forever. But the Germans will soon rise again. Europe is done for: England most of all countries. The war isn't over. Even if the fighting should stop, the evil will be worse because the hate will be dammed up in men's hearts and will show itself in all sorts of ways which will be worse than war. Whatever happens there can be no Peace on Earth.[2]

Lawrence's outburst might seem unbalanced, merely vindictive. But his forebodings were shared by others. What is more, such forebodings had begun to surface much earlier, even before the outbreak of war. We are sometimes told that the events inaugurated in August 1914 came out of a clear blue sky. No doubt that was how it felt to many people. But others had sensed an impending catastrophe. Or if that is too extreme a word, it can at least be said that there were those who in the period 1900-1914 sensed that they were witnessing the strange death of liberal England and that this was part of some wider shift, some seismic alteration in Western history. In this sense the 1920s might be said to have its beginnings in *fin-de-siècle*, in that decade's apprehension of an encroaching heart of darkness, of the stormy birth of a savage god whose strenuous cries would drown out Forster's plea, "Only Connect". The years preceding the Great War were "the treacherous years", as Henry James called them, and for him they brought to an end "the record of the long safe centuries"[3]. Although Robert Bridges' anthology of 1916, *The Spirit of Man*, tried to re-build connections to Forster's liberal spirit, the tone of Bridges' Preface, decent though it is, more than hints at the desperation underlying his enterprise.

> From the .... miseries, the insensate and interminable slaughter, the hate and the filth, we can turn to seek comfort only in the quiet confidence of our souls; and we look instinctively to the seers and poets of mankind, whose sayings are the oracles and prophecies of loveliness and loving kindness.[4]

Two years later, when the insensate and interminable slaughter came to an end, the victors felt little loving kindness for the defeated powers. In 1920 Bridges was ferociously attacked in the pages of *The Times* for daring to suggest that the humiliating terms forced on Germany at the Versailles Peace Treaty did not speak well for civilised values and would be unlikely to help the cause of peace. As Lawrence realised, and he was speaking before the Treaty had been signed, "this war isn't over". A year after his battering in *The Times*, Bridges wrote "Low Barometer", a poem whose title underlines the rough weather of contemporary history which the poem itself evokes:

> Some have seen corpses long interr'd
> Escape from harrowing control,
> Pale charnel forms – may ev'n have heard
> The shrillings of a troubled soul,

That wanders till the dawn hath cross'd
The dolorous dark, or Earth hath wound
Closer her storm-spredd cloak, and thrust
The baleful phantoms underground.

These emanations of what Bridges calls the "packed/Pollutions
and remorse of time" suggest an appalled vision very much at odds
with the sustaining liberal sentiments of *The Spirit of Man*. Or
rather, man's spirit now turns out to be tortured by "unhouseled
crime". This is a world of the comfortless dead. "That corpse you
planted last year in your garden,/Has it begun to sprout, will it
bloom this year/Or has the sudden frost disturbed its bed." Those
famous lines from *The Waste Land* also register a world haunted
by death, and this is undoubtedly one of the most powerful features of the 1920s, whether in the figures of the living-dead, those
thousands upon thousands of the war-wounded who stood at
street corners selling bootlaces off cardboard trays or who
tramped from town to town looking for the work they rarely
found; or who, more severely damaged – eyeless, or limbless, or
mental cases – were consigned to hospitals and nursing homes; or
whether we think of the lists of names upon the memorials
installed in every town and village throughout the U.K. The war
might not have come to Britain but death most certainly had.[5] And
with it had come a deep sense of vulnerability, of defences broken
down. Britain – or England – was no longer immune from the
demonic forces of history.

## II

Two qualifications are needed, however. In the first place, Britain
suffered less than other European nations. Though the numbers of
British service-men killed or wounded are appalling, France, Russia
and Germany lost many more. They also endured greater economic
hardship. Nor was it ever likely that Britain would have been
invaded. There were "back-door" scares (The Germans might use
Ireland as a staging post for invasion: hence, one of the claimed jus-
tifications for the whipped-up furore over Roger Casement), but
once the German navy decided to sit out the war there was precious
little danger the enemy would attempt a landing. Nevertheless
England in particular began to *look* different. Men enlisted in their
thousands and marched off to war, leaving behind them work which

would be done by women, by the old, by the infirm. Conscription only became necessary in 1916, by which time Haig and his generals had more or less exhausted the supplies of volunteers. Then again, half a million horses were shipped to France where they were wasted, either in ludicrous cavalry exercises, as at the battle of Loos, or in attempting to haul guns and supplies up the line to death. Woods were cut down, a loss over which Ivor Gurney grieves in "Possessions":

> Sand has the ants, clay ferny weeds for play
> But what shall please the wind now the trees are away
> War took on Witcombe steep?
> It breathes there, and wonders at old night roarings;
> October time all lights, and the new clearings
> For memory are like to weep.
> It was right for the beeches to stand over Witcombe reaches,
> Until the wind roared and softened and died to sleep.

This characteristic little poem, its note of loss blended in with protest and celebration, was written in 1919. The poem is really a lament for a lost England. And here I need to note that the second qualification I have to offer is that in the present study I am far more concerned with England than with the U.K.'s other constituent nations. I shall certainly be making mention of events in Ireland, Scotland and Wales; but in what follows the focus will be on England, because I know more about what went on in England during the 1920s and I don't want to risk generalisations about Britain as a whole which are either reductive or glib. Besides, I am fairly certain that the experience of war was different for each of the home countries, and to try to register, let alone account for, these differences would have led to a much longer book and not one I feel myself qualified to write.

Hence the fact that the writers I have so far invoked are writing about England. They are moreover writing about a very special kind of England: an England of rural circumstance. We are accustomed to thinking that the most anguished evocation of rural England belongs to the years succeeding the Great War. So it does. From the unbridgeable chasm separating now from then, from a wrecked, fallen world, successive generations have looked back to an England that seems in contrast one of primal innocence. The gross materialism of Edwardian England, the terrible poverty of millions (vast numbers of men who volunteered for war service in the autumn of

1914 were rejected on medical grounds, others because a constant diet of condensed milk and white bread had so rotted their teeth that they couldn't cope with army food), the strikes, the lock-outs, the city slums, to say nothing of the conditions which farm labourers had still to endure, the sleaze, (typified by the Marconi scandal) – these and other awkward actualities were soon forgotten or misted over in a prolonged soft focus recall of a time before the war.

The process was aided by the fact that at war's outset, High Command decided that the battles to come would be controlled by the cavalry. Exhortations to fight, in both prose and verse, were embroidered with images of individual heroism, of the knight-at-arms or, indeed, at play. Men were to break a lance in Life's Tournament, as Herbert Asquith urged in his war sonnet "The Volunteer", or, in Rupert Brooke's celebrated formulation, become swimmers into cleanness leaping. Either way, they were promised an escape from modernity. That was what such language implied. Asquith, Grenfell, and other of their generation and class might not have seen themselves as living in a sunlit, idyllic England, but they did persuade themselves that through chivalric warriordom they could return to it.

But the war was a confirmation of modernity. It was a machine war and men were fed to the machines. Julian Grenfell probably spoke for many when he dreamed of war – any war – as belonging to and somehow expressive of the cyclic processes of nature. "The naked earth is warm with spring" his poem "Into Battle" begins; and in the spring of the year red blood reigns in the winter's pale. "The fighting man shall from the sun/Take warmth, and life from the glowing earth." But other, wiser voices, understood or sensed how misguided was the ardency of Grenfell's words. For them the war not only opened the way to tragedy, it also wrote finis under a vision of England as the great good land. The anguish for a lost Eden, though it has often been presented as an exclusively post-war condition, begins earlier. The England Henry James evokes in "Within the Rim" (1915) isn't intended to be taken literally. James summons up an "ideal" pastoralism which has at its core a deeply conservative reading of social relations: rooted, mutually obliging, nourishing. I am not concerned here with questioning how closely the vision tallied with reality. I simply wish to note that with the coming of war James recognised that a vision which, whether literal or not, seemed to have permanent value, was bound to be obliterated. He writes:

Looking myself more askance at the dark hour (politically speaking I mean) than I after my fashion figured [England] as doing in the mass, I found it of an extreme, of quite an endless fascination to trace as many as possible of her felt idiosyncrasies back to her settled sea-confidence, and to see this now in turn account for so many other things, the smallest as well as the biggest, that, to give the fewest hints of illustration, the mere spread of the great trees, the mere gathers in the little bluey-white curtains of the cottage windows, the mere curl of the tinted smoke from the old chimneys matching that note, became a sort of exquisite evidence ... The vision was fed, and fed to such a tune that in the quest for reasons – that is, for the particulars of one's affection, the more detailed the better – the blades of grass, the outlines of leaves, the drift of clouds, the streaks of mortar between old bricks, not to speak of the call of child-voices muffled in the comforting air, became, as I have noted, with a hundred other like touches, casually felt, extraordinary admonitions and symbols, close links of a tangible chain.[6]

James's very syntax is here proof of the tangible chain, his slow-moving, leisurely accretion of detail a desire to hold onto the England which is nevertheless about to disappear.

Well, it might be said, nobody but an outsider could write with so innocent an eye about England. What James omits, or has no intimate personal access to, is the nation's complex, troubled internal history. For him the "blades of grass" epitomise a natural, cyclic, unending surety, whereas for John Clare, say, writing a century earlier, they symbolised enclosed, privatised, appropriated land, or, in a different trope, the rights of common people to fight back against the conspirators: "And still the grass eternal springs/Where castles stood and grandeur died." James's sense of tradition, of an unbroken history, is, however, very close to Pasternak's sense of Italy, as he recalls it from a pre-1917 visit in *Essay in Autobiography*.

I loved the living essence of historical symbolism, in other words the instinct which had enabled us, like house martins, to build a world, an immense nest made of earth and sky, of life and death, and of two kinds of time, time present and time absent. I understood that it was saved from disintegration by the cohesive forces contained in the transparently figurative quality of every particle of it.[7]

"The particulars of one's affection," "every particle": in each case details are somehow bound together by cohesive forces that are said to be history or the slow accumulations of history. James and Pasternak, feeling the earth begin to shift under their feet, empower their imaginations to evoke visions of survival, even of permanence. And in neither case does the writer allow himself to consider his reading of history as other than adequate. The particulars build to a whole, as they are meant to do in the visions of England which will recur throughout the *Four Quartets*, in which Eliot, like James and Pasternak before him, hopes to summon up "the living essence of historical symbolism." And James's appeal to "the child-voices muffled in the comforting air," both prefigures Eliot's "the hidden laughter/Of children in the foliage", and suggests a tangible, just-out of reach but perhaps recoverable Eden. Wholeness is imagined at historical moments when it is most under strain, and can perhaps be created only as mythic, by someone endeavouring to see steadily and whole – the terms Forster appropriated from Arnold for his own troubled musing over England at the close of Chapter 19 of *Howards End*. To see like this, is, I think, always to see back into a history from which the person doing the viewing feels somehow excluded by time and/or place: it *was* there, it *is* perhaps still there, but not where I am. As Gurney, exiled in wartime France, wrote in a magical little lyric, "Only the wanderer/Knows England's' graces".

It is easy enough to remark that there is a powerful mystificatory element at work in these sightings and soundings. But coming when they do, it is more important to note the deep disquiet which is inseparable from a yearning for wholeness, for as-yet unbroken tradition: for what has been made by time absent as well as present. And for James in particular there is a foreboding, amounting to near-certainty, that time future will wreck the great past. Pasternak may have felt the same way, but in 1956, when he wrote his essay, would have been foolish for him to have said so. His readers are left to infer it from the passion with which he writes of that "living essence".

A year after James's essay, Lawrence wrote to Lady Cynthia Asquith:

> When I drive across this country, with the autumn falling and rustling to pieces, I am so sad, for my country, for this great wave of civilisation, 2000 years, which is now collapsing, that it is hard to live. So much beauty and pathos of old things passing away and no new things coming: this house of the Ottolines – It is England – my God, it breaks my soul – this

England, these shafted windows, the elm-trees, the blue distance – the past, the great past, crumbling down, breaking
down, not under the force of the coming buds, but under the
weight of many exhausted, lovely yellow leaves, that drift
over the lawn and over the pond, like the soldiers, passing
away, into winter and the darkness of winter – no, I can't bear
it. For the winter stretches ahead, where all vision is lost and
all memory dies out.

It has been 2000 years, the spring and summer of our era.
What then will the winter be? No I can't bear it, I can't let it
go. Yet who can stop the autumn from falling to pieces, when
November has come in. It is almost better to be dead, than to
see this awful process finally strangling us to oblivion, like
the leaves off the trees.[8]

There are several reasons for quoting this. In the first place, the letter provides one of the first indications of what will become
Lawrence's settled conviction that the nation is "finished" and that
nothing is to be gained from trying to imagine a fresh start for it.
His earlier hope of creating a little communistic society somewhere
in England, which he had mooted in a letter of the same year to
Lady Ottoline Morrell, is now transferred to far-off places, although
of course making things new out of the rubble of the old will, for
others, become almost an *idèe fixe*, and therefore a crucial feature
of radical politics to which some of the young, and not so young,
were attracted in the post-war years. But Lawrence's apocalyptic
vision, his rejection of the Shelleyan optimism with which his letter
engages, will prove to have a strong appeal to others of the post-war
young. Second, his conviction that 2,000 years of history are now
breaking down is of a piece with that "cyclic" reading of civilisations
which is at the heart of Yeats's vision of history and which, as
Spengler's *Decline of the West* also testifies, typifies the tragic fatal-
ism notable in much post-war thinking about Europe. Third, as
James's essay reveals, Lawrence was by no means alone in reaching
for an image which will resonate with such cultural and historical
significance that it can stand for or even embody "England". This
requires further comment.

## III

"This England, these shafted windows, the elm trees, the blue distance." I have remarked elsewhere that at this period the elm tree
becomes almost an unofficial emblem of Englishness.[9] There is

16

early indication of this in William Morris's "Under an Elm Tree: or Thoughts in The Countryside" written in 1889, where Morris asks himself "What is the thought that has come into one's head as one turns round in the shadow of the roadside elm?" and answers, "A countryside worth fighting for, if that were necessary, worth taking the trouble to defend its peace." The period may be said to end with Edward Thomas's "As the Team's Head-Brass", written in May, 1916. Here, the poet sits "among the boughs of the fallen elm/That strewed an angle of the fallow" and talks to a ploughman from whom he learns that a blizzard has brought the elm down. The ploughman further tells him that

> "Only two teams work on the farm this year.
> One of my mates is dead. The second day
> In France they killed him. It was back in March,
> The very night of the blizzard, too. Now if
> He had stayed here we should have moved the tree."

The elm's fall is linked to, is in a way expressive of, the death of the ploughman's mate. A vast disruption of nature is discreetly symbolised in this conjunction; and Thomas's sombre, ruminative tone allows for a tragic sense of an ending. The poem concludes with him noting how

> The horses started and for the last time
> I watched the clods crumble and topple over
> After the ploughshare and the stumbling team.

Edna Longley comments on this ending that although the phrase "the last time" has ominous implications for the soldier-poet who will shortly be off to France, and at another level may prophesy "the social changes brought about by war", the main stress "is on an essential continuity: human progress is like that of 'the stumbling team.'"[10] Yet fear at the likelihood of discontinuity seems much more the defining stress here. "As the Team's-Head-Brass", like most of Thomas's poetry, and *pace* the view of many of his critics, is a war poem, not in the sense that it is a report from the front, but because it is filled with, is indeed prompted by, the poet's apprehensions of living within the rim of a tragic time.

This applies to the much-anthologised and seemingly innocent "Adlestrop." The poem was apparently written some five months earlier than "As The Team's Head-Brass," at the very beginning of

1915. You could not call it an elegy to a lost England, as you nearly can call the later poem, yet its very passion of recollection suggests a land now out of reach:

> And for that minute a blackbird sang
> Close by and round him, mistier
> Farther and farther, all the birds
> Of Oxfordshire and Gloucestershire.

The time was "late June", and that it should be "late" subtly hints at a time now gone forever.[10a] This is presumably why the poet remembers an otherwise meaninglessly trivial incident, when really nothing happened apart from an express train drawing up "unwontedly" at the bare platform: "No one left and no one came". The poem's opening line," Yes. I remember Adlestrop", suggests someone puzzling over why he *should* remember Adlestrop. Why has the name come to him? (He twice remarks that Adlestrop is "a name".) But then it suddenly becomes much more than that:

> What I saw
> Was Adlestrop – only the name
>
> And willows, willow-herb, and grass
> And meadowsweet, and haycocks dry,
> No whit less still and lonely fair
> Than the high cloudlets in the sky.

There is no full-stop after "only the name": memory flares in a surprised delight and as it catches, becomes particular, so the poem gathers up "the transparently figurative quality of every particle", to use Pasternak's lovely phrase. Here is a world, or as much of it as can be built by named shires and the widening circles of birdsong. This is a vision of a deep heart of England.

But it lasts "for a minute." The train will bear Thomas away to a quite other life; and, as the poem implies, express trains aren't for wayside stations. A momentary grace halted its iron progress through a sweet, especial rural scene, but the stop was unlooked-for and as a passenger on the train Thomas himself is allowed to do no more than glimpse an England which, however alluring, is for the most part hidden from him. Moreover, it is an empty place. We know that Thomas hugely admired William Morris – "Except for William Morris there is no other man whom I would sometimes like to have been" he told his friend Gordon Bottomley in 1908. And Stan Smith has noted that this admiration is to be connected with Thomas's own socialism.[11] He knew that the steadily emptying countryside not only meant the de-skilling of successive generations of craftspeople, but that it was part of the process of capitalism which made a mockery of a unified history, of a collective "England." That is why his search for a heart of England must always end in frustration, or in a tantalising glimpse of an all-but buried past, as in "Tall Nettles":

> Tall nettles cover up, as they have done
> These many springs, the rusty harrow, the plough
> Long worn out, and the roller made of stone:
> Only the elm butt tops the nettles now.
>
> This corner of the farmyard I like most:
> As well as any bloom upon a flower
> I like the dust on the nettles, never lost
> Except to prove the sweetness of a shower.

The voice broods over the private discovery of what is virtually a hidden history of rural England: it is entirely typical of Thomas that he should use the line-break "the plough/Long worn out" in order to emphasise an abandoned or lost or outmoded activity. (This is, as it were, discreetly underwritten by the "elm butt".) But whereas in *Howards End* Forster had used the dust stirred up by the motor car to symbolise a coming uniformity and, even, death to rural England, for Thomas the dust on the nettles is proof of a past that is still somehow securely there, though secret, unvisited.

It is inevitable that such intimations of a heart of England should often lead to whimsy. Not in Thomas, it must be said, in the first place because he has so powerful a sense of what he identified in William Morris: "the actual, troublous life of every day and toil of the hands and brain together"; and in the second place because he is keenly aware of himself as something of an outsider – by reason of class and his moment in history he looks in, on, and back to what he can never fully grasp. But for other writers of the period "England" is invoked in terms of the kind of *Country Life* chocolate-box pastoralism which still lingers on at our century's end. That is why Lawrence's story "England, My England" is so crucial, so powerful an imaginative critique of a then-dominant version of Englishness which even now has a certain glamour.

Lawrence first wrote the story in 1915 and revised it substantially after the war and in the light of that war's meaning. From

February to July of 1915 he and Frieda had been staying at Viola Meynell's aged cottage at Greatham, Sussex. The Meynell cottage was near another such cottage, called Rackham, which belonged to Percy Lucas, brother of E.V. Lucas, a minor man-of-letters. Neither brother was calculated to appeal to Lawrence, nor would Lawrence have been much impressed by the fact that at the time he and Percy met at Rackham Percy had joined the army. Nevertheless, "England My England" is much more than a satire on people Lawrence disliked. As F.R. Leavis remarks, it is triumph of the tale that Egbert (who undoubtedly shares some of Percy Lucas's characteristics) should command so large a measure of our sympathy. He is a dilettante, but he isn't weak; nor is he contemptible. He is, however, very much within the Bloomsbury mode of Englishness: untroubledly certain of his way of life, content with friends "of the same ineffectual sort as himself, tampering with the arts, literature, painting, sculpture, music." He has an especial interest in "old folk-music, collecting folk-songs and folk-dances, studying the Morris-dance and the old customs." And he and his wife, Winifred, live in Crockham cottage.

The cottage belongs to Winifred's father, a "man of energy" who "had come from the poor." Geoffrey Marshall is a "man of courage", with a "tough old barbarian fighting spirit", an "almost child-like delight in verse", and blood "strong even to coarseness." Lawrence sees Geoffrey Marshall very much as he does the older Crich in *The Rainbow:* a man of "robust, sap-like faith" which keeps him going. "And so he applied himself to his own tiny selection of the social work, and left the rest to the ultimate will of heaven ... sometimes, even from him, spurted a sudden gall of bitterness against the world and its make-up. And yet – he had his own will to succeed, and this carried him through."

Egbert has no such will, nor does he see the need for it. At Crockham he and Winifred seem out of the world.

> The timbered cottage with its sloping, cloak-like roof was old and forgotten. It belonged to the old England of hamlets and yeoman. Lost all alone on the edge of the common, at the end of a wide, grassy, briar-entangled lane shaded with oak, it had never known the world of today. Not till Egbert came with his bride. And he came to fill it with flowers ... That was Crockham. The spear of modern invention had not passed through it, and it lay there secret, primitive, savage as when the Saxons first came. And Egbert and Winifred were caught there, caught out of the world.

But their love begins to wear thin. Egbert won't do anything except in an idle, amateurish sort of way. The crisis comes when their youngest daughter trips over a sickle Egbert has carelessly left lying in long grass. Her leg is badly cut, she is inadequately treated by the local doctor, and eventually Geoffrey Marshall has to take charge, dipping into his own pocket in order to get the little girl into hospital in London where her life is spared, although it seems likely she will be left permanently lame.

Lawrence didn't invent the accident. In an article in which she rebuts the claim made by Harry T. Moore that the study of Egbert was based on her father, Barbara Lucas says that her sister Sylvia had been cut "cut in real life by a sickle," not a knife as Moore had claimed.[12] But she does not dispute that the accident had left Sylvia Lucas partially lame. It is not difficult to see why Lawrence should have seized on the accident. Adam and Eve worked in the garden of Eden. That was what kept it Edenic. But Egbert won't work. Hence, the symbolic importance of the abandoned sickle and wounded child. This is a sick heart of England or, if that puts the matter too stridently, it can at least be said that the story is wonderfully suggestive of failed potency among those who wish to embody or be seen to embody a culturally valid England which has in truth dwindled into mere antiquarianism: folk-song, morris dance, and so forth. No toil of the hands and brain together, not here.

In saying this I have again to guard against any suggestion that Lawrence merely satirises Egbert. On the contrary, he very surely evokes the man's attractiveness, his delicacy, even his courage. But his inability to imagine for himself any other life than that of "epicurean hermit" indicates the absence from his make-up of the "saplike" robustness that sustains his father-in-law. And so the story ends with his death in France.

> There had been life. There had been Winifred and his children. But the frail death-agony effort to catch at straws of memory, straws of life from the past, brought on too great a nausea. No, No! No Winifred, no children. No world, no people. Better the agony of dissolution ahead than the nausea of the effort backwards.

Egbert doesn't particularly believe in the cause of the war, but he volunteers anyway. His death is not tragic and perhaps, as Leavis suggests, Lawrence may wish to imply that "with him dies what he stands for."[13] But it is far more likely that deep in his bones

Lawrence knew that what Egbert stood for, though in one sense dead, was in another sense bound to linger on. The core might be eaten out, but the shell remained. And as we shall see in later chapters, he was right. The old order refused to disappear.


IV


In drawing on the image of an empty shell I have in mind Yeats's lines in "Ancestral Houses" (1921), the first of his "Meditations in Time of Civil War."

>                              now it seems
> As if some marvellous empty sea-shell flung
> Out of the obscure dark of the rich streams,
> And not a fountain, were the symbol which
> Shadows the inherited glory of the rich.

Yeats is here considering the country houses of the Anglo-Irish gentry, and his image ponders the likely hollowness of that political and social complex which they seemed to signify and to whose continuing vitality they supposedly testified. "Seems" does not say that the tradition *is* bogus but it undoubtedly leaves the way open for a final severity of judgement. The severity of Lawrence's judgement on Egbert doesn't depend on the need to uncover the emptiness of country-house politics, with their essentially pre-capitalist appeal to obligation as "naturally" incurred and fulfilled at all social levels. But Lawrence would have been aware that in the period leading up to the Great War there was an effort to re-animate such politics. It is unmistakably present in *Howards End*, where the house is offered as a "rooted" place, hopefully stabilising relations between its "natural" owners and the nearby farm. And although by the end of the novel we learn that the house will pass to the "natural" son of Helen Schlegel and Leonard Bast – the fruit of a relationship between an aspiring man of the people and an advanced intellectual – the sketchy, desperate symbolism of this undermines Forster's hoped-for connection of inner and outer life and of class reconciliation. Lawrence is far more radically alert to the actualities of class relationships and of the atrophying of the class from which Egbert comes.

There is a further point. Howard's End, the country house, though it is not at all grand, is nevertheless supposed to offer a vision of an essentially vital rural England in powerful contradistinction from the city. In this, too, Forster is aligned with the tradition of county-house politics: of that rooted "dwelling" to which Ben Jonson had appealed at the end of his great poem, "To Penshurst," and which had become a *raison d'être* of the tradition. By the early years of the 20th century this had dwindled into pastiche. The Decline and Fall of the British Aristocracy, which David Cannadine claims to be able to detect from 1870 onwards, probably happened at a far slower pace than he thinks; and even now I am far from certain that it makes sense to speak of its "fall": not, anyway, in a land where habits of deference are so deeply engrained that the English are content to think of themselves as subjects rather than citizens. Nevertheless, and for all Forster's attempts to revive it, the country house ideal becomes image – even hollow image – far more than substance during the years immediately prior to the Great War. And in Edwin Lutyens it found its perfect architect.

In the period between 1900-1914 Lutyens built houses across all of southern England. They range from the comparatively modest-sized Munstead Wood in Surrey to Castle Drogo in Devon. Lutyens also built north of the Wash (there are Lutyens houses in Scotland, and the restoration of Lindisfarne is famously his); but his genius feels most naturally to flourish in the southern counties. There are two reasons why this should be so. One, he used materials and styles which were deliberately but subtly eclectic and in which a kind of Georgianism could blend with elements of Gothic, of Norman, of Tudor, of Queen Anne. A brand-new Lutyens house gives the impression of being rooted in its place, of having always existed on that spot, of being as old as England. Two, Lutyens liked to work with the landscape gardener, Gertrude Jekyll. According to Jane Brown, Jekyll's procedure was never to impose on a garden but to allow nature to be "very carefully enhanced by art". Inherent in all gardens Jekyll worked on, for and with Lutyens, were, Brown says, "the Edwardian ideals – the fastidious wealth to patronize the finest craftsmanship in stone, brick and impressive baulks of oak, the time to tend and enjoy gardens where the clink of teacups and the crack of ball on mallet set the pace and it was easy to be amused, and the innocence to believe that it would all last forever."[14]

The combination of Lutyens and Jekyll was a powerful one, but what made them famous was the championing of their work in

*Country Life.* Jekyll introduced Lutyens to the journal's editor, Edward Hudson, in 1899, less than two years after Hudson had brought out his first issue, then called *Country Life Illustrated.* (It was an expansion of a not very successful paper, *Racing Life Illustrated.*) Hudson commissioned Lutyens to restore Lindisfarne; more importantly, perhaps, he asked the architect to build him a house at Sonning in Berkshire – Deanery Garden; and he praised and illustrated Lutyen's work in his magazine as well as recommending him to his friends and acquaintances. In short, Lutyens becomes *the* architect of *Country Life* and country life.

Such life, like the architecture which is its most evident expression, was a kind of pastiche. It pretended to continuity, to "rooted" values, even to a kind of blood lineage, of Saxon/Norman survival. There are very dubious motives behind these concerns, connected with fear of degeneracy, of the running-down of the stock which the city is supposed to prompt and hasten. This is one of those elements in late-19th century thinking which leads at different moments to calls, say, for the poorest city "specimens" to be segregated from the rest of the population and to the planning of garden cities. Hence, for example, the end-of-century proposal by the Reverend A. Osborne Jay "for the establishment of Penal Settlements which would solve the problem of heredity by wiping out the entire strain of [slum dwellers]"[15] And hence Donald Read's remark in *Edwardian England,* that the formation in 1899 of the Garden City Association was prompted by a desire to discuss and publicise the ideas of Ebenezer Howard, whose *Tomorrow* (1898) took as its central concern the "continuing in-flow of population from countryside to town," and the consequent rural depopulation. Four years after the founding of the "Association", the first garden city was started at Letchworth in Hertfordshire."[16]

Even *England, My England* takes for granted an "old" rural England of vital powers. After Egbert's and Winifred's marriage, Lawrence writes:

> The flame of their bodies burnt again into that old cottage, that was haunted already by so much by-gone, physical desire. You could not be in a dark room for an hour without the influence coming over you. The hot-blood desire of the by-gone yeoman, there in this old den where they had lusted and bred for many generations. The silent house, dark, with thick, timbered walls and the big black chimney-place, and the sense of secrecy. Dark, with low, little windows, sunk into

the earth. Dark, like a lair where strong beasts had lurked and mated, lonely at night and lonely by day, left to themselves and their own intensity for so many generations.

This voices the kind of intense belief in an ancient, buried but still tangible and vital England that can be found in Kipling's writing about Hobden the Hedger, the tutelary Englishman of *Puck of Pook's Hill* and *Rewards and Fairies*.

His dead are in the churchyard – thirty generations laid.
Their names were old in history when Domesday Book was made;
And the passion and the piety and the prowess of his line
Have seeded, rooted, fruited in some land the law calls mine.

"Some land." Kipling has in mind Bateman's, his house and grounds in Sussex. Bateman's operates as metonym for England. The link between Hobden and Kipling is a "law" which is not so much written on parchment as felt along the blood.

Kipling's verses were written in 1910, the year of the publication of *Howards End*. Forster's novel is much concerned with the legal struggle for ownership of a country house and in the end, as I have already noted, the choice of future inheritor reads as a rather desperate, liberal hope for reconciled interests. But then much in *Howards End* feels desperate, including the account of Margaret as the "natural" owner of the house. Here, she sees it for the first time.

There were the greengage-trees that Helen had once described, there the tennis lawn, there the hedge that would be glorious with dog-roses in June ... Down by the dell-hole more vivid colours were awakening, and Lent lilies stood sentinel on its margin, or advanced in battalions over the grass. Tulips were a tray of jewels. She could not see the wych-elm tree, but a branch of the celebrated vine, studded with velvet knobs, covered the porch. She was struck by the fertility of the soil; she had seldom been in a garden where the flowers looked so well; and even the weeds she was idly plucking out of the porch were intensely green. *(ch.23)*

This pallid, half-hearted, cliché-infested account of the garden at Howards End suggests Forster's largely theoretical concern with the country house theme. And "theme" is what it comes down to. Hence, the ruse of having the male Wilcoxes suffer from hay fever – their natural habitat is the city. As for London, Forster seems intent on writing the city off. At the beginning of Chapter 13, he acknowledges that "certainly it fascinates"; but, he continues:

> One visualises it as a tract of quivering grey, intelligent without purpose, and excitable without love; as a spirit that has altered before it can be chronicled; as a heart that certainly beats, but with no pulsation of humanity. It lies beyond everything: Nature, with all her cruelty, comes nearer to us than do these crowds of men. A friend explains himself: the earth is explicable – from her we came, and we must return to her. But who can explain Westminster Bridge Road or Liverpool Street in the morning – the city inhaling – or the same thoroughfares in the evening – the city exhaling her exhausted air? We reach in desperation beyond the fog, beyond the very stars, the voids of the universe are ransacked to justify the monster, and stamped with a human face.

Not much would be gained by point-scoring here. But Forster's opposition of country – good, healthy, to city – bad, inhuman, needs to be noted, as does his use of the by-then common assumption that the city, any city, is an inexplicable monster. And it is also important to remark that although Forster was the least bellicose of men and *Howards End* was in part an attempt to offer a vision of England and Germany connected through cultural values rather than divided by jingoistic nationalism, his shuddery withdrawal from the fact of the city can be linked to a habit of thought which would regard warfare itself as a glorious opportunity to escape from modernity, from what Rupert Brooke called "a world grown old and cold and weary, "inhabited by "half-men", those who, for Herbert Asquith, were typically clerks, "Toiling at ledgers in the city grey." Just like Leonard Bast. In short, decent liberal that he is, Forster is part of that developing complex of ideas (attitudes might be the better word) whose basic premise is that the modern city is a disaster, potential or actual, where the individual is bound to feel alienated. ("Nature, with all her cruelty, comes closer to us than do these crowds of men.")

## V

One of the formative experiences of the Great War, for officers and men alike – and I suspect for the V.A.D.s too – was that a sense of privileged and therefore alienated individuality was mistaken. Not that the experience of collectivity, and thus of the expansion of individual potentialities, was new to many of those who fought. Before the war they had after all been members of trades unions and some of them would have been active as socialists. But for their superiors, the officer class, it *was* new, and for the first time in British history collectivity therefore crossed class boundaries rather than being confined within them. Alienation, in other words, didn't have to be the defining experience of living among crowds of men. The city as the place of a crowd might offer new, enlarging possibilities for social living.

Nevertheless, the city was widely perceived to be a problem. Perhaps the ways of life it promoted and encouraged, the rage for material wealth, for profit, for the championing of conspicuous consumption – perhaps all these matters, and more beside, made for a heart of darkness that threatened to infect the healthy parts of the commonwealth. The language of taint, of fever, of fatal illness, is in fact common to the pre-war period, and lies just beneath the surface of *Tono Bungay*, Wells' searching novel of 1909, the rogue hero of which, Edward Ponderevo, is caught up by a dream of money so vast it leads to swindling on an international scale. It also involves the building for Ponderevo of a country-house as hideous as it is colossal. The novel is splendidly sardonic about country-house values. Wells' protagonist, Edward's nephew, George, remarks that "One hears a frightful lot of nonsense about the Rural Exodus and the degeneration wrought by town life upon our population. To my mind, the English townsman even in the slums is infinitely better spiritually, more courageous, more imaginative and cleaner, than his agricultural cousin." (Book the First: ch 3). Although George has agricultural workers in mind, the novel later deftly unpicks the habits of deference that make up rural society as a whole. When his uncle moves to Lady Grove, "a very beautiful house indeed, a still and gracious place, whose age-long seclusion was only effectively broken with the toot of the coming motor-car", George watches the vicar greet the house's new owners.

> He was a Tory in spirit, and what one might call an adapted Tory by stress of circumstances, that is to say he was no longer a legitimist, he was prepared for the substitution of new lords for old. We were pill vendors, he knew, and no doubt horribly vulgar in soul; but then it might have been

some polygamous rajah, a great strain on a good man's tact, or some Jew with an inherited expression of contempt. Anyhow, we were English and neither Dissenters nor Socialists, and he was cheerfully prepared to do what he could to make gentlemen of us ... So he was very bright and pleasant with us, showed us the church, gossiped informingly about our neighbours in the countryside, Tux the banker, Lord Boom the magazine and newspaper proprietor, Lord Carnaby, that great sportsman, and old Lady Osprey ... his wife regarded my aunt with a mixture of conventional scorn and abject respect, and talked to her in a languid persistent voice ... Encouraged by my aunt's manner the vicar's wife grew patronising and kindly, and made it evident that she could do much to bridge the social gulf between ourselves and the people of family about us. *(Book the Third: ch.2)*

*Tono-Bungay*, on which C.F.G. Masterman was to draw heavily for his study *The Condition of England*, is a powerfully persuasive novel about the anxieties lying just beneath the "vast smug surface" of English life in the early years of this century. These include such matters as cultural health, the unlikely survival of what Martin J Weiner has dubbed "The English Way of Life'", with its "myth of England essentially rural and essentially unchanging"[17], and the brute fact of money. For it is money, dirty money, too, which alone makes possible the continued existence of a way of life which pretends to know nothing of material needs. Hence, the vicar of Lady Grove's ambiguous welcome to the Ponderevos. And it is money which oils the wheels of the England whose uncertain journey towards the future Wells' novel chronicles. Hence George Ponderevo's recognition of that tendency towards what Thornstein Veblen had not long since called "conspicuous consumption": the upper levels of the social system, George realises, constitute "that multitude of economically ascendant people who are learning how to spend money ... With an immense astonished zest they begin shopping ... as a class, they talk, think, and dream possessions." (Book 3, ch 2). And hence the novel's ending, with George prepared to sell the new type of destroyer he has built to whichever power is willing to buy. This George of England is quite without patriotic fervour.

*Tono-Bungay* is a novel which disturbs the consoling dream of *Howard's End*. Its sense of an ending – for its closing pages with their image of "a squadron of warships waving white swords of light" surely prophesy war? – testifies to a deep pessimism that runs

28

like a hard, unyielding band of quartz under the loamy myth of an England endlessly nourished by rural circumstance. In this it may be connected to a sense of impending darkness which is not merely *fin de siècle* but also *fin du globe*. Expressions of that sense of an ending go back to the 1890s, but they find an almost definitive, gnomic utterance in Isaac Rosenberg's "A Worm Fed on the Heart of Corinth":

> A worm fed on the heart of Corinth
> Babylon and Rome:
> Not Paris raped tall Helen,
> But this incestuous worm,
> Who lured her vivid beauty
> To his amorphous sleep.
> England! famous as Helen
> Is thy betrothal sung
> To him the shadowless,
> More amorous than Solomon.

This poem must have been written at about the same time as "Break of Day in the Trenches". There, Rosenberg speaks out of a deep, sardonic sense that history offers no favours to those who think they are her favourites, those "haughty athletes/Less chanced than you for life." ("You" being the rat of "cosmopolitan sympathies" whom Rosenberg addresses throughout the poem.) "A Worm Fed" is a more sombre, rapt poem, but as deeply convincing in its insistence that England's betrothal to death isn't to be avoided. As with other civilisations, other falling towers, England is doomed.

Rosenberg was killed in action in France, on April 1st 1918. That same year Arnold Bennett published *The Pretty Lady*, his novel about war-time England. Towards the end of the novel the ambiguously named hero, G.J. Hoape, walks the streets of night-time London:

> He was in solitude, and surrounded by London. He stood still, and the vast sea of war seemed to be closing over him. The war was growing, or the sense of its measureless scope was growing. It had sprung, not out of this crime or that, but out of the secret invisible roots of humanity, and it was widening to the limits of evolution itself.

Understandably perhaps, Bennett's pessimism here is absolute. I see no reason to dissociate him from his protagonist's thoughts. Nobody after all could know if and when the war would end. Yet to deny that war came from "this crime or that" and to insist it sprang from "the secret invisible roots of humanity" is to deny war's material causes. We need, therefore, to recall that there were many who believed that the causes of the Great War were explicable and were rooted, not in some metaphysical "evil", but in forces which could be understood in social and political terms. James's "treacherous years" were not only those of an increasingly vulgar, desperate imperialism, nor of crass materialism alone; they were also a period in which a new, radical political consciousness was developing. If, as I have suggested, to understand the 1920s we need to remember the 1890s, we need in particular to remember that Yeats's "savage beast" was his version of the Nietzschean hatred for "littleness", an outraged response to the first stirrings of the beast Demos. And in England during the *fin-de-siècle* that beast began to shape itself out of such constituent elements as the New Woman, Trade Unionism, and growing numbers of radical political parties (the S.D.F., the S.L., the I.L.P., Anarchists, and so on). In the years before 1914 some of these acquired new names and even more threatening shapes: among them Suffragism, Fabianism, and the "triple alliance" of dockers, miners and transport workers. The coming of the war entailed a setback for the immediate aspirations of these groups, both separately and collectively; but it also strengthened their determination to realise their hopes. The sense of an ending for some marked for others the sense of a beginning. As the war ended people who embrace this consciousness were encouraged to believe that change was indeed possible.

It had after all been signalled in Russia by the events of February and then of October 1917. This is not to say that in Britain there was a widespread sense – whether of hope or fear – that violent, revolutionary overthrow of the old order was at all likely. (Which didn't prevent those who favoured the old order from doing their utmost to spread such fears as a means of justifying their clampdown on social dissidents or "bolshies", a word which enters the language at precisely this moment and which, according to the O.E.D at once comes to mean "left-wing, unco-operative recalcitrant".) But it is to say that in the aftermath of war the old "English way of life" was bound to be subjected to new, fiercely critical scrutiny. In 1920 Douglas Goldring published *The Black Curtain*, a novel set in the years immediately before and then during the war. I shall reserve detailed discussion of the novel for the next chapter, but it is relevant here to note that when its heroine, Anne Drummond, a "new woman", decides to leave her old home behind

30

her, she is self-consciously choosing to reject rural circumstance: she turns her back on her father's country vicarage and surrounding "world of trees and green grass."

> [Her parents] stood side by side on the doorstep of the vicarage – a pathetic, white-haired couple, touching in their innocence and goodness – and waved their hands to her as the wheels of the old vehicle scrunched the gravel of the drive. Anne felt a stab of pain as she looked at them. "What have I to do with you" she thought, "you queer old things! You've lavished all your love and care upon a complete stranger ... and now the stranger is going away from you."
> She waved her hand, and blew the old couple a kiss, just as the wagonette lurched into the road and turned the corner which shut them out of sight. And when she got into the train for London and felt it moving with her along the platform, something told her that she would never see either her home or parents again. She had broken with her past, her childhood and girlhood were over and her work was beginning. (ch.12).

Never such innocence again. Goldring's novel is dedicated to D.H. Lawrence, and its socialist fervour, although certainly not Lawrence's, belongs very powerfully to a post-war determination to reject the past, or at all events to reject that version of England which, from the far side of the war, now looked as culpable as it was unreclaimable. That was the England which Lawrence had told his Bloomsbury listeners was finished. From now on, the city would be the place of new growth, for creating democratic vistas. And it is, then, of obvious importance that it should be a young woman who is here rejecting that past and looking to the future. Anne Drummond is a fictional version of the revolt of daughters against parents which was so powerful a shaping force in the 1920s. As of course was the revolt of the sons.

## Notes on Chapter 1

1. *The Diaries of Evelyn Waugh*, ed. Michael Davie, Harmondsworth, Penguin, 1976, p. 206.
2. Paul Delaney: *D.H. Lawrence's Nightmare: The Writer and his Circle in the Years of the Great War*, Hassocks, Harvester, 1979, p. 385.
3. Henry James: *Within the Rim and Other Essays*, Collins, London, 1915.
4. Robert Bridges, *The Spirit of Man*, (preface), London, OUP, 1916.
5. For relevant statistics here see esp. Eric Leed, *No Man's Land: Combat and Identity in World War One*, London, C.U.P., 1979, esp. ch.5.

6. Henry James *Within the Rim*, pp. 25-31.
7. Boris Pasternak, *Selected Poems*, translated from the Russian by John Stallworthy and Peter France, Harmondsworth, Penguin, 1984, p. 19.
8. *The Letters of D.H. Lawrence*, eds. G.J. Zytavak and J.T. Boulton, Vol 2, London, C.U.P., 1981, pp 431-2.
9. See *Modern English Poetry: from Hardy to Hughes*, London, Batsford, 1986, pp. 53-5.
10. Longley (ed) *Edward Thomas: Poems and Last Poems*, London, Collins, 1973, p. 353.
10a As notebooks show, Thomas is drawing on an account of a train journey taken in June, 1914. For more on this, see my essay, "Discovering England: the views from the train," in *Literature and History*, vol. 6 no. 2, Autumn, 1997, esp. pp. 37-46.
11. See Stan Smith: *Edward Thomas*, London, Faber, 1986 esp. ch.1.
12. Barbara Lucas, "A Propos of England my England", in *D.H. Lawrence: Penguin Critical Anthology*, ed. H.H. Combes, Harmondsworth, Penguin, 1968, p. 428.
13. F.R. Leavis, *D.H. Lawrence, Novelist*, Harmondsworth, Penguin, 1964, p. 279.
14. *Lutyens: The Work of the English Architect Sir Edwin Lutyens* (1869-1944), Arts Council of Great Britain, p. 22. For more on this see my essay "The Sunlight on the Garden" in *Seeing Double: Revisioning Edwardian and Modernist Literature*, eds. Kaplan and Simpson, New York, St Martin's Press, 1996, pp. 59-77.
15. For this see my essay "From Naturalism to Symbolism," *Romantic to Modern: Essays*, Hassocks, 1982 and "Fitness and the *Fin de Siècle*", by William Greenslade, in *Fin de Siècle/Fin du Globe*, ed. John Stokes, London, Macmillan, 1992.
16. D. Read: *Edwardian England*, London, Longman, 1972, pp. 35-6.
17. Martin J. Weiner, *English Culture and the Decline and Fall of the Industrial Spirit, 1850-1980*, London, C.U.P., 1981, p. 55.

## CHAPTER TWO

# A RED DAWN

In November 1915 Sigmund Freud looked back to the outbreak of war which "had robbed the world of its beauties," and which was now destroying "the countryside through which it passed", as well as shattering "our pride in the achievements of our civilisation, our admiration for many philosophers and artists and our hopes of a final triumph over the differences between nations and races." Yet Freud was unwilling to despair. "When once the mourning is over, it will be found that our high opinion of the riches of civilisation has lost nothing from our discovery of their fragility. We shall build up again all that the war has destroyed, and perhaps on firmer ground and more lastingly than before."[1]

Three years later, with much of the Europe he loved in ruins, Freud was less optimistic. And certainly the post-war mood in Germany and Austria hardly supported his hope that what the war had destroyed could be re-built. Dada is a most significant expression of this mood, its brutal anti-art, anti-culture shock-tactics a contemptuous rejection of values and assumptions which were held to have been dominant in Berlin and Vienna before the outbreak of war. Given that those who upheld such values had shown themselves powerless to oppose war's coming – had even welcomed it – a break with the past seemed inevitable, at least to the young writers, artists and intellectuals whose challenge to the old order had begun with the events they staged at the Café Voltaire in Zurich, in 1916, and which in the immediate post-war years culminated, in John Willett's words, in "a utopian, near anarchist Expressionism."[2]

It hardly needs saying that Expressionism isn't a recognisable feature of English cultural life in the post-war years. There is, for example, a world of difference between the Berlin Dada fair of 1920 and the Sitwells' *Façade*. And although some of the woodcuts Paul Nash worked on in the early 1920s suggest the influence of German contemporaries, that influence was neither deep nor long-lasting. This is not to disparage Nash. The work he produced as an official war artist includes some memorable, even great art, especially, "We Are Making A New World"; and the famous letter to his wife of November 1917, in which he sets down his impressions of the front-line, is a key document of protest against the prolongation of the war: "I am no longer an artist interested and curious, I am a messenger who will bring back word from the men who are fighting to those who want the war to go on for ever. Feeble, inarticulate, will be my message, but it will have a bitter truth, and may it burn their lousy souls."[3]

This is also the moment of Ivor Gurney's sonnet "To the Prussians of England," which he sent in a letter to his friend Marion Scott, on October 12th, 1917:

Our silly dreams of peace you put aside
And Brotherhood of man, for you will see
An Armed Mistress, braggart of the tide
Her Children slaves, under your mastery.
We'll have a word there too, and forge a knife,
Will cut the cancer threatens England's life.

The poem so shocked Scott that Gurney had to reassure her that she wasn't its target. Nevertheless, he insisted, he did care about "liberty for Englishmen," and he thought it more important that "The Duke of Bilgewater should respect and sympathise with Bill Jones than that the sun should never set on the British Empire..."[4]

Perhaps Scott read into Gurney's poem the violent revolutionary feelings which at that very moment were being turned into action in Russia. Forging a knife to cut England's cancer: was that a threat, promise, or merely rhetoric? Probably something of all three. We know, even if we choose to forget, that men – officers as well as rankers – who came together in the Great War, *did* turn towards radical politics and that they *did* look with angry contempt at those who kept them fighting. We know, though for years the facts were hidden, that both during and immediately after the war there were several mutinies among British troops.[5] In due course I shall comment on ways in which the moment to which Nash and Gurney testify was prolonged in the years after 1918. And yet as the war clouds lifted they revealed the Duke of Bilgewater still safe in his saddle. The world had been totally altered by the Great War and yet, paradox of paradoxes, it was also possible to feel that nothing

had changed, not in England, anyway. Elsewhere, people gathered together fragments to shore against ruin. But in England "it still goes on", to quote the title of a play which Robert Graves wrote at the end of the decade.

Graves was training his sights on an older generation, that generation of fathers who, having urged their sons to war and vehemently proclaimed the need to fight on "to the very end," could see nothing in either words or actions for which they needed to apologise. There is no doubt that the smug complacency which enraged Graves is a remarkable component of much post-war writing by the older generation. Looking back over the decade from the vantage point of 1940, Orwell noted that "even more than at most times, the big shots of literary journalism were busy pretending that the age-before-last had not come to an end. Squire ruled *The London Mercury*, Gibbs and Walpole were the gods of the lending libraries, there was a cult of cheeriness and manliness, beer and cricket, briar pipes and monogamy"[6]. This chimes with Wyndham Lewis's claim, made in 1937 in *Blasting and Bombardiering*, that well before November 1918, Ford Madox Hueffer had told him: "One month after [the war's] ended, it will be forgotten. Everybody will want to forget it – it will be bad form to mention it."

Still, even if we believe Lewis's account of Hueffer's remark – a tall order – he is plainly wrong to add that "This worldly forecast was verified to the letter."[7] And this is not merely because of the many memoirs and novels about the war, most of which came out in the later 1920s, all of them replete with anguished remembering, but because, unbelievable as it may now seem, almost as soon as the Armistice was agreed some writers chose to recall the war in exactly the terms in which it had been anticipated. No doubt these writers provided desperately needed consolation for thousands of widows and bereaved mothers. Herbert Hayens' boys' novel, *Play Up Queens*, ends with a roll-call of the careers of those sixth-formers whose adventures had filled the novel's pages. "It is impossible to follow their fortunes here," Hayens writes: "we know only that Manton's name is inscribed on the Scroll of Honour, and that the words opposite it run, 'Killed in Action.' The men of his company, who were proud of him, relate that he died with a whimsical smile in his eyes, and the words, 'Play Up, Queens,' on his lips".[8] The novel was published in 1920.

When Ernest Raymond's boys' novel for adults *Tell England* was published two years later, it became an immediate and huge best-

seller. (My 1930 edition informs me that the novel was reprinted 14 times in 1922, 6 times in the following year, and that it went through numerous further reprints and impressions during the decade.) It, too, ends with death on the battlefield. We are given the closing page of a diary in which the novel's hero, Rupert Rey, notes that "I may be whimsical tonight, but I feel that the old Colonel was right when he saw nothing unlovely in Penny's death; and that Monty [the padre] was right when he said that Doe had done a perfect thing at the last, and so grasped the holy grail. And I have the strange idea that very likely I, too, shall find beauty in the morning." [Penny and Doe are Rupert's school friends][9] "Whimsical": "fanciful or playful." J. M. Barrie sets the tone for this.

The huge popularity of *Tell England* is very revealing. It shows how deeply large numbers of people wanted to believe not only that the war had been a good war but that the public school values so inextricably associated with it were inherently worthwhile, and had survived untarnished. In other words, pre-war England was still alive and well. But was it? In his report on the Condition of England in 1922, *England After the War*, C.F.G. Masterman claimed to be fearful of the damage the war had done to the middle and upper classes. The best of the younger generation of the privileged had been killed, maimed or ruined. Tens of thousands of families, formerly in comfortable circumstances, had been bereaved of their sons and heirs, while high taxation and financial loss compelled many to sell their estates and belongings. This was gloomy news, at all events if, like Masterman, you feared that the harm done to the privileged classes wasn't so much the cutting of a cancer but the amputation of a healthy and crucial limb. Yet in his personal account of *The Nineteen Twenties*, written in 1945, Douglas Goldring counters Masterman's diagnosis by remarking that "we can now see that this burden [of suffering and loss] as in the present war, was very unevenly shared. The bulk of the propertied and professional classes, although suffering some discomfort and temporary loss of income, soon recovered from their country's ordeal."[10] And Douglas Jerrold's *Georgian Adventure*, the autobiography he published through the 'Right' Book Club in 1937, speaks of the immediate post war period as a time of "getting back to 1914....After the march of armies, the wriggling of martinets. Instead of the swift footsteps of youth to lead us on to the new era, the patient shuffling of elderly politicians spelt its doom before it was born....No wonder no one, not even on the editorial staff of *The*

36

*News of The World*, knew whether we were going on or going back."[11]

Going back, if *Mr Prohack* is anything to go by. The chortling, intendedly good-natured hero of Arnold Bennett's novel, published in 1922, is a monster of unctuous complacency, yet there is no suggestion that Bennett finds anything wrong with him. Consider for example, this passage on Mr Prohack's relationship with his son, Charlie.

> Charlie had gone to war from Cambridge at the age of nineteen. He went a boy, and returned a grave man. He went thoughtless and light-hearted, and returned full of magnificent and austere ideals. Six months of England had destroyed these ideals in him. He had expected to share in the common task of making heaven in about a fortnight. In the war he had learned much about the possibilities of human nature, but scarcely anything about its limitations. His father tried to warn him, but of course failed. Charlie grew resentful, then cynical. He saw in England nothing but futility, injustice and ingratitude. He refused to resume Cambridge, and was bitterly sarcastic about the generosity of a nation which, through its War Office, was ready to pay studious warriors anxious to make up University terms lost in a holy war decidedly less than it paid to its street-sweepers. Having escaped from death, the aforesaid warriors were granted the right to starve their bodies while improving their minds. He might have had sure situations in vast corporations. He declined them. He spat on them. He called them "graves." What he wanted was an opportunity to fulfil himself. He could not get it, and his father could not get it for him. While searching for it, he frequently met warriors covered with ribbons but lacking food and shelter not only for themselves but for their women and children. All this, human nature being what it is, was inevitable, but his father could not convincingly tell him so. All that Mr Prohack could effectively do Mr Prohack did, – namely provide the saviour of Britain with food and shelter. Charlie was restlessly and dangerously waiting for his opportunity. But he had not developed into a revolutionist, nor a communist, nor anything of the sort. Oh, no! Quite the reverse. He meditated a different revenge on society. *(ch.5 "Charlie": section II).*

I shall return to the nature of Charlie's revenge. Here, I want merely to note that Mr Prohack's self-satisfied demeanour is fully approved by his author. There is nothing to put daylight between them. *Mr Prohack* is a novel which perfectly exemplifies that smug complacency against which Graves and other returning "warriors" raged. Charlie may seem to be a radical – wanting to help make heaven in a fortnight – but he also thinks that as an ex-soldier resuming his studies he's entitled to be better paid than a street-sweeper. But then again, to call the war in which he fought "a holy war" and to call him a "warrior" is, as the tone makes clear, to deny that either needs to be taken seriously. Nor is there any need to take seriously ex-warriors reduced to begging at street corners, "human nature being what it is."

Later in the novel we encounter this human nature in the flesh:

> Crossing a street, the car was held up by a procession of unemployed, with guardian policemen, a band consisting chiefly of drums, and a number of collarless powerful young men who shook white boxes of coppers menacingly in the faces of passers-by.
>
> "Instead of encouraging them, the police ought to forbid these processions of unemployed," said [Mrs Prohack] gravely. "They're becoming a perfect nuisance."
>
> "Why!" said Mr Prohack, "this car of yours is a procession of unemployed."
>
> (ch. XIII "Pure Idleness" section II)

It is worth setting against this a remark of A.C. Ward's, in his 1930 study of *The Nineteen Twenties*, that

> Through four years the soldiers had been 'beloved Tommies', credited with undying courage and every virtue. Once the panic was over, the 'beloved Tommies' became, in the mouths of their one-time sentimental and hysterical admirers, loafers and lazy wastrels concerned only to draw 'the dole' (unemployment benefit paid by the state). Political extremists were quick to seize upon this fuel of disillusion and distress, which promised a first-class blaze in the interests of world-wide Communism.[12]

Bennett's comedy is meant to dissolve feelings of bitterness. It is of a piece with this that Mr Prohack's son should meditate a revenge on society far different from revolutionary communism. Charlie plans to become an engineer. "Revenge?" Well, in so far as this acts as a rebuke to his father's dream of Charlie as some sort of a cultured layabout, yes. But in so far as it deflects attention away from the festering dissatisfaction of thousands upon thousands of his real-life counterparts, hardly. Some of these would indeed become communists. Others would go in different directions. But as Bennett's uneasy, bad-faith comedy unintentionally reveals, many of the younger generation were united in an appalled awareness of the prevailing attitudes of civilian society, especially the attitudes of those elders who had urged them to war in the first place. And this does much to explain the rejection of that society and of those elders which, although it took many forms, was one of the distinguishing characteristics of the decade.

It is of course a commonplace that each generation is in revolt against its predecessors. But the generation which went to war in 1914 could feel that it had done exactly what the older generation required of it. The shock of awakening that followed was not, therefore, simply to the gap between a romantically conceived-of battle of noble warriors and the brutal realities of mass warfare; far more important was a dawning recognition among the young of the fallibility, even culpability, of their elders.

In this context it is worth noting Miles Malleson's plays *D Company* and *Black 'Ell*, published in 1916 and seized by the police as "A deliberate Calumny on the British soldier." According to Raphael Samuel, Malleson "had joined up enthusiastically at the beginning of the war, but was invalided out and became a war resister. (A later pacifist play of his, *Paddy's Pools,* was one of the few left-wing dramas to become a normal part of the amateur dramatic repertory.)" In *Black 'Ell*, the play's hero describes an incident when he came within earshot of the German lines and heard "a man there, a Socialist or something, I suppose, talking against the war....They got furious with him....He said he was going to refuse to kill any more, and they called him traitor and pro-English and they've probably shot him by now....Well you can shoot me...because I'm not going back ....I'm going to stop at home and say it's all mad. I'm going to keep on saying it... someone's got to stop sometime ... somebody's got to get sane again...."[13]

Malleson's detestation of the collective "insanity" of those who championed war is close to Wilfred Owen's characterisation of the murderous intent of an older generation of war mongers in his "Parable of the Old Man and the Young." At the end of Owen's reworking of the story of Abraham and Isaac, the old man defies the angel's call "Lay not thy hand upon the lad,/Neither do anything to him..." "But the old man would not do so, but slew his son,/And half the seed of Europe/ one by one." After such knowledge, what forgiveness.

From bitter loathing to despair can be a short step, and one that Ward thinks also characteristic of the 20s. He goes so far as to call the 1920s A Decade of Despair. "Military success followed by impoverishment and moral bankruptcy can only be described as victory if that word is used in a spirit of tragic fantasy," he remarks; and a little later adds that as the 1920s went on so "the mood of despair deepened."[14] Despair for some had come with the end of the war. Despair of Europe, as in Pound's famous formulation of its being reduced to "an old bitch gone in the teeth/... a botched civilisation"; or as in Eliot's subtler evocation of decay in "Gerontion", with its lamentation of lost purpose, vitality, passion, its "Thoughts of a dry brain in a dry season." Despair of England, as in Lawrence's *Kangaroo,* where the protagonist, Summers, sails away and "There was snow on the Downs like a shroud. And as he looked back from the boat, when they had left Folkestone behind and only England was there, England looked like a grey, dreary-grey coffin sinking in the sea behind, with her dead grey cliffs and the white, worn-out cloth of snow above." (ch 12.)

Despair such as this takes for granted a death which can't be denied simply by the pretence that old forms have life, that "it still goes on." Even Galsworthy tinkers with this perception, in a play of 1924 to which he gave the revealing title *Old English.* The central character, Sylvanus Heythorp, is an aged, enfeebled entrepreneur, Geoffrey Marshall on his last legs, you might say, who has done his best to fight off various attempts to take over his company, "The Island Navigation Company". But now fellow directors want to bring him to book over some shady financial dealings. He dies before he can be undone. But with him dies any real hope of rescuing the company: island navigation, with all its robust if dubious methods, is on the rocks. Heythorp, "Old English", may be thought of as a more red-blooded version of Mr Prohack. The play's last words are spoken by Old English's devoted Irish maid: "The grand old fightin' gintliman!" she says. "The great old sinner he was!" Leave aside the tactlessness of having an Irish maid *in 1924* express such devotion to the kind of bullish Englishman Heythorp is meant to be. (Or is Galsworthy offering here an image of reconciliation so soon after the Troubles?) What remains is a sense of "Old English" as combination of Fighting Temeraire and Squire Allworthy. *This* England is now as good as dead.

But it wouldn't of course lie down. Douglas Jerrold, as we have seen, was convinced that in the aftermath of the war the old order came out of retirement and carried on as though nothing had happened. *Mr Prohack* implies that, "human nature being what it is", little changed between 1912 and 1922. Yet it was just this insistence – or desperate hope, or forlorn wish – that gave such an edge to the revolt of the young against the old. And it is here that the true radicalism of the decade begins to emerge. Even among those for whom revolting behaviour amounted to little more that *ersatz* flings or night-club frolics there was a quite new sense of confronting and affronting elderly parties. Hence, John Betjeman's studied rudeness to his father, Evelyn Waugh's to his, the Sitwells to theirs; and instances could be multiplied. There is no point in doing so, however: that way lies the world of William Hickey and the Bright Young Things. The behaviour of Betjeman *et al* is of small importance compared with events taking place elsewhere, even if those events appeared to give licence to such behaviour. We are customarily asked to accept that the "despair" of the Bright Young Things, because it is apparently authentic, justifies their behaviour. But they weren't usually out of work, and, if they were, jobs of a not-too demanding kind could be found for them, or, failing that, money, a legacy or a loan. Nor were they made to suffer "on state-doles, or showing shop-patterns/ Or walking town to town sore in borrowed tatterns/Or begged," as Ivor Gurney noted so many ex-soldiers having to do. ("Strange Hells")[15] And as Douglas Goldring remarked, "come the General Strike, most of the Bright Young Things joined the despised professional middle class in rallying to the Government standard and [they] kept the essential services running by supplying 'blackleg' labour."[16]

Goldring's commentary on the decade is crucial, because he lived through it, and his writings of the period bear important witness to a little told story: a story not of despair, but of resistance, even of vision. It was Goldring who, in the course of a collection of essays called *Reputations,* published in 1920, provided an explanation for the vast numbers of volumes of poetry that appeared during the war years:

> If any student of English life wishes to gain an insight into the real meaning of the Public School spirit, that poisonous anachronism on which our country still prides herself, he cannot do better than study a handful out of the countless vol-

umes of war verse which it has produced. For our Public School system, in its effort to turn out every little Englishman "a thoroughly manly young fellow," succeeds brilliantly in stunting the growth of his thinking apparatus. It preserves him as an intellectual adolescent living in a fairyland of chivalric illusion, with a blind trust in the doctrine enunciated in the reactionary newspapers. Many of these Public Schoolboy soldiers must have gone straight from the cricket-field and the prefect's study to the trenches, in a kind of waking dream. Their mental equipment for withstanding the shock of experience was as useless as the imitation suit of armour, the dummy lance and the shield of an actor in a pageant. It was their false conception of life, their inability to look at facts except through tinted glasses of one particular colour, which rendered the poems of so many young subalterns so valueless as literature, so tragic and accusing as human documents. For they accuse the age which permitted and gloried in an educational system so monstrously unfair to its victims, and they accuse the schoolmasters who have acquiesced in perpetuating it.

Goldring will allow only a very few war poets claims to distinction: "Alan Seeger, Wilfred (sic) Sorley ... and some honest and effective verse ... by Siegfried Sassoon, Robert Graves and Osbert Sitwell."[17]

As far as I know, this is the first really hostile account of those sad, slim volumes of public-school verse which tumbled from the presses during the war years, many of them serving as memorial collections; and although it soon became commonplace to attack the public school's ethos of glory-in-death, Goldring's criticism is important not merely for its wit (the image of the public-school soldier as an actor in a pageant is cruelly accurate), but for its vehemence. You have only to compare what he has to say with Forster's sardonic account of the 1925 exhibition of Sir John Singer Sargent's war paintings to see how different, how "bookish," Forster seems, although as we shall see, he turns this to his own advantage. "I have a suit of clothes. It does not fit, but it is of stylish cut. I can go anywhere in it and I have been to see the Sargent pictures at the Royal Academy." This is how Forster's essay, "Me, Them and You" begins, and it is characterised by that quizzical, slightly arch manner which he affected in much of his writing. Forster loathed the public school ethos, as his accounts of Charles Wilcox in *Howards End* and Ronnie Heaslop in *A Passage to India* make clear; and in this brief essay he turns his attention to Sargent's war-painting, "Gassed", in order to show how it participates in the lie that "it is possible to suffer with a quiet grace under the new conditions." Who are the sufferers?

> A line of golden-haired Apollos moved along a duck-board from left to right with bandages over their eyes. They had been blinded by mustard gas. Others sat peacefully in the foreground, others approached through the middle distance. The battlefield was sad but tidy. No one complained, no one looked lousy or over-tired, and the aeroplanes over head struck the necessary note of the majesty of England. It was all that a great war picture should be and it was modern because it managed to tell a new sort of lie. Many ladies and gentlemen fear that Romance is passing out of war with the sabres and the chargers. Sargent's master-piece reassures them.

Yet although Forster's tone may here seem inadequate to his theme, it is carefully calculated. Inadequacy is the point. "Me, Them and You" is about class. "Them" are the ladies and gentlemen free to wander about the Royal Academy, and in his stylish suit Forster, however much he may want to be "Me", knows he is one of "Them". "You" meanwhile "had been plentiful in the snow outside (your proper place)" but appear in the Academy exhibition only on canvas. For You are among the gassed. And in the final brief paragraphs Forster turns to address "You." The gulf between "Them" and "Me" may be wide he says, but "wider still is the gulf between us and You." And he then poses the question:

> What would become of our incomes and activities if you declined to exist? You are the slush and dirt on which our civilisation rests, which it treads under foot daily, which it sentimentalises over now and then, in hours of danger. But you are not only a few selected youths in khaki, you are old men and women and dirty babies.... The misery goes on, the feeble impulses of good return to the sender, and far away in some other category from the snobbery and glitter in which our souls and bodies have been entangled, is forged the instrument of the new dawn.[18]

I do not pretend to know what Forster means by this last sentence. He probably didn't know himself, although the "new dawn" may well gesture to a socialist future. For what he *did* know was that the visible, street-corner misery of many ex-soldiers could connect to a possible radicalised politics which, the failure of the 1924 Labour Government notwithstanding, would herald the new day.

By 1925, when Forster wrote, "Me, Them and You," much had happened to suggest that if the days of the public-school ethos weren't over they were certainly numbered. This is not so much to give credence to Masterman's belief that the code and traditions of the ethos had been lost in the mud of Flanders as to say that immediately after the war a new political aggression became evident among working-class people – "You" – and those sympathisers who were drawn from "Them and Me."

In 1920 the Communist Party of Great Britain was born. Admittedly it had at first few members and took some time to become a significant force. But the very fact that it began existence in that year suggests a new militancy among the disaffected. And while the Party might lack members it certainly didn't lack sympathisers. They included the dockers who in the spring of 1920 refused to load arms onto ships bound for Poland, where they were intended to be used against the Red Army. They also included the miners who struck in October that same year. There was the emergence of the *The Daily Herald* as a mass-circulation newspaper of the left.[19] In the immediate post-war years those of Forster's class who looked for a new dawn had every reason to suppose it was coming and that socialism would both help to bring it into being and become its chief beneficiary. The future in fact belonged to socialism. I shall defer a fuller discussion of this until Chapter 5. My present concern is with a number of novelists who were aware, as the Bennett of *Mr Prohack* was not, that the war had changed things and that writers needed to recognise this, to account for it and, perhaps, to imagine what might come of the change.

## III

Looking back on the period, Goldring remarked that

> Those of us who were in our early 'thirties when the war ended had to carry on our professional activities amid the wreckage of the past, but under the moral obligation, imposed by *l'honneur du métier*, to do what we could to prepare the way for the future. Weeds grew apace in the Waste Land, rank growths of greed, corruption and brutality, but the flowers and the fruit native to the soil still contrived a precarious blossoming. In order to protect them we were forced to become politically-minded at the expense of our art.[20]

Goldring is here probably offering a coded apology for his own writing in the 1920s, much of which is unashamedly propagandist. *The Black Curtain* is a case in point. Goldring published this novel in 1920 complete with dedication to D.H. Lawrence, with whom he was at the time on friendly terms and about whom he had written both perceptively and generously in an essay, "The Later Work of D.H. Lawrence," included in *Reputations*. Lawrence is a difficult writer, Goldring says, "and the chief effect of *The Rainbow* affair seems to have been to cause him to retire more deeply into himself." He then examines the poems of *Look! We Have Come Through*, and remarks that "Many mystics have tried to deny sex altogether, but Mr Lawrence sees in the bodily union of men and women the central mystery of human life, a mystery indissolubly connected with every real religious impulse of mankind, a symbol of an ultimate spiritual consummation."[21] These words are echoed at the moment in Goldring's novel when its protagonist Philip Kane and his girlfriend make love and Philip feels that "The joy of his possession made him long for the joys of a more spiritual possession, a deeper intimacy, a true mating."[22]

*The Black Curtain* also carries an echo of the furious attack Lawrence had directed against the bohemian London of *Women in Love*. Philip is friendly with a minor poet, Lawrence Reilly, whose poems are apparently a mixture of Verlaine and Dowson, and who eases his way into polite society as part of a campaign to make himself a known writer. Philip bumps into him by chance at a restaurant where a "nigger band" is playing. "Reilly was having supper with Mr and Mrs Caldwell and Lady Ermyntrude Dimmock. Caldwell was a man of considerable means, and combined a taste for literature and the arts with some business ability. He was one of that class of men with plenty of capital at their disposal and a university training behind them, who so frequently drift into publishing." (ch. 7)

So far, so Lawrentian. But *The Black Curtain* is more importantly about envisaging a possible socialist future for England and, who knows, for the western world as a whole; and Lawrence would hardly have been likely to care for that, even though he did offer his play *Touch and Go*, to "A People's Theatre" project with which Goldring was closely concerned. This project developed out of the desire of Herbert Morrison, then secretary of the London Labour Party, to create cultural initiatives modelled on the German SDP. "The efforts of literary-minded branch secretaries were seconded by the publication of play-scripts intended for use in and around the Labour movement and for the propagation of the Socialist idea." Goldring's anti-war play, *We Fight for Freedom* (1920) was a People's Theatre text, and Raphael Samuel quotes what I assume to be a publisher's blurb for it which extols its "terrible exposure of the effects of war on the sex instinct," as well as its "plea for tolerance and clear thinking on the subject." The play's heroine, Margaret Lambert, the daughter of a clergyman, is engaged to Captain Henderson, a public school type who "fights for freedom." Henderson returns from two years in the trenches to discover that Margaret is in love with another man – a socialist. "In a fit of passion" Henderson spikes Margaret's champagne and seduces her. Her family now hope she will do the respectable thing and marry Henderson, but she holds out for her socialist lover. Unfortunately for her and their love, he won't avenge her. Instead, he suggests that Henderson is more to be pitied than hated. "Punishment for the crimes of soldiers – even for 'atrocities' – ought to be visited not on the tortured devils who actually commit them, but on the heads of those who made the war .... Those are the real criminals."

It is difficult to imagine how *Touch and Go* would have fitted in with this or with other plays for a People's Theatre such as *Captain Youth* by Ralph Fox ("a romantic comedy for all socialist children") or Hamilton Fyfe's *The Kingdom, The Power and the Glory* ("an attack on kings, queens and emperors, and ... therefore working-class propaganda").[23] Presumably Goldring persuaded Lawrence to let him have the play, but Lawrence's preface, written like the play itself while he was waiting for the passports which would take him and Frieda out of England, shows how uneasy he felt about the project's intentions.

> A nice phrase: "A People's Theatre." But what about it? There's no such thing in existence as a People's Theatre: or even on the way to existence, as far as we can tell ....
> A People's Theatre. Since we can't produce it, let us deduce it. Major premiss: the seats are cheap. Minor premiss: the plays are good....
> The seats are cheap. That has a nasty proletarian look about it. But appearances are deceptive. The proletariat isn't poor. Everybody is poor Except Capital and Labour....
> A People's Theatre shows men, and not parts. Not bits, nor bundles of bits. Whole bunches of roles tied into one won't make an individual. Though gaitors perish, we will have men.
> Although most miners may be pick-cum-shovel-cum-ballot implements, and no more, still among miners there must two

or three living individuals. The same among the masters. The majority are suction tubes for Bradburys. But in this Sodom of Industrialism there are surely ten men, all told. My poor little withered grain of mustard seed, I am half afraid to take you across to the seed testing department![24]

The apparently gratuitous mention of miners and masters comes in because Lawrence has in mind what he calls "The Strike situation." Early in 1919 the Miners Federation had demanded a six-hour day, a thirty per-cent increase in wages and nationalisation of the mines. (During the war years the mines had been under effective government control, as had the railways). The government rejected the miners' demands and the miners voted to strike. Lloyd George bought time by agreeing to set up a Commission which would examine both wage demands and the question of ownership of industry. There were compromise agreements on both sides, but throughout 1920 the miners were becoming increasingly angered by the government's failure to offer a sufficient wage increase; on the 16th October they finally struck. The railwaymen and transport workers threatened to follow them. The strike was called off after two weeks because the government, faced with this threat from the Triple Alliance, announced a temporary six-month wage increase. (The following year they de-controlled ownership of both mines and railways, as they had been planning to do, and wages went back down again.)[25]

Lawrence is therefore writing at a moment of crisis, when, as he himself said, "a new wind is getting up. We call it Labour *versus* Capitalism."[26] And this is the wind which Goldring attempts to ride in *The Black Curtain*. I am not considering the novel here as a work of art so much as a remarkably interesting document, an often intriguing blend of fact and fiction, plainly of importance to any adequate understanding of the immediate post-war years. Goldring is not an especially gifted novelist – I doubt if his decision to become "politically minded" means that the expense of art cost him very much – but *The Black Curtain* is a significant work for at least two reasons. In the first place it is keenly alert to issues of the day and of how they can be read. Secondly, its socialism links it to novels to be considered in Chapter Five, although whereas they are set in an imagined future, Goldring's deals with the immediate past and present, and at its close it offers no more than a glimpse of a new dawning, whereas they are confidently prophetic.

47

The novel begins in pre-war Europe and ends with the Armistice. The opening pages are taken up with Philip Kane's chance meeting in a restaurant in Barcelona, where he has for some years worked as a correspondent, with a Russian exile, Smirnoff. Smirnoff is known to the habitués of the restaurant as a gifted musician. Accordingly, the orchestra leader offers Smirnoff his violin and begs him to play. Smirnoff reluctantly obliges.

> The mobile Russian face, which had but little of feature of modelling, which in repose was ordinary enough, seemed now suddenly to become transfigured with a kind of ecstasy. In the upturned eyes, the rapturous expression of mingled love, sorrow, courage and aspiration, Philip recognised the real character of the man with whom he had just been chatting; recognised in him a type which he had rarely before encountered, the type of the idealist. What it was that Smirnoff had chosen to play he did not know .... It was something quite simple – a revolutionary air in which despair and sorrow yielded to a triumphant soaring hope. All the agonies of the proletarian class the world over were expressed in it, their longing for deliverance, their faith in the future." *(p. 21)*

Back in London, Philip goes to an art exhibition. (From Goldring's brief description it seems that the work on the show may be Vorticist, although Kandinsky's theories are mentioned.) But he is repelled by the sterility of both the works and the people he meets in the gallery. "Their minds were hard, arid, and it seemed to Philip that they had cut themselves off from the Life Force which alone can invigorate art, and that nothing they did could possibly matter because they had no spiritual roots." (p. 48)

Luckily for him, however, he meets a young woman called Anne Drummond who shares his view of the exhibition's worthlessness. Afterwards, over tea, she tells him that "'All this has nothing to do with life or anything that's real. These people have no religion and no politics – therefore, from my point of view, they don't exist. They are like figures painted on a stage back-cloth; there is nothing behind them!'" (p. 49). She then announces to Philip that a new world order is about to be born. "'The Revolution will come in Russia first,' she said, 'and from Russia it will spread to the rest of the world, in time. It will come to England last of all.'" (p. 54).

Who is she, Philip wonders. Anne obligingly tells him the history of her political education. At school she had made friends with a girl called Nancy O'Connell. (A nod in the direction of Nancy

Cunard and Daniel O'Connell perhaps? As we shall see, events in Ireland are part of Goldring's story, and Anne is as daringly unconventional as Nancy Cunard was by 1920 known to be.) Nancy's father is "vicar of a large parish in the London docks area". (Shades of Margaret Lambert). Concealing Nancy's true character from her parents, [Anne's father is also a vicar, but in rural Dorset] Anne had paid a long visit to the vicarage in Dockland, where her education in 'views' appeared to have been completed. During the weeks she had spent with Nancy she had made friends with enthusiastic young men at I.L.P. meetings, had assisted at the birth of a trade union of tailoresses and generally run amok as a suffragist, socialist and priestess of the internationale." (p. 54)

This opening section of the novel is set is 1913, and we gather that Anne is in her early twenties. She must therefore be recalling episodes in her life from 1908 or thereabouts. The suffragists were far more radical than their sister suffragettes and although mostly working-class they included among their numbers some who were of middle-class origins. But because they were representative of working-class interests, suffragists inevitably had much to do with the Trade Union movement and, faced with the indifference or plain hostility of the men, began their own unions.[27] As to the work of Dockland priests, this had been a feature of late 19th century and early 20th century Labour history. At the time of the 1889 Dock Strike the dockers, it is true, had found a champion in Cardinal Manning and an opponent in Temple, Bishop of London; but the East End Missions and the work of such radical priests as Stewart Headlam, Arnold Toynbee and Scott Holland meant that, as Henry Pelling notes, many Labour Churches were formed in the last years of the 19th century and "It is difficult at times to distinguish between their activities and those of the I.L.P., between the political and the religious, for they were closely connected."[28] In calling Anne's friend Nancy a "priestess of the internationale", Goldring may want his readers to understand that she enthusiastically identifies with the song composed by Eugéne Pottier for the Paris Commune in 1871 and adopted by French socialists early in the 20th century (and sung by other socialists), or that she attended or was in favour of the meetings of international socialists which women certainly did attend in the pre-war years, and to which they made important contributions.[29] Either way it doesn't much matter. All we need to recognise is that Anne Drummond represents energies and radical commitments that were emerging in women's movements before 1914.

Not surprisingly, Philip is much impressed by her. "He regarded politics as unclean and hideously tedious, was attracted by the little he knew of socialism, and was by temperament an internationalist." (p 59) He is even more impressed by Anne's readiness to smoke a cigarette and by the unabashed ardour of her love-making. (I put this as sympathetically as I can, although the scene in question, where "the sex instinct" is celebrated is both mawkishly conceived and very badly written.) Philip now becomes an ardent supporter of women's causes. When one of his women friends says that she wishes women were free, he tells her how much he agrees. "'Then men would be free too. As it is, women are forced to work off their subjection to the social ordinances of the opposite sex. That is why marriage is so often a joint servitude instead of an alliance of free souls.'" To which remark a male friend replies "'You've both been reading *Love's Coming Of Age* .... I can always detect traces of that pernicious work.'" (p.77) The significance of his words would not have been lost on readers in 1920, but they perhaps need explaining to readers of a later decade for whom *Love's Coming of Age* has not only ceased to be a radical work, but has ceased to be read at all.

Edward Carpenter's treatise had first been published in 1896. It was then made up of six papers: "The Sex passion", Man, the unknown", "Woman, the serf", "Woman in freedom", "Marriage: a retrospect", Marriage: a forecast – the free society", and a concluding paper on "the early star and sex worships." Other papers were added to the editions of 1906 and the sixth edition of 1909, and these were included in the Methuen pocket editions of 1914 and 1915. In having his characters refer to and more or less quote verbatim from *Love's Coming Of Age,* Goldring is not merely identifying an emergent element of immediate pre-war thought with which Carpenter's work was closely associated, he is also providing further evidence of Lawrence's importance to him and to others of his generation. For as Emile Delavenay shows in his *D.H. Lawrence and Edward Carpenter: A Study in Edwardian Transition,* Lawrence was deeply indebted to Carpenter's best-selling work. Although Delavenay oversteps the mark in trying to establish *The Rainbow* and *Women in Love* as fictional re-workings of Carpenter, he is right to argue for Lawrence's indebtedness to certain of Carpenter's arguments and even his adoption of the terms which point the arguments.[30] Such arguments continued to have potency in the years following the war. That was why Lawrence mattered so deeply to the generation which came of age in the 1920s, and it was why they still read Carpenter. (The 1923 edition of *Love's Coming Of Age* added new papers.)

This is not, however, to say that Philip and Anne are more aptly thought of as belonging to the later decade. Goldring is pretty good at establishing that they are of their moment. Even Anne's refusal to commit herself to Philip (unlike, say, Wells's Ann Veronica, that free spirit who ends in un-ironised married bondage) – even this is recognisably pre-war, and not just because Forster had made a heroine out of the unmarried mother, Helen Schlegel. The new woman as one free of the trammels of marriage was a fact of the time. Besides, in the pre-war period a growing number of young (middle-class) women rejected their parents' way of life. The quickest way out of Grantchester was usually via art school; but for obvious reasons politics also provided a passport to freedom. With the coming of war that was soon the preferred option. It is therefore plausible for Anne to spend the summer of 1915 with her parents in their rural Dorset parsonage before heading for the east end of London where she is to act as secretary to "the newly formed Workers' Peace Federation". And to return to the passage already quoted in Chapter 1, which indicates just how momentous her decision is: "when she got into the train for London and felt it moving along the platform, something told her that she would never see either home or her parents again. She had broken with the past, her childhood and girlhood were over and her work beginning." (pp. 124-5) In committing herself to radical work Anne necessarily moves from country to city. From living in the past to working for the future.

Neither in fact nor fiction was this popular work. During the war the Suffrage movement was as split as the Labour Party over the question of support for or opposition to the war effort; those who organised resistance to military conscription had a hard time of it, as Thomas Kennedy shows in his study of the No-Conscription Fellowship, *The Hound of Conscience*. Supporters of the movement were "insulted, hounded, hated, humiliated and imprisoned."[31] These things happen to Anne.

Meanwhile, Philip's own political awakening is under way. He begins to wonder whether the "U.D.C. people" might not be right about the war. (The Union of Democratic Control argued from and for an internationalist understanding of how the war had come about.) "How came it that England, of all countries, was in alliance with the infamous Tsardom, with a government which was one of the greatest iniquities of the modern world? Would it be possible to wage an honest, disinterested and noble war for the sacred cause of liberty, in conjunction with such a shameful ally?" (p. 130). Philip does not at this stage pretend to know the answer. But the reader of 1920 is of course in a position to provide it. And the abruptly introduced radical peer, Lord Midhurst, also knows the answer. He tells Philip that after the war "'the world will break itself up I suppose, and be fashioned anew. I shall see what my grandfather saw, but this time the revolution will be in Russia, in Germany – and perhaps in England. But certainly in Russia' .... 'And what do you think will happen in England?' Philip asked. 'I don't think we shall get off without something approaching class war,' the old man replied." (pp. 148-9).

Midhurst then goes on to tell Philip that he has just been reading "a little book which contains the gospel of an Irish revolutionary of 1848 on the subject of land nationalisation." He quotes from the book, which was, he tells Philip "written by an inspired but embittered hunchback named James Finton Lalor, for a paper called *The Irish Felon.*" The passage he quotes foresees world revolution; Midhurst concludes his reading by saying that "'I fancy that somewhere in Europe – if not in Ireland then in Russia – we may both live to see part of that prophecy fulfilled .... And history, on the whole, seems to be on the side of the people ...'" To which Philip replies that "The world is ripe for a new gospel.'" (pp. 150-151).

Shortly after this meeting Philip receives a commission from a Liberal newspaper to go out to France. His messages are severely censured but

> the things that he saw and heard, though he could not give utterance to them, remained engraved on his mind. When at last, at the time of the Russian revolution, he could bear his enforced passivity no longer, he came back to England with a fixed purpose. He would fight in the rank and file of the revolutionary army; take his stand with the 'objectors', and do his best to bring the orgy of murder to an end. *(p. 176)*

He goes to an anti-war meeting and discovers that Anne is on the platform. The meeting is broken up by the British Patriots' Union and Anne knocked to the floor. Philip rushes to her side, only to find her being helped to her feet by none other than Ivan Smirnoff. Anne recovers and the three of them leave, although not before Anne has told a police sergeant that "'When you men realise that you belong to the working classes and refuse to persecute your brothers and sisters, we may have a free England'" (p. 185), a remark bound to carry a certain frisson to readers in 1920, by which time there had been police strikes in London (in 1918, before the end of the war,) and in Liverpool (in 1919). The strikes had been called because of the government's refusal to allow policemen to join or form a union. The Liverpool strike led to rioting and the intervention of troops.[32]

Philip and Anne now resume their relationship, but Anne rebukes Philip both for his lack of commitment to the ideas he claims to believe in – "'you cultivate your fine feelings ... and play first with the idea of being a hermit, and then with that of being a new kind of husband'" (p194), and because he wants to turn their companionship into marriage as "a safeguard against me ever worshipping other gods but you. You have the possessive instinct! That's why you want a child. Another safeguard!'" (p. 195). Her deepest fear, however, is that "'Every male baby born this year will belong automatically to the 1937 class unless we exert ourselves to save them. If men and women don't want to waste their time bringing up cannon fodder for the profiteers to murder in the next war they'd better wake up *now*.'" (p. 194)

Anne speaks here for many of Goldring's readers, for whom the war to end wars had instead made further wars seem more inevitable. Will Dyson's hauntingly prescient cartoon, drawn at the time of the Versailles treaty, eloquently reveals the same fear. In this cartoon, published in *The Daily Herald*, the politicians who have carved up the world and determined Germany's crippling reparations are seen descending the steps of the famous railway carriage. As they do so, one of them says "Somewhere I hear a child crying." In the bottom left-hand corner of the cartoon a small baby sits forlorn, round its body a sash bearing the legend, "Class of '39".

*The Black Curtain* does not end in despair. Though Anne is dead – imprisoned for her part in yet another anti-war meeting, she dies in childbirth on November 11th 1918 – Smirnoff tells Philip to "'Remember that in Russia our victory is assured.'" Philip replies:

> "In England the changes will come, no doubt, but they will come slowly, imperceptibly. In twenty years time we shall recognise Lenin as a respectable figure for history books. In twenty years those who to-day are denounced as Bolsheviks

will be recognised as a political party with a chance, in some distant future, of realising a part of its programme. And we shall have much to do in the next twenty years to achieve even that result."

But Smirnoff rejects such gradualism. "'Even while we speak," he says to Philip, "'the Dawn is with us!'" "Night was defeated," the novel ends, "and the red Dawn – cold, terrible, relentless, but bearing with it the promise of the new day – was breaking at last over the desolate world. 'Come, my friend,' said Smirnoff, 'God himself has given you your answer! Let us rest now, for we must work.'" (p. 239-40).

*The Black Curtain* is no masterpiece but nor is it to be dismissed as a piece of woeful propagandising. Goldring pays careful attention to how his main characters, Philip and Anne, have come to be as they are: each is involved in matters of sexual and political radicalism whose origins can be traced to pre-war England but whose realisation has to wait for the post-war years. And he astutely recognises that although the anti-war movement regularly provoked violent opposition throughout the war and at its end, with the result that all the pacifist I.L.P. MPs were defeated in the 1918 general election, by 1920 a gathering revulsion against the war began to show itself in popular thinking and therefore in results at by-elections. Arthur Marwick notes that "As more and more people, in the years after 1918, began to see the whole war as a ghastly mistake, the men who at the time had suffered persecution for that same belief emerged as leaders of public opinion."[33] Ramsay MacDonald lost his seat in 1918. In 1924 he became Prime Minister of the first Labour Government. Moreover, against the cynical hedonism which, we are regularly assured, defines the 1920s, we need to set the "red Dawn", under whose skies Goldring connects events in Ireland and Russia as evidence of an approaching new day. As we shall see, his vision was far more widely shared than has customarily been allowed; and its generous hopes both offset and, I would say, provide a necessary criticism of the Bright Young Things, who saw nothing to be done. Only later would Goldring come to feel that what he had imagined as a new dawn was in fact a false light in the east.

There is a further point. Goldring's vision might not have been generally endorsed by an older generation, but among them were at least two novelists whose best-sellers of the immediate post-war years add substance to it and with which it needs to be contrasted. The first of these, A.S.M. Hutchinson's *If Winter Comes*, appeared in August 1921. By June of the following year it had gone through no fewer than twenty-nine printings, and although after that the frequency of reprints slowed, it remained one of the most widely-read novels of the decade. It is not hard to understand why. *If Winter Comes* is a love story which touches on any number of political and social issues; and while its Galsworthy-like appeasement of those who at one time seem to be the correctly identified villains undoubtedly suggests Hutchinson's desperate desire to face all ways, there is by the end of the novel a sense that the new day dawning may be anticipated with confidence, even with eagerness.

Like Goldring, Hutchinson begins his story in the years before the war and ends it in war's immediate aftermath. And as Goldring sees pre-war England harbouring seeds of future discontent and therefore of eruptive change beneath the nation's smug or "safe" surface, so Hutchinson tries to offer a disenchanted account of the period before 1914. Neither novelist, that is, adopts a reading of the fall from innocence into experience which, as I have already pointed out, has regularly (dis) formed English ways of thinking about pre-war England and may even seem (or be held) to define them.

The protagonist of *If Winter Comes,* Mark Sabre, whose name perhaps suggests his antiquated, chivalric outlook on life, is trapped in a loveless marriage to "the Dean of Tidborough's only daughter," Mabel. Mabel has no curiosity about anyone who is not of her class and she is particularly indifferent to the lives of working-class people. "It never occurred to her that any of these people had homes, and it never occurred to her that the whole of the lower class lived without any margin at all beyond keeping their homes together, or that if they stopped working they lost their homes .... The only fact she knew about the lower classes was that they were disgustingly extravagant and spent every penny they earned." (Bk 1 ch. 4) Mabel is presented as an entirely unsympathetic character. That she does not share her husband's bedroom is not therefore to be read as a sign of her political emancipation. Hutchinson may intend us to see in Mabel's decision to deny Mark her body a hint of that pre-war sexual emancipation which, so Paul Thompson notes, included for many women the right to introduce into conventional marriage "freedom of bargaining to the best advantage." Thompson refers to "The most advanced new marriage manuals, such as Maud Braby's *Modern Marriage and How to Bear It*" as encouraging trial mar-

riages, wild oats for women, toleration of infidelity and "the deliberate fostering of male friendships for married women."[35] But
Mabel is simply indifferent to her husband, although it has to be
added that this is as nothing compared with her author's loathing
of her.

Mark, on the other hand, is puzzle-headed, quizzical; and he is
uncomfortably aware that all is not well with England. The junior
partner in a firm of "Ecclesiastical and Scholastic Furnishers and
Designers", he undertakes to commission and publish for the firm a
series of textbooks for use in schools, and himself writes the one on
history. We are told that this is scorned by the public schools but
much favoured by "lesser" schools. Mark then decides to write an
account of "England", and in the early summer of 1912 he sets to
work. "Kings were to enter this history but incidentally, as kings have
in fact been but incidental to England's history. It was to be just
'England'; the England of the English people". Sabre's "England" is,
then, the England of what Rudyard Kipling had in 1910 called the
nation of the "mere uncounted folk". (In the poem which introduces
*Rewards and Fairies*.) The opening sentences of Sabre's Book, we are
informed, tell its readers that "This England is *yours*. It belongs to
*you*. Many enemies have desired to take it because it is the most glorious and splendid country in the world. But they have never taken
it because it is *yours* and has been kept for *you*." "You" are of course
the English people and "you" will guarantee that "England will continue. Your England. *Yours*". (Bk I., ch. 6 iv)

The hectic note of this belongs authentically to pre-war England;
but its appeal in post-war England was bound to be strong because
it assuaged the feelings of deep distrust about whether "your
England" had in fact survived the war. At the same time it insists on
the survival of the kind of "single nation" version of England which
in the immediate post-war years might well have been thought to be
under threat from the "Red Dawn" as well as from the obvious signs
of discontent, anger and class schism which show themselves in the
many strikes and other evidence of working-class militancy in those
years. In other words, Hutchinson's novel is calculated to draw on
and minister to fears which, while they undoubtedly existed before
the war, were that much more credible after it. Such fears were
bound to include male fears of what women's new-found freedom
might mean: hence, the (betraying) presentation of Mabel.

Mabel is contrasted to Nona, the upper-class love of Mark's life
who is, however, married to Lord Tybar, "debonair and attractive of

countenance to a degree" (Bk 2 Ch I iv). We later learn that in his role as landlord Tybar turns out of his house one of Sabre's fellow workers, Twyning. Twyning tells Sabre, "'The lease is out and the whole damned house and everything I've put in to it goes to one of these lordlings – this Lord Tybar – just because one of his ancestors, who'd never even dreamt of the house, pinched the land it stands on from the public common and started to pocket ground rent.'" (Bk 2, ch. 2, ii). Still later, we are given additional evidence of the unfeeling corruption of those who "own" England, when Mabel's friend, the fashionable clergyman Mr Boom Bagshaw, announces his plans for a Garden Home, where "'We shall have no poor .... No ugly streets. No mean surroundings.'" When Mark protests at this, Boom Bagshaw replies that "'if people thought a little less about their duty towards the poor and a little more about their duty towards themselves, they would be in a great deal fitter state to help their fellow creatures, rich or poor." (Bk 2, ch. 2 viiii).

This part of the novel is competently handled. Boom Bagshaw's remarks might seem strictly incredible, but after all the pre-war years were ones where, as Paul Thompson notes, "the open display of wealth was an essential element in the upper-class style of life. Wealth, birth and manners constituted the three prime qualifications for commanding obedience and respect from others."[36] These certainly influence Sabre, the puzzle-headed Englishman. When Twyning bursts out with loathing at a certain baronet's having left in a will, "a million and three-quarters," Sabre rejoins that the man must have earned it.

> 'Earned it. *Earned it!* I tell you who earned it. His employees earned it. That's who earned it. Not Sir James Cotton-Spinner Money-Spinner Coates, Bart.'
> At once Sabre stiffened for capitalism. 'Well, he paid his employees for earning it, didn't he?'
> 'Paid them! What did he pay them? Are any of them going to leave a million and three-quarters do you suppose?'
> Violence, venom, hatred was in Twyning's voice and appeared in spittle at the corners of his mouth; and the venom disgusted Sabre, and the horrible spittle disgusted him and made him loathe the class of mind that had such venom and such habits." *(Bk 3 ch. I. vi).*

A little later Sabre says of the suffragettes that he detests their methods, thinks they're monstrous and indefensible, but that "their horrible ways are bringing the vote a jolly sight nearer than it's ever been before." (Bk 2. ch. 2. iii). Sabre, in short, is offered as a typical middle-of-the-way Englishman in all his vulnerability, his liberal decencies and limitations. Although Hutchinson's novel is never mentioned in George Dangerfield's *The Strange Death of Liberal England* (1935), Hutchinson's protagonist represents exactly those qualities whose "extinction" Dangerfield's book eloquently studies. Mark even seems to be the embodiment of grievously limited common sense in his reaction to the Irish crisis of July, 1914:

> Austria, and then Germany, made a not bad attempt on public attention by raking up some forgotten sensation over a stale excitement at a place called Sarajevo; but on the 26th, Ireland magnificently filled the bill again by the far more serious affair of Nationalist Volunteers landing 3,000 rifles and marching with them into Dublin. Troops fired on the mob, and the House of Commons gave itself over to a most exciting debate on the business .... It was delicious. *(Bk 3, i)*.

In fact, *The Times's* leading article for July 27th, 1914, was headed "Grave News From Ireland," and began: "The grave news which we publish this morning from the European capitals is accompanied, we are sorry to say, by very serious intelligence from Ireland". It ended by predicting the probability of civil war.[37] Nevertheless, Sabre's light-hearted response to the crisis seems perfectly proper so long as he is presented as a character who, however, sympathetically conceived, is revealed in all his puzzle-headed limitations.

Unfortunately, Hutchinson throws his subject away. With the onset of war Sabre becomes a character to take on trust: his point of view now carries authorial approval. We are told that his history of England "had arisen out of his passionate love for all that England had meant to him," that in all Shakespeare "no passage had moved him in quite the same way, whenever he recalled it, as Richard II's 'Dear earth, I do salute thee with my hand,'" and that despite weak health he wants nothing so much as to volunteer for the army. Given Sabre's cast of mind this is plausible, as is his emotional recitation to Nona of John O'Gaunt's speech, and her reciting to him Rupert Brooke's "If I should die." (Mark is seeing more of her now that her husband has inevitably gone off to war, where he will gain the V.C. and later be killed in action.). What *isn't* plausible is that after the war Sabre should have no qualms about the war's conduct, nor about the motives of those who prolonged it; nor that in 1919, when the novel ends, he should have nothing to say about Ireland, nor about events elsewhere, Russia especially. True, he is ill, but then Nona, whom he is shortly to marry — some complicated plotting has seen Mabel divorce him for supposedly fathering a child on another woman — tells him that "'England, your England that you loved so, [is] at peace, victorious; those dark years done. England her own again. Your dear England, Marko." (Bk 4, ch. 8 ii). She adds that he will now be able to resume the writing of his book on England. No, he tells her, it cannot be, he is too ill. But we know that he'll recover and will write the book.

In a sense, Hutchinson's novel is Sabre's book. An account of England which attempts to say something about splits and divisions ends up by endorsing an entirely soft-focus account of a united nation. "The dark years done." It may be excusable for Nona to think that – although as we have seen, D. H. Lawrence would have been quick to deny her optimism – but it isn't excusable for a novelist writing in 1920/21 to allow the remark to stand unopposed, unless we are intended to read it ironically, and there is nothing in the novel's concluding pages to encourage such a reading. These pages are nevertheless unintendedly ironic. Events of the immediate post-war years made plain that, Red Dawn or no, the day dawning was a great deal bleaker than the novel will admit for millions of those men and women whom Sabre the historian-cum-liberal politician addresses as the mere uncounted possessors of England. On the other hand, it is easy to see why the consoling note on which Hutchinson's novel ends should have found favour with so many readers. Even Ireland is cancelled; the "troubles" wiped clean from the closing pages.

This may be why C. E. Montague's *Disenchantment* also established itself as a best-seller soon after its publication in 1922. Montague's novel was probably the first to offer a critical account of the conduct of war: of the bland pieties of the church, of the lying and distortions of the press, of the shortcomings of the military topbrass. (For which, very like Goldring, he blamed the public-school ethos, with its "gallant, robust contempt for 'swats' and for all who invented new means to new ends and who trained and used their brains with a will.") But despite the novel's scorn for those who gloried in and profited from the war, and for all its rejection of what is called "'the hero stunt, the sob story, all the darling liqueurs of war emotionalism, war vanity, war rant and cant of every kind", Montague does not identify with Goldring's militant socialism. He detested the "failure to be merciful" of the victors, and was rightly contemptuous of those especially clamorous champions of the policy that Germany Should Pay who had fought their war battles exclusively on the home front. But *Disenchantment* opts for a kind of quietism, a belief that somehow – but how? – domestic virtues can make their way in the post-war world, can even embody a model of the social value of reconciliation which, more than anything else, Montague appears to have believed was the only hope. And in this very English way, his fiction connects with the work of other writers, especially perhaps women. As C. J. Fox has noted, Montague was a strangely contradictory figure: "Though the chief ideologue of a famous Radical paper [Montague had a key post at the *Manchester Guardian*], he was in many ways a Tory, suspicious of reformist abstraction. Love of humanity he considered a rarefied emotion starved of the direct sensuous vision that fosters love of family; and country."[38]

It seems appropriate, then, to note that Yeats's famous remark, "The best lack all conviction while the worst/Are full of passionate intensity", appeared at precisely this time and that for an older generation the immediate post-war years were inevitably years of bewilderment, or of lack of conviction. Hutchinson and Montague were older than Goldring. Indeed, Montague, born in 1867, was only two years younger than Yeats, and looking back to his youth Yeats described himself in his *Autobiographies* as having been "in all things pre-Raphaelite". The transition to the world of wrecked post-war Europe was bound to be traumatising; and I do not wonder at Montague's desire to turn against the passionate intensity of those he would have been entitled to regard as "the worst."

But the belief that *therefore* the best should lack conviction seems to me deeply debilitating. It makes possible the all too commonly respectful account of much satiric writing of the decade whose pose of languid indifference has customarily been taken as a mark of disenchanted sophistication, whereas what it actually betrays is a disabling triviality. This is emphatically not the case with Evelyn Waugh's early novels, but it is the case with, for example, Aldous Huxley's and with William Gerhardie's *Polyglots* (1925). In his introduction to the re-print of Gerhardie's novel, Michael Holroyd remarks that "Beneath the compulsory conviviality of wartime party-going runs a current of melancholy, and this, together with many farcical episodes and philosophical speculations, is interwoven with a number of powerful anti-war passages."[39]

Here is one such passage. The protagonist, whose name is Captain Georges Hamlet Alexander Diabologh, is at this point railing against those "particularly women, and more particularly old women", who glorify war.

> 'I remember', I continued, 'an hotel in Brighton where I stayed two weeks before joining up in the so-called Great War. The inevitable old ladies with their pussy cats were by far the worst of all. They talked in terms of blood. They demanded the extermination of the whole of the German race; nothing less, they said, would satisfy them. They longed to behead all German babies with their own hands for the genuine pleasure, they said, that this would give them. They were not human babies, they argued, but vermin. It was a service they desired to render to their country and the human race at large. They had a right to demonstrate their patriotism. I was not a little shocked, I must confess, at this tardy display of Herodism in old, decaying women. I told them as much, and they called me pro-German. They discovered unpleasant possibilities in my name that had slipped their attention heretofore – a serious oversight. A danger to the realm.[40]

Powerful? The tone of would-be comic disdain is struck by many young writers-as-satirists of the 1920s. It's easy to imagine Diabologh's words in the mouth of one of Noel Coward's world-weary matinée sophisticates. But Diabologh obviously isn't the slightest shocked by what he recounts. It's all terribly or frightfully amusing. It is also a far cry from Kipling's great story, "Mary Postgate", where an English lady companion watches a German airman, whose plane has crashed into her garden, gradually die. "Again the head groaned for the doctor. 'Stop that!' said Mary, and stamped her foot. 'Stop that, you bloody pagan!'" [41] Kipling here provides a truly shocking insight into the black hatred and feral energies which did much to promote and keep alive war. Such hatreds, such energies, were hidden behind the public mask of civilized western society, of the England for whom the young should gladly consent to die. It was from the appalled recognition of this that some, at least, of the younger generation turned. Hence, the urgent note of *The Black Curtain* and its rejection of those temporising visions of England to which Hutchinson and Montague subscribe, although neither endorses the glib reading of an untroubled nation set out in *Mr Prohack*, nor the studied vacuity of Gerhardie's novel.

*The Polyglots* typifies a kind of satire peculiar to the 1920s. Such satire does not proceed from savage indignation. Rather, in a weary manner it rejoices in its own acceptance of having seen through the hollowness of post-war, "modern" life. There is, it suggests, no alternative but to accept an invitation to Trimalchio's feast. And this is the version of the 1920s we are so frequently sold as the definitive account, "as though life at that time was all parties and holidays"[42] while people waited for the end. But for others, equally young, there *were* alternatives. *The Black Curtain* suggests as much. Here, however, I need to make a final point. Goldring and his protagonist were both mature men by the time the Great War began. Others came to maturity as it dragged on. Among them was Alick West. West is representative of numbers of men and women whose histories have been written out of the standard accounts of the 1920s but whose considered turning against their fathers is of far greater significance than Betjeman's rudeness – all of that tie-twanging and mossy teeth – or Waugh's casual insolence.

West sat out the war in Germany, where he was trapped as a student in August, 1914. With the coming of the Armistice he was free to return to his well-heeled home and to a father waiting for him to decide how he would map out his life.

> At last, one evening early in January, 1919, when I had been at home rather more than a month, my father said to me, 'Well, my dear lad, what are you going to do with your life?' I said again that I wanted to write. 'What will you live on? he asked me. I said that I could manage on the money my mother had left me, and that I ought to be able to make a little more by writing. There was no reason, my father said, why I shouldn't write; but wouldn't it be wise to have a second string to my bow .... There was nothing like having a good University degree behind me, so why not go to Oxford?[43]

West writes with some restraint in his autobiography about the growing tensions between himself and his father; but his widow told me that in fact it was far more fraught than the published version implies. He was threatened with being thrown out of the family house if he wouldn't do his father's bidding. He eventually compromised by agreeing to go to Trinity College, Dublin, but from then on West would steer towards the rejection of those values his father stood for and which he expected his son to adopt. By the end of the decade he had become a Marxist. In the early 30s he joined the Communist party.

West's journey from upper-middle-class cushioned incuriosity to first a cultural then political awakening, was in large part followed by two contemporaries of his who at that time did not know of each other's existence, although later they became close friends. Douglas Garman came of wealthy parents: his sister Mary would marry Roy Cambell and be added to the list of Vita Sackville-West's many lovers. At the end of the war Garman was called to the house of his favourite grandfather, keeper of the family's fortune. The best port was sent for and the young man asked how, being now of age, he proposed to spend his life. There were apparently three alternatives: the law, the church or government. Garman said he wanted to be a writer. "Yes, yes," his grandfather said. "But what are you going to *do*?" Be a writer, Garman repeated. The port was sent away and Garman was told that if he persisted with so foolhardy a scheme he would be cut off without a penny. As the young man had money of his own – some of which he would use to help fund *The Calendar of Modern Letters* – his grandfather's act was far from coming as a decisive blow. But it did mean that from then he would be estranged from the family elders. Garman was soon active in radical politics and like West he would find his way into the Communist Party in the 1930s.

Then there is the example of George Thomson. At the end of the war the man who would become one of the greatest classical scholar of his generation was in his final year at Dulwich College. By day he drilled with the O.T.C. But at night, unkown to his parents, he changed into the uniform of the Gaelic Youth League and trained with the local cell.[44] After a glittering undergraduate career at Trinity College, Thomson turned down the chance of a fellowship in order to take up a post as a classical lecturer at Galway College. There he immersed himself in radical Irish politics as well as translating the whole of Aeschylus into Irish.

Such stories could be multiplied. There is for example Patrick Hamilton's rejection of *his* domineering father, both as writer and as political *savant*. Hamilton senior was an incompetent historical novelist as well as a dyed-in-the-wool tory. Hamilton junior was to become one of the finest novelists of his generation, his radical fictional methods expressive of his developing political radicalism. Like the others mentioned here, Patrick Hamilton would choose to join the Communist Party.[45] This is not to suggest that in the years immediately after the war English middle-class youths were typically transformed into political radicals. But for many who wanted to be writers, the seeds of their future radicalism were dropped into ground unwittingly prepared by an older generation; and these young writers and intellectuals, who did not accept the account of their time offered by the Gerhardie-ites, define a very different 1920s from the one with which we are familiar. The men whose early careers I have sketched were prompted by concerns which led ineluctably to political engagement and therefore and inextricably and *in all senses* to a recognition of the need for radical forms of art. To be a writer was, for each of them, to be radical: the two terms become virtual synonyms.

Aldous Huxley spoke for them all, perhaps, when he told his father that *Antic Hay* "was written by a member of what I call the war generation for others of his kind & ... it is intended to reflect – fantastically of course, but none the less faithfully – the life and opinions of an age which has seen the violent disruption of almost all the standards, conventions and values current in the previous epoch." I am not persuaded that Huxley is a particularly important writer of the period, but these words bear clear testimony to a new spirit of revolt among the young and the reasons for it. For those who tried to maintain there had been no such "violent disruption", the young would be likely to nurture a special contempt. Hence, I imagine, such rebelliousness as characterises the schoolboy and undergraduate careers of Edward Upward and Christopher Isherwood, both of whom were eager to reject their upbringing and, in particular, the class snobbishness of their mothers.[46] But it was not just sons who were turning against their parents' generation. Goldring's Anne Drummond is far more representative of a new kind of woman than Hutchinson's Nona. And while Mabel Sabre undoubtedly represents qualities of an older generation of women of whom Mrs Isherwood was a type, in the post-war period that type was to have a hard time of it, with daughters as well as with sons.

## Notes on Chapter 2

1.  S. Freud, "Transience" in *The Penguin Freud Library 14,* ed. A. Dickson, London, 1985, pp. 289-90.
2.  J. Willet, *The Weimar Years: A Culture Cut Short,* London, Thames and Hudson,

1984, p. 9.

3. Quoted by John Ferguson in *The Arts In Britain In World War One*, London, Staines and Sell, 1980, p. 105.

4. *The Letters Of Ivor Gurney*, ed. R.K.R. Thornton, Manchester, Carcanet, 1991, p. 348 and pp. 353-4.

5. For information about such mutinies, see *inter alia*, G.D.H. Cole & R. Postgate, *The Common People* 1746-1946, London, Methuen, 1946, pp. 546-548 and F.W. Becket and Keith Simpson (eds) *A Nation in Arms : A Social Study of the British Army in the First World War*, Manchester, Manchester University Press, 1985, esp. pp. 226-229.

6. George Orwell, *Collected Essays, Journalism and Letters*, Vol 1, 1920-40, Harmondsworth, Penguin, 1970, p. 555.

7. Wyndham Lewis, *Blasting And Bombardiering*, London, Calder and Boyers, 1967, p. 185. (The book was first published in 1935).

8. H. Hayens, *Play Up Queens*, London, Collins, 1920.

9. Ernest Raymond, *Tell England*. In *The Return To Camelot: Chivalry and the English Gentleman*, London, 1981, Yale, Mark Girouard draws attention to a number of plans for war memorials and church memorial windows which celebrated "knights in armour": of these, perhaps the most astonishing is Adrian Jones's memorial to the Cavalry of Empire, in Hyde Park. (See Girouard pp. 291-293).

10. D. Goldring, *The Nineteen-Twenties*, London, Nicholson and Watson, 1945, p. 23.

11. Douglas Jerrold, *Georgian Adventure*, London, The 'Right' Book Club, first published 1937, 1938, pp. 227-8.

12. A.C. Ward, *The Nineteen-Twenties*, London, Methuen, 1930, pp. 6-7.

13. Raphael Samuel in *Theatres Of The Left* eds. Samuel, MacColl and Cosgrove, London, Pluto, 1985, pp. 24-5, and Andrew Davies, *Other Theatres: The Development of Alternative and Experimental Theatre in Britain*, London, Routledge, 1987, pp. 99-100.

14. A.C. Ward, op. cit. pp. 6-7.

15. Ivor Gurney, *Collected Poems*, ed. P. J. Kavanagh, London, O.U.P., 1982, p. 141.

16. Douglas Goldring, *The Nineteen-Twenties*, op. cit., p. 24.

17. Goldring, *Reputations*, London, Chapman and Hall, pp. 103-4.

18. E.M. Forster, "Me, Them and You," in *Abinger Harvest*, London Edward and Arnold, 1936, pp. 27-30.

19. George Lansbury had created the *Daily Herald* in 1912. During the war it became a weekly newspaper but with the coming of peace it reverted to daily publication and soon established itself as a mass-circulation newspaper of the left, for which many intellectuals wrote on both political and literary and artistic matters. According to C.L. Mowat, its circulation by 1920 was 333,000, although an advertising boycott caused financial problems. But by the early 30s only *The Daily Express* sold more copies. See C.L. Mowat *Britain Between The Wars, 1918-1940*, London, Methuen, 1968, (1st edn. 1955) pp. 20 & 245.

20. Goldring, *The Nineteen-Twenties*, p. 66. In his autobiography, *Odd Man Out: The Autobiography of a "Propaganda" Novelist*, London, Chapman and Hall, 1935, Goldring makes plain his detestation of the war and his conviction that "my job as a man of letters [was] to plunge into the fray on the side of peace..." p. 254.

21. *Reputations*, pp. 71 and 75.

22. Douglas Goldring, *The Black Curtain*, London, 1920, p. 63. Future references to the novel will be identified by page references after the quotations.

23. Raphael Samuel, *Theatres of the Left* op. cit. pp. 23-6. Samuel's excellent account of the project is essential to an understanding of socialist energies as they sought direction and focus in the post-war years.

24. D.H. Lawrence, *Phoenix 2: Uncollected, Unpublished And Other Prose, Writings,* eds. Warren Roberts and Harry T. Moore, London, Heinemann, 1968, pp. 289-291.

25. For a full account of these events see Henry Pelling, *A History Of British Trade Unionism,* Harmondsworth, Penguin, 1963, esp pp. 162-5.

26. *Phoenix* 2, op. cit. p 291. The play itself was written before the 1919 strike, when Lawrence was living in Ripley, and was presumably prompted by what he observed there. Goldring heard about the play in 1919 and wrote to Lawrence, offering to produce it. For this and other details of the relationship between Lawrence and Golding at this moment, see Mark Kinkaid-Weekes's biography of Lawrence.

27. More of this is to be found in Jill Liddington and Jill Norris, *One Hand Tied Behind Us: The Rise of The Women's Suffrage Movement,* London, Virago, 1978.

28. Henry Pelling, *The Origins of the Labour Party,* London, MacMillan, 1954, p. 142.

29. Such meetings are easy to confuse with congresses of Anarchist Internationals, for both included women – sometimes the same women. For this, see George Woodcock, *Anarchism,* Harmondsworth, Penguin, 1963.

30. Emile Delevany, *D.H. Lawrence and Edward Carpenter: A Study in Edwardian Transition,* Heinemann, London, 1971, esp. pp. 99-110.

31. Thomas C. Kennedy, *The Hound of Conscience: A History of the Non Conscription Fellowship,* 1914-1919, Fayetteville, U.S.A., 1986, p. 286.

32. For this see Henry Pelling, *A History of British Trade Unionism,* op. cit. p. 61.

33. Arthur Marwick, *The Deluge: British Society and The First World War,* Harmondsworth, Penguin, 1967, p. 87.

34. A.S.M. Hutchinson, *If Winter Comes,* London, Hodder and Stoughton, 1921. All future references will be by book and chapter nos.

35. Paul Thompson, *The Edwardians: The Remaking of British Society,* London, Paladin, p. 243.

36. Ibid. p. 21.

37. *Documents From Edwardian England,* (ed. Donald Read), London, Harrap, p. 318. Read's *Edwardian England, 1901-15, Society and Politics,* includes a useful chapter, "Irish Home Rule," on the Irish crisis from an English point of view. London, Harrap, 1972.

38. C.J. Fox, "Reaching for Heaven: The Legacy of C. E. Montague," *London Magazine,* April/May,1991, pp. 94-106.

39. William Gerhardie, *The Polyglots* (originally published 1925), preface by Michael Holyroyd, Oxford, O.U.P., 1987, p. x.

40. Ibid. pp. 24-5.

41. "Mary Postgate" was written in 1915 and published in *A Diversity of Creatures,* 1917.

42. David Craig and Michael Egan, "Decadence and the The Crack-Up: Literature and Society in the Twenties and Thirties," in *The Radical Reader,* eds. S. Knight and M. Wilding, Sydney, Wild and Woolley, 1977, p. 11.

43. Alick West, *One Man in his Time: A Personal Story of This Revolutionary Century,* London, Allen and Unwin,1969, p. 51.

44. For information about both Garman and Thomson I am indebted to the reminiscences of their widows.

45. There will be more to say about Patrick Hamilton in a later chapter. I might also note here the transformation of Montagu Slater from his early years at Millom and education at Oxford to the radicalising experiences of work as a cub-reporter in Liverpool in the early 1920s. And Hubert Nicholson's *Half My Days And Nights: A Memoir of the 1920s,* London, Autolycus, 1982 (first published 1941) is a fascinating account of the radicalising of a journalist and writer from Hull, "striving to be a witness to my times."

46. For this see Katherine Bucknall's introduction to Christopher Isherwood & Edward Upward: *The Mortmere Stories,* London, Enitharmon Press, 1994, esp. pp. 10, 11, and 17.

CHAPTER THREE

# WOMEN AFTER THE WAR:
# THE FAMILIAL and THE FERAL

That the events and consequences of 1914-18 included radical changes to women's lives is a truth long established. In the immediate post-war years women over thirty were for the first time able to vote. By the end of the decade all women over the age of 21 were enfranchised. Many women who had found new freedoms during the war years, often by becoming wage earners, refused to give up those freedoms. New modes of dress, of hair-style, new modes of behaviour, of smoking in public, of going unchaperoned to dances and parties: these were among the outward signs of a change which between them suggested the possibility of further changes, still greater freedoms.[1] There was, for example, Marie Stopes' *Married Love* (1922) and the first birth-control clinics; there was the marketing of the disposable sanitary napkin, which Alison Light suggests "was in its own way as powerful an event as increasing female education or shifts in the employment market."[2]

There is one important qualification. Most of these changes, these new freedoms, applied to women in the broad range of the middle class. This chapter is therefore much more concerned with them than it is with working-class women, whose lives were on the whole circumscribed in ways that war had not greatly altered. Working-class women appear to have shown no great initial enthusiasm for their newly-won enfranchisement and many seem not to have used the votes to which they were entitled. To say this is to *not* to ignore or underestimate the energies of significant numbers of working-class women in their efforts to change their own lives and the lives of those like them; it is simply to say that these efforts spent themselves for the most part in forms that lie outside my discussion.[3] Here, it is relevant to note that in 1930 Virginia Woolf was asked to provide an introduction to a collection of memoirs put together by

69

members of the Women's Co-operative Guild, and published as *Life As We Have Known It: By Co-operative Working Women*. Woolf's "Introductory Letter to Margaret Llewelyn Davies", who edited the memoirs into book form, is a tactful, astutely phrased admission of the gulf that separates her from the women whose writings make up the book itself. She begins by recalling an occasion in 1913 when she had attended a meeting of the Guild and had been made to realise that she was "a benevolent spectator. I [was] irretrievably cut off from the actors. I [sat there] hypocritically clapping and stamping, an outcast from the flock." Seventeen years later, and despite the vote, she admits she still knows little of the kind of women whose lives are described in *Life As We Have Known It*. "These voices are beginning only now to emerge from silence into half articulate speech. These lives are still half hidden in profound obscurity. To express even what is expressed here has been the work of labour and difficulty."[4]

I have no wish to follow up whatever class assumptions lurk within the phrases "half articulate", "half hidden", "even what is expressed here". I want merely to remark that as far as I am aware there is in the post-war decade very little published writing by working-class women, whereas in the same decade a mass of radical writing by middle-class women begins to appear.

## II

First, though, I need to discuss some writing about women by men. This may seem perverse until we recognise that a number of key writings by women during the period are in part at least a form of response or even resistance to men's writing. But then the writing by men I have in mind is itself an implicit or even explicit response or resistance to that sensed change in women's roles and expectations which the war years did so much to initiate. A glance at Arnold Bennett's work will help to make the point. Before the war Bennett had written a number of novels intensely sympathetic to women locked into loveless or sexually frustrating marriages. Of these, *Leonora* (1903) and *Whom God Hath Joined* (1906) are of most value. The latter in particular is a very impressive study of a painful divorce. Yet by the time of *The Lion's Share* (1916) Bennett had begun to treat women's issues – here focused on suffragism – in exactly the same would-be genial but reductive and eventually dismissive comic spirit that Wells had adopted in

*Ann Veronica*. Men may plead for women but women may not fight for themselves.

After the war Bennett and Wells were regarded as back numbers by younger writers, men and women both. Their "realism" was as out of date as their views of women. And certainly a crucial feature of novels of the 1920s is their abandonment of realism for fantasy and other non-realistic modes, a matter to which I shall return. Yet for all that the technique of the younger male writers might be self-consciously *avant-garde,* and as such imply a rejection of novelists of the pre-war generation, few if any were at ease with new women. A deep anxiety underlies or is to be found within much writing by men during this period, and one of the ways it shows is in the depiction of women gone feral. In this context, the title poem of Charlotte Mew's *The Farmer's Bride* (1916), has an especial significance.

It is difficult to know just how widely the volume was read but there is no doubt that *The Farmer's Bride* made a considerable impact on those who did read it. Hardy was a great admirer. He described Mew as "far and away the best living woman poet – who will be read when others have been forgotten", and asked her up to visit him at Max Gate. Other admirers included Hugh Walpole, Robert Bridges, and Lady Ottoline Morell, who predictably invited Mew to Garsington; Virginia Woolf wrote in 1920 that she found *The Farmer's Bride* "very good and interesting and unlike anyone else."[5] It seems unlikely that anyone moving in literary circles would have remained unaware of Mew, especially as the 1916 volume was re-printed with eleven additional poems in 1921. (There would be a further edition in 1929, a year after she killed herself.)

The title poem is a monologue spoken by the farmer.

> Three summers since I chose a maid,
> Too young maybe – but more's to do
> At harvest-time than bide and woo.
>     When us was wed she turned afraid
> Of love and me and all things human;
> Like the shut of a winter's day.
> Her smile went out, and 'twasn't a woman –
>     More like a little frightened fay.
>         One night, in the Fall, she runned away.
>
> "Out 'mong the sheep, her be," they said,
> Should properly have been abed;
> But sure enough she wasn't there
> Lying awake with her wide brown stare.

So over seven-acre field and up-along across the down
    We chased her, flying like a hare
    Before our lanterns. To Church-Town
        All in a shiver and a scare
    We caught her, fetched her home at last
        And turned the key upon her, fast.

    She does the work about the house
    As well as most, but like a mouse:
        Happy enough to chat and play
        With birds and rabbits and such as they,
    So long as men-folk keep away.
    "Not near, not near! her eyes beseech
    When one of us comes within reach.
        The women say that beasts in stall
        Look round like children at her call.
        *I've* hardly hear her speak at all.

    Shy as a leveret, swift as he,
    Straight and slight as a young larch tree,
    Sweet as the first wild violets, she,
    To her wild self. But what to me?
    The short days shorten and the oaks are brown,
        The blue smoke rises to the low grey sky,
    One leaf in the still air falls slowly down,
        A magpie's spotted feathers lie
    On the black earth spread white with rime,
    The berries redden up to Christmas-time.
        What's Christmas-time without there be
        Some other in the house than we!

        She sleeps up in the attic there
        Alone, poor maid. 'Tis but a stair
    Betwixt us. Oh! my God! the down,
    The soft young down of her, the brown
The brown of her – her eyes, her hair, her hair!

It's possible that "The Nuptials of Attila" is somewhere behind "The Farmer's Bride", although Meredith's poem is a far more violent treatment of a woman who goes mad and murders her husband on their wedding night. When soldiers break in the following morning they find her "humped and grinning like a cat,/Teeth for lips ... [combing] her hair with quiet paws." In "The Farmer's Bride" the young wife flees from her husband's sexual demands and is described in a way that identifies her not with a wild cat but with a hunted animal: a leveret in her shyness, her fears, and her "soft, young down." The poem may also owe something to John Masefield and, after him, the Dymock poets. It was Masefield who early in the century brought back into English poetry the use of idiomatic speech, and although the date of Mew's poem cannot be decided, it was probably written sometime between 1900-1914, by which time the Dymock circle had established itself.[5a] But to mention possible debts is in no sense to play down the originality of this remarkable poem, its uncovering of the woe that is in marriage, and its revelation of a woman escaping from sexual bondage, no matter how kindly that may be meant, into a wilderness that has at its heart an implacable rejection of men. The poem turns on its head the jovial convention by which the farmer takes a bride and at once seals a marriage and social relations that affirm stability.

As Val Warner notes, mental illness is a theme which recurs throughout *The Farmer's Bride*. Mew's sister Freda and brother Henry (died 1901) both became incurably insane and were committed to institutions, and Mew's own suicide – she killed herself by drinking half a bottle of lysol – followed her voluntary entry into a nursing home for neurasthenia.[6] If we add that there is good evidence for believing Mew to have been deeply in love with and rejected by the novelist May Sinclair, it becomes clear that hers was a tragic life. And it is of course possible to read her poems in the light of that tragedy. Yet "The Farmer's Bride" also seems to set in a train a number of works in which women become feral creatures. It may be no more than one of those weird accidents of history that Mary Webb's *Gone to Earth*, published in 1917, has as heroine a girl who bears a close resemblance to Mew's Farmer's Bride. Yet the coincidences are notable. Hazel Woodus is born "in bitter rebellion" to a Welsh gypsy woman who hated "marriage and a settled life ... as a wild cat hates a cage." Hazel herself fears the entrapment of marriage because, pursued though she is by two different men, her real affinity is with the "unfenced wild", the longing for which she inherits from her mother. She goes to "her bridal in a funeral wreath," accompanied by the animals she loves, including a one-eyed cat and a fox. At the end of the novel, released into the woods by her husband who has come to understand she is not for domesticity, she is pursued by hounds and eventually leaps to her death, "Foxy" in her arms.

*Cold Comfort Farm* has made it well-nigh impossible to look back at Mary Webb's novel with anything other than derisive laughter. But for all the doom-laden tushery, the wurzel-gummidge dialect, the amateur-writing-school descriptions – "The stately May morning, caparisoned in diamonds, full of solemnity that perfect beauty wears, had come out of the purple mist" – despite all these faults, Webb is in touch with a subject that will help to explain both her novel's popularity with women readers and the anxiety that surely underlies some men's writing of the period. To understand why we have only to look at the following moment. It comes when Hazel has forlornly agreed to become Edward Marston's wife and is introduced to his mother.

> It was characteristic of Mrs Marston's class and creed ... that she did not consider Hazel in the matter. Hazel's point of view, personality, hopes and fears were non-existent to her. Hazel would be absorbed into the family like a new piece of furniture. She would be provided for without being consulted; it would be seen that she did her duty, also without being consulted. She would become, as all the other women in this and the other families of the world had, the servant of china and the electro-plate and the furniture, and she would be the means by which Edward's children came into the world .... Mrs Marston forgot, in this summing up, to find out whether Hazel cared for Edward more than she cared for freedom." *(ch. 11).*

It would not, of course, be difficult to find such protests against enforced domesticity in earlier novels. But what gives this its edge is the fact that in 1917 it was possible to feel – or fear – that women who cared for freedom might at last be able to achieve it. That was another thing the "treacherous years" had been moving towards. Financially, politically, and, yes, sexually, women were beginning to take liberties.

Hence, I suggest, David Garnett's odd little tale, *Lady Into Fox*, published in 1922. This is about a young woman called Silvia Fox who, shortly after her marriage, "in the year 1879 to Mr Richard Tebrick," does indeed turn into a fox. It takes some time for her to become truly feral. At first her husband continues to take her to bed, to dress her in womanly clothes, to wash and feed her as though she is human; and he tells her that "However you may be changed, my love is not." The fox initially responds to these ministrations as though "she was still his wife, buried as it were in the carcass of a beast but with a woman's soul."[7] But nature will out. The name Silvia Fox is as laden as Hazel Woodus: these are creatures of the wild woods. Tebrick's wife is soon longing for her freedom. Tebrick drinks to drown his sorrows. Then he "would be a beast too like his wife, though she was one through no fault of her own, and could not help it. To what lengths he went then in that drunken humour I shall not offend my readers by relating, but shall only say that he was so drunk and sottish that he had a very imperfect notion of what had passed when he woke the next morning." (p. 38). Bestiality? Perhaps not, but it isn't difficult to decode this passage as implying that women's sexuality is naturally animalistic whereas men are driven to depravity. (By women, of course.)

Silvia Fox gains her freedom and is eventually killed by hounds, hunted to her death like Hazel Woodus. But there is a difference. Garnett's tale suggests that lady-into-fox leads inevitably to tragedy. Webb's novel, on the other hand, makes plain that Hazel's death comes about because men won't grant her her freedom. Contented domesticity would in both cases have averted tragedy; but *Gone to Earth* does at least outline how such domesticity is a kind of prison cage. *Lady into Fox* implies that the real prison cage is the feral nature in which women are trapped and from which they perhaps can't be freed, no matter how solicitous their menfolk happen to be. When Silvia is trying to dig her way to freedom, Tebrick hauls her back.

> They stayed there for a minute facing each other, he on his knees, and she facing him the picture of unrepentant wickedness and fury .... it was her eyes that held his, with their split pupils looking at him with savage desperation and rage....
> "What is this, Silvia?" he said very quietly, "what is this? Why are you so savage now? If I stand between you and your freedom it is because I love you. Is it such a torment to be with me?" But Silvia never moved a muscle. *(p. 55)*

Lifted out of context this scene could easily be thought of as a domestic spat between husband and wife in some realist story; but then, of course, given its author and the cultural position he occupied, the writing's bias in favour of Mr Tebrick would plainly look unacceptable. David Garnett was a member of the Bloomsbury group and a friend of Virginia Woolf. He could hardly commit himself to the view that the true brick of a husband was opposed by a wife whose savage unreasonableness alone explained her desire for freedom. Change lady into fox, however, and such opposition might be explicable, even though the implication of lady as fox – that is, as possessed of a bestial nature – might take some explaining.

This is probably the major reason for Garnett's decision to write fantasy. Fantasy has its uses. It registers its author's claim to be a modern; and it also allows for the expression and probing of anxieties which in any other form would stand exposed as decidedly unmodern. These considerations have a bearing on another novel of 1922 – that in so many ways key year – David Lindsay's *The Haunted Woman*. Two years earlier, the publication of *A Voyage to Arcturus* had seemed to hold out the promise that Lindsay would become one of the most important writers of the post-war period.[8] *A Voyage to Arcturus* deserves its status as a classic, even though I suspect that it is among the most unread books of the century. But Lindsay's brilliant debut led nowhere much. *The Haunted Woman* was lukewarmly received and its author's career was as good as over, despite the publication of a further three novels before his death in 1945. (Two more have been issued since then). None of his novels has sold well. [9]

In his Introduction to the 1987 Canongate Classic re-print of *The Haunted Woman,* John Pick says that, reacting to the poor sales of his first novel, Lindsay chose to "accommodate his vision to the conventional novel." His next fiction is set, therefore, "not on a remote planet but in hotels and a country house in Sussex, and the characters are not archetypal figures moving in a symbolic landscape but ladies of leisure, stockbrokers and the like."[10] But this is to underestimate the strangeness of Lindsay's novel. True, its heroine, Isbel Loment, seems at first an unexceptional woman. She and her aunt drift in a restless, bored fashion from hotel to hotel while waiting for Isbel's marriage to a youngish Lloyd's underwriter, Marshall Stokes. Lindsay however soon hints at a deep dissatisfaction in Isbel's life: and her prickly behaviour can be read as the token sign of an emptiness which comes interestingly close to a moment in that canonical text of 1922, *The Waste Land*. Sitting beside her fiancé in his expensive car as they embark on a journey into Sussex, Isbel's "first exhilaration faded .... Nature always had this effect on her. Streets, shops, crowds, any form of human activity, enabled her to forget herself, but natural surroundings threw her back on her own mental resources, and then the whole emptiness and want of purpose of her life loomed up in front of her." (p. 15) This is the accidie of contemporary living so memorably evoked by the woman in "A Game of Chess" who asks her lover "Why do you never speak. Speak./What are you thinking of? What thinking? What?", and by the typist who is "bored and tired."

In saying this I do not intend to suggest that Eliot and Lindsay were aware of each other's work. It is rather that by indicating an emptiness at the heart of "modern woman" – in which, as we shall see, they are joined by others – both men may well be betraying an anxiety that women are in fact *not* bored and that their condition is certainly not to be treated, rectified or cured by conventional means – that is, by masterful love. Such love is, however, offered Isbel. She and her fiancé go to see an Elizabethan manor house, Runhill Court, situated deep in the Sussex countryside. Marshall thinks it might do for them after their marriage. There, Isbel meets the court's owner, an older man called Henry Judge. She also hears about the "lost" rooms of the house, and through Judge finds herself able to enter these rooms and within them talk to him in a manner which she likens to "a *spiritual* lesson." "'Let me interpret for you.'" Judge says. "'Isn't your feeling that during the short time we have spent here together we have been enabled temporarily to drop the mask of convention, and talk to each other more humanly and truthfully? Isn't this what you feel'" Isbel agrees and adds, "'The air here seems different. It's nobler, and there's a sort of music in it ...'" (p. 87)

The heart of England as the heart of the shires. We have been here before. As I suggested in Chapter 1, pre-war writing is thronged with such identifications. Kipling had written of Hobden the Hedger, his tutelary spirit of the Sussex countryside, that "the passion and the piety and prowess of his line/Have seeded, rooted, fruited in some land the Law calls mine." The land he had in mind was that on which stood Bateman's, the "Jacobean house of stone in a lonely valley" which he had chosen for himself and his family, and which he kept free of modern improvements.[11] But post-war England is separated by an unbridgeable abyss from a dream of continuity which, however forlornly, Kipling and others nourished. Alone with Judge in the lost rooms of Runhill Court, Isbel may imagine herself in love with him and even committed to a "noble, uplifting union with a man of unique character." But she is too much a woman of her time to risk the "social catastrophe" of a broken engagement.

Nevertheless, she is granted a vision of the world she has lost. In the secret part of the house, and accompanied by Judge, she hears music: "a simple, early English rustic air – sweet, passionate and haunting. The sonorous and melancholy character of the instrument added a wild, long-drawn-out charm to it which was altogether beyond the range of the understanding and seemed to belong to other days, when feelings were more poignant and delicate, less showy, splendid, and odourless..." (p. 136) Then, looking from a glass-less window onto a sunlit landscape with "an indescribable fresh, sweet smell, as of meadow-grass, turned-up earth, and dew-drenched flowers", she catches sight of the musician: "only his head, the upper half of his back, and one out-stretched leg were visible; but the leg was encased in a sage-green trouser, tightly cross-gartered with yellow straps, the garment on his back resembled .... a purple smock, and the hair on his hatless head fell in a thick, bright yellow mane as far as his shoulders." (pp. 140-141).

Although it is autumn when Isbel visits Runhill Court, the vision she has and the music she hears is, as she says to Judge, "'like the voice of spring'.... 'You are tortured, but you don't know what is happening to you.'" (p. 143). What seems to be happening is that she and Judge are drawing together; but at that moment "the sun went in, the wind ceased, and every sound stopped, as if cut off by a screen .... Judge's upraised arm fell slowly to his side, as he mechanically shrank back." (p. 151) At the same moment the vision beyond the window fades and is replaced by the familiar autumnal landscape.

This is the crisis. The novel's *dénouement* is taken up with Isbel's breaking off her engagement to Marshall, her attempt to return to Judge only to find that he has been discovered in an upstairs room of Runhill Court, dead of a cerebral haemorrhage (this will have occurred at the moment when he shrank from her), her subsequent decision to accompany her aunt to the Riviera – a much favoured spot for footloose women in the 1920s, both in fact and fiction – and, finally, the hint that she will after all resume her relationship with her former fiancé. In other words, the dream of an English idyll, powerful though its attractions are, cannot be sustained. We are left alone with our day.

Even the most sympathetic account of *The Haunted Woman* is likely to make it appear as at best a throw-back to the fantasy world of George MacDonald, while at its worst it seems no more than an exercise in soggy nostalgia. Yet this is to be less than fair to the novel's myth-making power. Lindsay's imagination is deeply conservative, but his apprehension of the insufficiencies of the present undoubtedly testifies to a widely-shared feeling of some terrible break with the past engendered by the war. It also typically tries to locate that past in an ancient Englishness, and *maleness,* which stretches as far back as the anglo-saxonry of Hobden the hedger. (Judge says to Isbel that the musician they can both see "'looks like an ancient Saxon come to life'") (p. 141) This attempt to uncover an English line is a matter with which Ivor Gurney is also engaged, as we shall seem in a later chapter; and it very powerfully shapes the myth-making of *The Waste Land* as well as the later *Burnt Norton* and *East Coker*. Which is not to say that the three writers were in any way reliant on each other. It is, however, to remark that the deep sense of horror implanted by the events of 1914-18 was not exhausted by the millions of lives then lost nor even by the beggaring of nations. The war made for a deep psychic, wound, a sense of catastrophe, one of whose expressions, as we have seen, was Lawrence's bitter taunting of his Bloomsbury associates, "England is finished," and another of which was, as Lindsay's novel suggests, a new sense of rootlessness, the appropriate metaphor for which is Isbel's life of hotel rooms, both in England and out of it.

A similar restlessness afflicts the women of Douglas Goldring's *The Merchant of Souls*[12]. And as with *The Haunted Woman* so here, the blame may lie with post-war man. The novel's opening pages are taken up with the talk between two sisters, young "society" women, who are discussing the previous night's dance. Joan Verschoyle says, "'I thought the men you had here last night were rather a weak-kneed lot, Betty. The post-war young man isn't the equal of his sisters.'" (p. 16) Betty, who at 29 is the older of the two, agrees, even though she includes among her friends "the men who were writing the better kind of successful novel and successful play and contributing to the more important of the monthly reviews. It was a world which made a way of escape from her other world; the world of disillusioned soldiers, emotionally exhausted by the strain of war, of diplomats and politicians, of effeminate and disappointed young men, weakly vicious and dully corrupt." (p. 20)

But then she goes to a garden party where she meets "a young man from Australia who wrote in the style of Miss Amy Lowell and declaimed his own outpourings". This is probably intended for Jack Lindsay, who had by then arrived in London and immediately set about making himself known in literary circles. More importantly, she is introduced to Everard Powis, a man who seems full of a strange charm and, as his name suggests, power. They arrange to have lunch together. There, he tells her that the age is full of superficial people, afraid to be in touch with their feelings: "'that is why people live on the surface – cowardice.'" As for Betty: "' for some unknown reason you pretend to be cynical when you are not. I should think, if the truth were known, that you were rather emotional than otherwise; warmhearted but nervous of being yourself.'" (p39).

It appears that Everard is the man to rescue her from a life of triviality, of endless parties – Betty's equivalent of Isbel's life of hotel rooms. But it then turns out that he is a cold-hearted seducer of a well-known "society" woman, Bianca Carson, now married but still pining for Everard. Even so, Betty follows him to the south of France where he has bought a fortress "for a song". Bianca is also there, with her husband, although he soon returns to England. There is no point in further detailing the plot of what is in most respects a silly novel. It's enough to say that Everard emerges as a combination of devil and vampire, causing the deaths of Bianca's small son and of Bianca herself. (Having spent the night in Everard's bed Bianca dares to return home, dares, that is to try to break his spell.) By the end of The Merchant of Souls Betty, who has come to conceive a great hatred for Bianca, sells herself to Everard. She will no longer live in her father's house and we are told that Everard has successfully destroyed her interest in everything but himself. "'Wars, murders, diseases, Communism, the League of Nations, Geneva, had lost their significance.'" (p. 243) As we have never seen her showing the least interest in these things it's difficult to know why they should now be introduced, unless we are to understand that Betty has exchanged the possibility of social commitment for a life of enclosed hedonistic slavery.

And this is indeed the point. The novel's thesis seems to be that in post-war England men let women down. They are either occupied with establishing themselves as "society" successes – writers, dramatists, and what not, all fit for gossip columnery but bereft of seriousness, of vision[13] – or they are sexual inadequates. Everard's power comes from his sexual predatoriness and his refusal to allow the women he holds in his grip to live apart from him, to be in any way committed to social or political issues. (The south of France, here as in The Haunted Woman, is a convenient metaphor of escape from a world of wider responsibility.) Betty is even led to deny sorority – she turns away from her sister and from Bianca – as she becomes hopelessly in thrall to Everard. It is of course entirely possible to read into The Merchant of Souls a deep anxiety about women's sexuality. Once awakened might it not prove destructive of domestic arrangements? But it is also possible, perhaps even necessary, to see Goldring's often preposterous novel as an attempt to grapple with issues raised by an altogether greater work of fiction.

Lawrence's novella *The Fox* was published for the first time in 1923, although Lawrence had finished a version of it in 1918. In the course of several adulatory pages devoted to the story, F.R. Leavis says that when at its close Ellen March feels that "she ought to do something, to strain herself in some direction," it is proper that her lover, Henry, who has by now killed the woman friend with whom Ellen has set up a farm, should insist that all responsibility be relinquished to him. "She had to be passive, to acquiesce, and to be submerged under the surface of life." But even Leavis is struck by possible objections to this, so he adds: "We may think of normative conclusions that occupy Lawrence elsewhere, but the psychological truth of *The Fox* is so compelling, and the close belongs so much to the concrete specificity of the situation presented, that the tale can hardly seem involved in any questionable generality of intention."[14]

Leavis presumably has in mind *The Plumed Serpent,* about whose intention even he has his doubts. "In its sustained intentness *The Plumed Serpent* as a whole rings false", he says.[15] Since this intentness includes the denial that women are entitled to any sexual pleasure other than that which they manage to provide for their menfolk, "false" is likely to appear a weasel word to those readers for whom *The Plumed Serpent* breathes an atmosphere of evil. I do not suggest that *The Fox* is an evil tale but I do think that its exploration of "natural" values touches on dark and troubling matter. Graham Holderness is a good deal closer to the truth of the matter than Leavis when he remarks that Henry's victory in winning Ellen March is her defeat. That this is at least partly Lawrence's meaning is plain from a passage near the tale's end which Holderness quotes to good effect.

> The inner necessity of his life was fulfilling itself, it was he who was to live....
> .... Her black eyes gazed upon him with the last look of resistance. And then in a last agonised failure she began to grizzle, to cry in a shivery little fashion of a child that doesn't want to cry, but is beaten from within, and gives that little first shudder of sobbing which is not yet weeping, dry and fearful .... She would never leave him again. He had won her. And he knew it and was glad, because he wanted her for his life. His life must have her. And now he had won her. It was

what his life must have
But if he had won her, he had not yet got her.

Henry is in position to fulfil himself because he has killed his opponent, Jill Banford. This episode belongs to additional work
Lawrence put into the story which in 1918 had ended with Henry,
having announced his intention of marrying Ellen and perhaps having persuaded her to accept him, returning as required to his army
camp on Salisbury Plain. He leaves frustrated because he is by no
means sure that Ellen won't renounce him for her continued life
with Jill. In the 1918 version Lawrence convincingly establishes the
strong attractions and repulsions at work between all three characters. But then he wants to force the issue to a crisis and resolution.
Henry returns from camp and as good as murders Jill. He chops
down a tree at which she has been labouring, certain that she won't
respond to his half-hearted request that she move out of the way –
she is, as he knows full well, bitterly resentful of his presence on the
farm and of his managing to do work that is beyond her. And once
she is dead he can take possession of Ellen.

Holderness is quite right to reject Leavis's suggestion that
Henry's love for March is "essentially disinterested". As he says,
this amounts to an extraordinary mis-reading of the tale. Henry's
love, if that is what it can be called, is entirely *self-interested*.
Holderness points out that Henry "is a hunter who seeks to make
March his quarry; when he conceives the ambition of marrying
March he is holding a dead rabbit in his hand; and March herself
resembles that rabbit when Henry, to secure his objective, destroys
his rival in an act of bestial revenge and murder."[17]

But this murderous, ruthless certainty hinges on the identification of Henry with the fox. In *Gone to Earth* and *Lady into Fox* it
was women who had turned feral and who ended by being pursued
and killed. In Lawrence's tale, however, it is the man who is identified with the feral; and he is the pursuer. At the beginning of the
tale the women's farm is plagued by a dog fox who regularly steals
their chickens. On one occasion March comes face to face with it.
"So he looked into her eyes, and her soul failed her. He knew her,
and was not daunted." (p. 89). Then Henry arrives, out of the
dark. "To March he was the fox. Whether it was the thrusting forward of his head, or the glisten of fine whitish hairs on the ruddy
cheek-bones, or the bright, keen eyes, that can never be said; but
the boy was to her the fox, and she could not see him otherwise."
(p. 93)

Henry proposes to Ellen, she more or less accepts, and then he hears the two women discussing him in their bedroom. Jill tells Ellen that Henry must be after the farm and that he'll despise her for giving into him. He picks up his gun and steals out into the night:

> And suddenly it seemed to him England was little and tight, he felt the landscape was constricted even in the dark, and that there were too many dogs in the night, making a noise like a fence of sound, like the network of English hedges netting the view. He felt the fox didn't have a chance .... He knew the fox would be coming. It seemed to him it would be the last of the foxes in this loudly-barking, thick-voiced England, tight with innumerable little houses. *(p. 121)*

To escape this he must get away to Canada, and after the killing of Jill that is where he plans to take Ellen. Of this, Holderness remarks that "However strongly the moralising narrator endorses and confirms Henry's hopes, the realism of the tale's art cannot deny the validity of March's resistance; and the tragic sadness of the conclusion is the only proper consummation to the tragedy of the tale."[18] Holderness has in mind here what he argues is an irresolvable conflict between on the one hand the "social" world of Ellen's ordinary existence, "in a specific time and place", and, on the other, the symbolically realised "natural" values of "emotional and instinctive experience."[19] I don't necessarily disagree with this, but it is important to note that in his attempt to resolve the issue the narrator is forced into some bullying and highly abstractive and generalised statements. Ellen has reached after happiness. That won't do at all.

> And women? – what goal can any woman conceive, except happiness? Just happiness for herself and the whole world. That, and nothing else. And so, she assumes the responsibility and sets off towards her goal. She can see it there, at the foot of the rainbow. Or she can see it a little way beyond, in the blue distance. Not far, not far.
>
> But the end of the rainbow is a bottomless gulf down which you can fall forever without arriving, and the blue distance is a void pit which can swallow you and all your efforts into its emptiness and still be no emptier. You and all your efforts. So, the illusion of attainable happiness.
>
> Poor March, she had set off so wonderfully towards the blue goal. And the farther and farther she had gone, the more fearful had become the realisation of emptiness. An agony, an insanity at last. *(p. 156)*

The objection against this has to be that March hasn't been shown to be in pursuit of happiness and that anyway to apply to her a statement as vast as "women – any woman" is precisely to deny the "specific time and place" which Holderness argues for. It also makes a mockery of the Leavisian claim for Lawrence's "concrete specificity of the situation presented." Yes, in the tale as we have it until Henry's return to camp there has indeed been a balancing of the symbolic and realistic modes, of the "natural" and the "social"; and yes, Lawrence does there manage to make entirely convincing the women's social register, their desire for independence, their touching inadequacies as farmers, their small pleasures and rather more substantial anxieties. But at the tale's ending this poise is replaced by an insistence that the fox, the hunter, is in the right of it. I agree with Holderness that, as we see her at the end of the tale, Ellen is still struggling for independence. But the terms in which Lawrence accounts for this struggle make clear how far he is from wanting us to sympathise with the ambition, even if we can still sympathise with her. What she thinks she wants isn't what she needs. So at least we are to understand. It is as though Lawrence is anticipating an answer to Freud's famous, yet unasked, question.

> And she was so tired, so tired, like a child that wants to go to sleep, but which fights against sleep as if sleep were death. She seemed to stretch her eyes wider in an obstinate effort and tension to keep awake. She *would* keep awake. She *would* know. She *would* consider and judge and decide. She *would* have the reins of her own life between her own hands. She *would* be an independent woman to the last. But she was so tired, so tired of everything. And sleep seemed near. And there was rest in the boy. *(p. 157)*

For all that Lawrence provides access to the strength of Ellen's desire for independence, there can be no doubt that the Fox will succeed; his will-power is the stronger, he is the more authoritative of the two. The tale's very last remark is given to him. He has told Ellen she'll feel better when they have started their new life in Canada. "' Yes, I may. I can't tell,'" she says. "'I can't tell what it will be like over there.' 'If only we could go soon!' he said, with pain in his voice." (p. 158)

Although Paul Fussell does not discuss "The Fox" in his study of *Abroad: British Literary Travelling Between the Wars*, he regards Lawrence as the first of many writers who left England after 1918 in order "to escape something hateful at home."[20] The allure of "abroad" was certainly very great; but for women that didn't necessarily mean escape with a man. It might mean escape *from* a man or men, as the flight to Paris of Violet Trefusis and Victoria Sackville-West suggests.[21] The episode isn't typical – nothing to do with Victoria Sackville West is that – but it is important to note that women in the post-war years could well choose to combine going abroad with maintaining or even discovering independent life styles. *That* was what women wanted. And the fear of such independence can be felt as undeclared fears in Garnett's, Lindsay's and Lawrence's writing, no matter how different in other respects they might be. Only Goldring acknowledges that women's new-found freedoms might legitimately lead to a wider sphere of involvement. This has a bearing on what comes next.

## III

In June, 1920, Nancy Cunard noted in her diary that she was cursed with a "shocking super sensitiveness. Oh how often indeed have I cursed that, and now more than ever – it stands in the way of everything, distorts my life and makes me almost impossible to live, get on with I should say. Hidden, it's even worse, this gnawing and probing and exaggerating and lacerating state of mind. I seem to want too much, hence a mountain of unhappiness."[22] *The Fox*, with Lawrence's approval, would have condemned Cunard's confession for its mistaken belief in an achievable happiness. Others, more robustly cynical, may be imagined as seeing in it merely the complaint of a poor little rich girl. Yet although there is an element of posturing in these diary jottings they also hint at Nancy Cunard's desire to do something worthwhile with her life; and this deserves to be taken seriously.

She was born in 1896 to wealthy parents and for most of her life had access to money. Her early years, as the daughter of a dull, aristocratic landowner and a beautiful, restless and intelligent American woman half his age, seem to have been spent without much parental love although with plenty of excitement. This increased when Lady Cunard left her husband to set up as an independent woman in London and, then, mistress of the young Thomas Beecham. In November, 1916, acting more or less on a whim, Nancy married Sydney Fairburn, "handsome and agreeable, a first-class cricketer and a gallant soldier." The marriage, contracted in all the haste typical of war-time marriages, was a predictable disaster. Fairburn had no interest in the arts or intellectual matters, whereas in the month of their marriage seven of Nancy's poems were included in the first of six anthologies to be published by the Sitwells. One of her poems, called "Wheels", gave the anthologies their name.

Also at this time Nancy became friendly with Sybil Hart-Davies, whom she would later call "my liberator". Cunard's biographer, Anne Chisholm, says that the two young women's close friendship "made some of their friends and relations uneasy; they were said not to be a good influence on each other." And she adds that this was the moment when Nancy read Norman Douglas's *South Wind,* a novel which Lawrence hated, and that "The conversations and eccentricities of a group of expatriates on Capri dabbling in intellectual and sexual experiment may not seem powerful enough to help liberate someone today, but it had a distinct effect upon Nancy. She began to feel certain that life was full of possibilities, and that her marriage need not confine her forever."[23]

Sorority is an essential part of the story of new women. And although Nancy's social position and wealth might be thought to have cosseted her and freed her from the constraints affecting other women – and men, too – she learnt to shift the mountain of unhappiness by confronting those constraints. Sexual freedom was not to be considered apart from other freedoms. Another diary event for 1920 records "How hidden and remote one is from the obscure vortex of England's revolutionary troubles, coal strikes, etc. So much newspaper talk does it seem to me and yet – is it always going to be so?" Chisholm takes this to show how seldom "Nancy looked outside herself and her immediate surroundings .... Mostly, Nancy was interested in herself."[24] But that isn't how I read the entry. Its interest surely lies in what Nancy Cunard feels – guiltily perhaps – hidden and remote from. Besides, her words reveal an intuitive awareness that strikes and revolutionary troubles aren't *merely* newspaper talk. The troubles Nancy will have had in mind here include those already referred to in this book: the dockers' refusal to load arms intended to aid Poland and the White Russians, even though the Government was supporting Poland against Soviet Russia; and the bitter dispute between government and miners and railwaymen about wages and conditions of labour.[25]

Betty Verschoyle's sexual enslavement coincides with her loss of interest in social and political matters, including Communism and the League of Nations. Cunard's restlessness, her uncertainty about what to do with her life and her dissatisfactions with the social world in which she moved, has its echoes in Betty's discontents of and, for that matter, those of Isbel Loment. In 1920 Nancy moved to Paris. But according to Chisholm, she remained for several years part of the London scene. "In England it was the time when the legend of the twenties was being formed; and the legend of Nancy as an archetypal twenties girl took shape simultaneously. Indeed, the style and behaviour of girls such as Nancy were a basic ingredient of twenties mythology, both at the time and afterward."[26]

So much the worse for mythology. There is all the difference in the world between the aimless socialites and debutantes who fill the pages of Evelyn Waugh's *Diaries* of the 1920s and Cunard, (who incidentally makes no appearance in their pages until the end of the decade). And while I do not doubt that her life-style, her sexual independence, her drinking and smoking, her pleasure in a wide variety of friends, could be and was exploited by the gossip columnists, the fact is that her hunger to be more serious resulted in a growing commitment to radical politics. This included, and may have been partly prompted by, further strong ties with women such as the young American writers Janet Flanner and Solita Solano, whom she met in Paris in 1923. It was certainly furthered by her affairs with the communist poet Louis Aragon and Henry Chowder, the American black musician and composer with whom she compiled the famous anthology *Negro,* eventually published in 1934.[27] To treat Nancy Cunard as an archetypal flapper is to dishonour a brave and good person.

There is, though, an opposing danger: that of making her political radicalism seem exceptional. Among many young women who got abroad in the aftermath of the war, especially to Paris, sexual freedom and adventure were, if not the only lures, at all events powerful ones. And why not? As Paul Fussell remarks, there is a strong inducement to flee from the kind of control which closes pubs and regulates sexual behaviour, especially when, he might have added, those who exercised such control were members of an older generation which their disenchanted juniors held accountable for the recent catastrophic war.[28] Besides, Paris was as hospitable to art as it was to independent women, and if these women were artists so much the better.[29] I shall return to this, but first I want to consider the example of an independent woman who was neither

87

writer nor artist but who in the 1920s was determined to find a life for herself beyond England, and who discovered it in commitment to radical politics. What follows is anecdotal, but I have no reason to doubt its essential truth.

When I met the widows of George Thomson, Alick West and Douglas Garman, I wanted to find out as much as I could about what had turned the three young men towards radical politics. The women had come into the men's lives at different moments. Elizabeth West, Alick West's second wife, was not greatly interested in his politics, although she obviously much admired her husband's literary criticism. By comparison, Katherine Thomson, a distinguished musicologist, shared with George Thomson a passionate commitment to radical activity. The two of them had been largely responsible for setting up the Clarion Singers in Birmingham in the 1930s. They staged amateur performances of Mozart from the back of a lorry and persuaded professional composers and friends to help them bring music to working people. Paddy Garman, like Liz West, was a second wife. She had married Douglas, she said, after her return to England in 1933. I wondered where she had been before that, but she wasn't particularly keen to tell me. Not that there was anything to hide about her past, but her main concern was to set straight the record of her husband's life and especially the part he had played in the founding and running of the *Calendar of Modern Letters*, which she felt had been under-estimated. Only reluctantly, therefore, would she agree to talk about herself.

She had been in North Germany in the early 30s, helping with the work of a newly formed union of seamen. But then Hitler came to power and she was advised that it would be too dangerous for her to continue with her union activities. Hence, her return to England. "So you were away for what – two or three years?" I asked. But Paddy explained she had got to Germany not from England but from China. A hair-raising journey it had been, too, by train. All the way across China she had been forced to hide under her seat to escape the attention of Chang Kai Shek's guards. Why? Oh, because she had been working for a communist newspaper in Shanghai. Shanghai? Yes, she said, she had gone to Shanghai after escaping from Peking, where she had also been working on a communist newspaper. Peking was in the path of Chang Kai Shek's army. She had got out in the nick of time. But how had she got to Peking? From Moscow, she explained. She had been working in Moscow when she had been told that volunteers were needed in Peking to

88

help staff a newspaper there. So she decided to go. And what was she doing in Moscow? Ah, well, she had been working in London as a stenographer – her word – feeling more than a little bored with life, when one morning she had seen a notice in a daily newspaper offering work in Moscow to people with her skills. So she applied and was accepted. That was all there was to it.

I don't suppose that *was* all but it was more than enough to be going on with. I had one further question. "Weren't you at all lonely in Moscow?" I asked. "Oh, no," Paddy said, "there were plenty of us there, at the time." In other words, young English women, who had never before left home, had chosen to go to Moscow during the early to middle years of the 1920s, in order to use whatever skills they had to earn a living and, perhaps, assist in making a new world. This isn't a point to be over-emphasised but neither should it be ignored. Of the women Paddy met in Russia, some must have gone for adventure, some because anything that got them out of England would be good; and I have no reason to doubt that others went because they wanted to see the future and find out at first hand whether it was working. Paddy Garman's wasn't false modesty. She genuinely did think that while what she had done might have been unusual it wasn't at all exceptional. Her experiences in Russia and China confirmed her in a life-long commitment to socialism. This may be thought the real-life equivalent of the fictional Anne Drummond's committed socialism. It also finds a counterpart in the commitment to radical causes of other women at that same time, for example Winifred Holtby, who in 1926 went to South Africa and who while there helped to set up a Black Workers Union.[30]

As Nancy Cunard's experiences show, you didn't have to travel as far afield as Moscow or South Africa to develop this commitment. Paris would do. Paris in fact did well enough for many young women of the period, especially those trained as artists. Art School was the quickest way out of Manchester. It had begun to look that way as early as the 1890s, although Alison Thomas rightly notes that such appearances could be deceptive. In *Portraits of Women: Gwen John and her Forgotten Contemporaries*, Thomas surveys the more or less thwarted careers of four women art students who trained at the Slade in the 1890s. Three of the quartet, John herself, Edna Clarke Hall, Gwen Salmond and Ida Nettleship went off to Paris, yet despite the fact they were all highly talented, none had what can be called a successful career. After producing five children by Augustus

John, Ida Nettleship died young. Gwen Salmond married Ivor Smith and surrendered her career to the task of bringing up two sons in poverty. As for Gwen John, a major artist by any standards, her extraordinary life would probably have been much the same whenever and wherever she had been born.[31]

This is not, however, to under-estimate the importance of her move to Paris, nor of her meetings with, among others, Rilke, Jacques Maritain and Rodin. Pre-war Paris was uniquely a city where artists gathered, women artists among them. Nina Hamnett, who had lived there for a short while before 1914, couldn't wait to return once the war was over. She was tired of London, and bored with the Westminster Technical Institute, where she taught life-drawing. "I waited anxiously for the term to finish and decided to go to Paris as soon as I could." Lack of a passport was easily resolved, lack of money more of a problem, but by March, 1920, Hamnett was once again in her favourite city and "so pleased to be back in Paris that, during the daytime, I walked about by myself, visiting all the places I had been to before the war."[32]

Nina Hamnett's love of Paris, her knowledge of its artists, and of the cafés, bars, bistros and studios which were their habitual haunts, makes her a prime candidate for at least a walk-on part in Jean Rhys's *Quartet*.[33] Yet as far as I know none of the women in that novel is based on her, and Rhys's biographer, Carole Angier, doesn't include Hamnett among the women artists Rhys drew on for her characters. Some of these are taken seriously. For example, Miss De Solla, introduced as "a painter and ascetic", who makes occasional brief appearances, lives in a smelly but peaceful studio "behind a grim building where the housewives of the neighbour-hood came to wash their clothes" (p. 8), and is in Paris as a dedicated artist. According to Angier she is based on "Violet Dreschfield, an English sculptress who exhibited in Paris from 1929."[34] By comparison Lois Hedler plays at being an artist. Her husband, "H.J.", with whom the novel's protagonist is having an affair, has enough money to buy her a studio apartment. There she paints portraits and entertains "interesting" people.

*Quartet* comes out of Jean Rhys's unhappy love affair with Ford Madox Ford, but it is a mistake for Angier to argue that Lois is therefore "based" on Stella Gibbon, the Australian artist with whom Ford was living at the time he met Rhys, just as it is wrong to assert that "There are several women artists in Jean's Paris novels and stories, and I think they're all based on Violet

Dreschfield."[35] This is to ignore the quality of a writer's imagination and to do considerable injustice to Rhys's inventiveness. In particular, Angier will not credit Rhys's recognition that women artists were drawn to Paris because it was everything England – including London – wasn't.

Of course numbers of the young women who went to Paris as artists were not expecially serious about their careers and had only minimal talent. (The same is true of numbers of the young men who landed there with the intention of becoming writers.) So what? Post-war London wasn't without its bohemian element, as we shall see in the next chapter; but it couldn't compare with Paris. Nor could its greyness, of inner and outer weather, compare with the French city's glitter. Above all, London couldn't offer the same freedoms, the realisable possibilities of independence. Post-war Paris was crucial in helping to shape a generation of women artists who learnt habits of independence from their experiences there (and – in the case of Evelyn Gibbs at least – Italy). One of them, Nan Youngman, has hanging in her house a painting she made at the end of the second World War. The title, "Le Départ," perfectly fits the heartfelt yearning for the light and warmth which wait, so you feel, beyond the railway station along whose empty platforms you look towards a brightening sky.[36]

Going abroad didn't necessarily bring these women artists success, but it did help to make possible their determination to take seriously their lives as artists. Not all of them would have agreed with the American Natalie Barney that in England "nothing is for women – not even the men."[37] But Barney, who settled in Paris in the 1920s and who, as Ezra Pound remarked, got more out of life than was ever perhaps in it, typified the kind of energy, even joy, that seemed possible in Paris and which drew to it, among others, the painters Eileen Agar, Kathleen Hale and Nan Youngman, and the sculptor Gertrude Hermes.[38] Most of the women artists returned to England in order to find work and, less certainly, a measure of success. But Paris or, as in the examples of Barbara Hepworth and Evelyn Gibbs, Rome, had changed them. The experience of abroad gave them a new confidence, a certainty of the propriety of independence, a sense that they might be able to make a life – a studio – a room – of their own.

Virginia Woolf's famous essay first appeared in 1928. It is based on two papers she read to the Arts Society at Newnham and the Odtaa at Girton in October, 1928, and its subtle, sinuous argument is directed at young women about to leave Cambridge's sheltering climate. Hence a plea that comes towards the end of the essay, where Woolf voices her hopes that the women to whom her remarks are specifically addressed will go on to write books, "hesitating at no subject however trivial or however vast."

> By hook or by crook, I hope that you will possess yourselves of money enough to travel and to idle, to contemplate the future or the past of the world, to dream over books and loiter at street corners and let the line of thought dip into the stream. For I am by no means confining you to fiction. If you would please me – and there are thousands like me – you would write books of travel and adventure, and research and scholarship, and history and biography, and criticism and philosophy and science.[39]

Virginia Woolf could have pointed to very recent examples of such writing. That year Enid Welsford, who had been appointed to a lectureship in English at Newnham in 1927, won the British Academy's Rose Mary Crayshaw prize for her book on *The Court Masque*; and in 1927 Helen Waddell had published *The Wandering Scholars*, one of the century's indubitably great works of historical scholarship. Also in 1927, the London publishing firm of Gerald Howe Ltd began its monograph series on *Representative Women* under the general editorship of Francis Birrell. Among its first planned titles were *Aphra Behn* (by Vita Sackville-West), *Cristina of Sweden* (by Ada Harrison), *Jane Welsh Carlyle* (by Willa Muir), and *Elizabeth Barrett Browning* (by Irene Cooper Willis).

Such examples could be multiplied, and although they do not amount to a radical revision of Virginia Woolf's contention that women have been all but absent from history, they do at least show that in the 1920s women were becoming visible in spheres that had by and large seemed exclusively reserved for men. (As *Representative Women* shows, this included the re-discovery of women *in* history.) They even had their own club, The Cavendish Club, which had been started by ex-V.A.D.s in 1920. "The burdens of domesticity", which Augustus John admitted had thwarted the careers of women artists of his generation, were less often picked up by a later generation of women, whether artists, writers, or scholars.[40] Nancy Cunard's refusal to do her mother's bidding, to make a proper marriage and to stay in England, may be the most spectacular rebellion, but it is by no means the only one. For such women, as for the men, the 'civilisation' which had permitted and then encouraged the events of the war had forfeited all rights to respect. This is hinted at in a fragment of conversation in *Quartet,* where Lois Heidler says to Marya that she finds "Sensitiveness ... an unmitigated nuisance." By sensitiveness she means prudishness, old maidishness, the circumscribed lives of women left indoors: "'Clergymen's daughters without any money. Long slim fingers and all the rest. What's the use of it? Those sort of people don't do any good in the world.' Well, don't worry,' answered Marya. 'They're getting killed off slowly.'"

The impoverished lives of spinster daughters was hardly a subject new to fiction in the 1920s. But it took on new urgency with the much-touted and frequently repeated statistic of the nation's 2,000,000 superfluous women, a figure produced by the census of 1921. In her invaluable essay on "The Spinster in Women's Fiction of the 1920s," Maroula Joannou quotes from an unsigned editorial in the *New Statesman* for September 29th, 1921, the writer of which thinks it "absurd" for the press to make so much of "'superfluous women', or 'thwarted women,' as though 'superfluous', 'thwarted', and 'unmarried' were convertible terms .... Who, indeed, is to decide what is a thwarted life? Was Swift's a thwarted life? Or Ruskin's? If so, it seems clear that thwarting may be merely a means to a completer fulfilment."[41] Given that the lives of both men ended in madness, although Swift may have suffered from Alzheimer's disease, these are scarcely well-chosen examples. Nevertheless, the point stands. The pathos of the sisters in Katherine Mansfield's "The Daughters of the Late Colonel" attaches to their being trapped in an outmoded way of life.

> If mother had lived, might they have married? But there had been nobody for them to marry. There had been father's Anglo-Indian friends before he quarrelled with them. But after that [Josephine] and Constantia never met a single man except clergymen. How did one meet men? Or even if they'd met them, how could they have got to know men well enough to be more than strangers? One read of people having adventures, being followed, and so on. But nobody had ever fol-

lowed Constantia and her. Oh yes, there had been one year at
Eastbourne a mysterious man at their boarding house who
had put a note on the jug of hot water outside their bedroom
door! But by the time Connie had found it the steam had
made the writing too faint to read; they couldn't even make
out to which of them it was addressed. And he had left next
day. And that was all. The rest had been looking after father,
and at the same time keeping out of father's way. But now?
But now? The thieving sun touched Josephine gently. She
lifted her face. She was drawn over to the window by gentle
beams ...[42]

The story's delicate symbolism deftly points the sisters' wasted
lives: even after his death, they are terrified to enter their father's
room, terrified of opening his writing table, his chest of drawers, his
wardrobe; and when, once and once only, they dare to intrude on
that tyrannically powerful male preserve, "bigger flakes of cold air
fell on Josephine's shoulders and knees". (p. 110). This is the snowy
death of love, of vital warmth. And yet the sisters are entirely confined by domestic arrangement. The sun's beams may draw
Josephine to the window but as the tale ends she "stared at a big
cloud where the sun had been." (p. 127) The sisters are marked for
cold, for defeat.

There is a similar sense of desolation at the end of the story,
"Miss Brill." Miss Brill is a spinster whose timid pleasures are
centred on Sunday afternoon walks in her local park. The story is
set on one such afternoon of sun but coming chill. "Miss Brill was
glad she had decided on her fur .... Dear little thing! It was nice to
feel it again. She had taken it out of its box that afternoon, shaken
out the moth-powder, given it a good brush, and rubbed the life
back into its dim little eyes." (p. 199). In the park she overhears
two young people talking contemptuously about her. "'It's her fu-
fur which is so funny,' giggled the girl." (p. 206) Miss Brill goes
back to her "little dark room – her room like a cupboard – and sat
down on the red eiderdown. She sat there a long time. The box
that the fur came out of was on her bed. She unclasped the neck-
let quickly; quickly, without looking, laid it inside. But when she
put the lid on she thought she heard something crying." (p. 207).
This is a tale where lady doesn't turn into fox. The symbolism of
approaching winter, of the dilapidated fox fur and of the red eiderdown, hints at unrealised desires which, while they may not be
sexual will, so we understand, be withheld from this single woman
in her "little dark room."

These stories may look vulnerable to the charge that Mansfield's imagination is nourished by a reactionary conviction that women need men and marriage if they are to achieve happiness. But actually her subject here is the pathos of the necessarily incomplete lives of women who can conceive of completeness in no other way than through marriage. And as the women she writes about have acquired no skills that offer them the chance of truly independent lives, how else can they conceive of freedom?

With Mansfield's near contemporary, Ivy Compton-Burnett, matters are rather different. Her novels typically dramatise the hell that families make of their lives together. Imprisoned in marriage and domesticity, her women frequently become ogres of tyrannical control, their egotism flowering as through the acquired postures of matriarchy. Alison Light puts this very well when she notes that "Compton-Burnett's project bespeaks a traumatised sense of being and of conduct; an ontology characterised by the refusal to engage with any notion of wider social involvements or place." But as Light adds, this project can "be made by readers into an enhanced cultural or social position." In other words, Compton-Burnett's families can be prized as representing a cultural idiom, "one which could start to take pleasure in being cut off, and find in feelings of estrangement new and desirable forms of privilege."[43]

I have no quarrel with this. Yet is should be said that for other novelists of the decade who share Compton-Burnett's project, the family as hell could never be mistaken as the repository of forms of privilege. The difference between Compton-Burnett on the one hand and, on the other, Christopher Isherwood and Patrick Hamilton, is as much to be explained in terms of the men's relative youth as in terms of gender. Compton-Burnett was born in 1884, both Hamilton and Isherwood twenty years later. They came to maturity as members of the post-war generation and might be expected to reject the fathers – literal or metaphoric – who, for all their eager endorsement of the war, nevertheless expected obedience and respect after it. But it was easier for men to break away than it was for women; and for women of Compton-Burnett's generation and class it was especially difficult.[44]

Hence, I suspect, the almost diabolic relish she brings to her depiction of what might be called monstrous matriarchs. The first of these occurs in the first of her fully achieved novels, *Brothers and Sisters*, 1929. Of the two earlier novels, *Dolores,* written before the war, was never afterwards referred to by the author, and *Pastors and Masters*, 1925, is a dry run for the future work. Early on in *Brothers and Sisters*, Sophia, who has managed to marry the man of her choice – he will turn out to be her natural brother – is caught in the gesture of passing "her hand over her children's hair, and they looked up to her and smiled. It had not occurred to them or to her, that they might not adapt their mood to hers."[45] Sophia endlessly acts out her role as mother: "'My children,' said Sophia, 'my boys and girl, I have a great anxiety to bring on you today. Dear Father is not well, dear ones, not well and strong as he used to be. There may come a time when we feel we may not have him with us much longer.'" (p. 107) What Sophia has to say is true; how she says it in one sense falsifies the children's relationship to her, in another binds them in hoops of steel. For "Sophia in her extreme moments, when she suffered more than most, never ceased to listen to herself." (p. 106) She knows exactly how to play the tragedy queen. Indeed some of her speeches bring her very close to Florence Lancaster in Noel Coward's *The Vortex*, a play I shall touch on in the next chapter.

It is a weakness that Compton-Burnett should wish so often to explain Sophia – as though she is afraid her readers won't understand what is going on. For example, after her husband's death we are told that Sophia "seemed to give little thought to the sacrifice" of her children's youth. "Seems? Nay, mother, I know not seems." The remark is then stretched to a whole paragraph.

> She overstressed the significance of widowhood, magnified her married happiness, and forgot what she had daily taken into account during her husband's life, that his feeling was for the personality she presented as herself. It stood simply that her children could not leave her while her widowhood was young. She regarded their share in her sorrow less as a claim on her sympathy than as a support of their duty; and their married life as, even in their own thoughts, subordinate to the ending of her own. *(p. 151)*.

This is a perfectly competent resumé of what the novel makes us see, but in view of the success with which Compton-Burnett dramatises Sophia's endless self-representation it is difficult to understand why she bothers – unless, that is, she means explanation to be exculpation. Alison Light sees Compton-Burnett's fiction "as speaking directly to the reshaping of English cultural life after the war, able to confront the explosion of ideals about domestic life and family, sentiments which had been as dramatically undermined as the nation's ideals of manhood."[46] If this is so, it follows that Sophia is a figure of pathos as much as an embodiment of domestic tyranny: trying for all she's worth to stand firm for her sense of matriarchy even as she feels the ground shifting beneath her. The problem with this, however, is that we don't get much sense out of how or why she might feel this shift; and there is no evidence for it within the novel itself. Although the war is mentioned we are given little sense of larger pressures weighing on the novel's main characters. The fears seem to be more the author's than the characters'.

Or it may be better to suggest that Compton-Burnett feels the need to explain Sophia's stance while at the same time resenting the fact that she has to do so. Which is to say the Compton-Burnett is probably more caught up in the pleasures of Sophia's kind of tyranny than even she senses is proper. Hence, those anxious qualifiers. Hence, seemed.

The tyranny works, of course, because of the close confinement to the house of the male characters. True, we are told that the younger son, Robin, "who was granted the need for a livelihood, was about to leave Oxford for a government office routine, and was to have the compensation of a London life for the sacrifice of any talents that might be his." (p. 31). But neither the office life nor the sacrificed talents makes an appearance in the novel; nor does the need to earn a livelihood seem very real. Robert Liddell correctly notes of Compton-Burnett that her novels are about "the horror that can lurk behind the façade of the respectable upper-middle class English home,"[47] but Alison Light is equally correct to rebuke him for suggesting in his full-length study of the novels that this is human nature.[48] On the contrary, it is the behaviour of those who wish to preserve the fabric of family stability in the only way they know how and in the face of all-too perceptible structural damage. Tyranny is only needed when acquiescence can't be guaranteed.

Here, then, we can bring into consideration a sonnet by Elizabeth Daryush.

> Children of wealth in your warm nursery,
> Set in the cushioned window-seat to watch
> The volleying snow, guarded invisibly
> By the clear double pane through which no touch
> Untimely penetrates, you cannot tell
> What winter means; its cruel truths to you

Are only sight and sound; your citadel
Is safe from feeling, and from knowledge too.

Go down, go out to elemental wrong,
Waste your too round limbs, tan your skin too white;
The glass of comfort, ignorance, seems strong
To-day, and yet perhaps this very night

You'll wake to horror's wrecking fire – your home
Is wired within for this, in every room.

I am not sure of the dating of this poem – it may be early 1930s.[49] But the "wrecking fire" could easily be an expression of the developing paranoia of those who in the 1920s feared the imminence of revolution. (A fear about which I shall have something to say in Chapter 5.) Even if we take "wrecking fire" not as a metaphor of class-conflict – that is, even it doesn't mean that the wiring introduced by working men who were called on to provide electricity for the houses of the wealthy is deliberately faulty – such fire threatens the safety of the family house and is to be connected to "elemental wrong", a phrase which puns brilliantly on the snowy weather and fundamental social ills. And as the poem's formal inventiveness breaks the molds of resolution, consolation, closure (it obeys none of the received forms of the sonnet and the concluding half-rhyme is as abrasive as the syntax of the final two lines which don't, for all the appearance of a closing couplet, act as one), so the meaning insinuates itself as one that threatens to wreck all sense of well-being initially associated with the children of wealth cocooned in their nursery warmth, as Sophia's children may at first seem to be.

Daryush's great sonnet even more potently perhaps than *Brothers and Sisters* speaks to those middle-class fears Light sees Compton-Burnett's work as addressing. Such fears were fed from many different sources and include not only the threat of class-upheaval but also, as I have noted, changing possibilities for women. Compton-Burnett seems to discount these, unless we see in Sophia's clinging to her role an underlying and not-to-be mentioned dread that women who ought to be like herself were finding different roles to play. As indeed in the post-war years they were able to do. In 1919 Oxford admitted women to full membership of the university; and although Cambridge was not prepared to go that far, it did in 1921 pass "Graces", as a result of which women graduates were given degree titles. In 1919 the first woman barrister was called to the bar. (Thirty more followed in 1920.) Women began to be elected to the house of commons. In 1923 the Matrimonial Causes Act provided that adultery by either spouse should be sufficient cause for divorce. If we add that in the previous year Marie Stopes had lectured a crowded Queen's Hall on the desirability of birth control, by which time she had established her birth-control clinic in London's east end, it is apparent that the early 1920s provides hard evidence that women's causes – including the right to take control of their own lives – were being materially advanced by legislative as well as other means.

But it is also apparent that these advances were made into predominantly hostile territory. The enemy might be falling back but it could still deliver powerful counter-blows, as for example happened over the harrying by the church – anglican as well as catholic – of Marie Stopes. (And as we shall later see, after the disastrous reverse of 1926, the forces of reaction became far more confident and more determined to fight back.) Besides, it would be absurd to deny that for many middle-class women marriage and family still operated as the socially approved model of fulfilment.

This is why Sylvia Townsend Warner's *Lolly Willowes* is so important an intervention. For in this first novel, published in 1926, Townsend Warner profoundly subverts orthodoxy. She does so in regard both to the novel's content and its form: the one is in fact inconceivable without the other. *Lolly Willowes* is a truly radical work. It begins as a realistic novel, and in its opening pages provides the history of a family. This is a reassuringly familiar mode.

> When Fancy Willowes had grown up, and married, and lost her husband in the war, and driven a lorry for the Government, and married again from patriotic motives, she said to Owen Wolf-Sanders, her second husband:
> 'How unenterprising women were in the old days! Look at Aunt Lolly. Grandfather left her five hundred a year, and she was nearly thirty when he died, and yet she could find nothing better to do than settle down with Mum and Dad, and stay there ever since.'
> 'The position of single women was very different twenty years ago,' answered Mr Wolf-Sanders. '*Feme sole*, you know, and *feme couverte*, and all that sort of rot.'
> Even in 1902 there were some forward spirits who wondered why that Miss Willowes, who was quite well off, and not likely to marry, did not make a home for herself and take up something artistic or emancipated. Such possibilities did not

occur to any of Laura's relations. Her father being dead, they took it for granted that she should be absorbed into the household of one brother or another. And Laura, feeling rather as if she were a piece of family property forgotten in the will, was ready to be disposed of as they should think best.[50]

Fancy Willowes sees herself as an emancipated spirit of the 1920s, although Townsend Warner's sly humour establishes her as an *ersatz* version of such emancipation – "married again from patriotic motives" – and to a man called Wolf-Sanders! Nevertheless, this passage might well seem to be setting us up for the kind of study of claustrophobic family life out of which Ivy Compton-Burnett would make her compelling fictions. But from the start there is something odd about Lolly, something not quite reassuring. We are told that her father yearned for a daughter. "A stuffed ermine which he had known as a boy was still his ideal of an enchanted princess, so pure and sleek was it, and so artfully poised the small neat head on the long throat. 'Weasel!' exclaimed his wife. 'Everard, how dare you love a minx!'" The infant Laura "seemed his very ermine come to life." Shortly afterwards he goes out hunting.

> But he came back home after the first kill. "'Twas a vixen, he said. 'Such a pretty young vixen. It put me in mind of my own, and I thought I'd ride back to see how she was behaving. Here's the brush.' *(p. 13)*

Later, Laura is described as having eyes "which were large, set wide apart ... diluted black," and a brown skin. As for her education, she reads among other things Glanvil on witches (p. 24), and Nicholas Culpepper, which encourages her to rove "the countryside for herbs and simples, and many were the washes and decoctions that she made from sweet-gale, water purslane, cowslips, and the roots of succory." (p. 31) She is, in other words, feral, even foxy, as well as witch-like.

After her father's death Lolly leaves the family's country house and goes to live in London with her brother, Henry, and his religious wife, Caroline. She is now required to meet men of the legal profession, "Their jaws ... like so many mouse-traps, baited with commonplaces. They made her feel shy and behave stiffly." (p. 55). In this atmosphere Laura grows increasingly witch-like. "Her face was beginning to stiffen. It had lost its power of expressiveness, and was more and more dominated by the hook nose and the sharp chin. When Laura was ten years older she would be nut-crackerish." (p. 59) Life settles into a routine "that with a few modifications for the sake of variety or convenience served [Henry and Caroline, their children and Laura] for the next fifteen years." (p. 65). This is the family trap. On holidays Laura "would have liked to go by herself for long walks inland and find strange herbs, but she was too useful to be allowed to stray." (p. 66) The mode is still predominantly realistic: this is the unsurprising tale, for the most part unsurprisingly told, of a family and its history.

Then comes the war. Laura "continued to do up parcels until the eleventh day of November 1918." On that day she returns to Henry's house as usual. "She felt cold and sick, she trembled from head to foot .... All the hooters were sounding .... she thought the walls of her room were shaking at the concussion, like stage walls. She lay down upon her bed, and presently fainted." (p. 70) Her sister-in-law diagnoses influenza. (It should be noted that in the aftermath of the war a particularly virulent form of "Spanish or septic" influenza became pandemic and ended by killing many more millions than had all the battles of the previous four years.)[51] But Lolly's collapse has also to be read as a breakdown, an inner revulsion at her life of routine activities, which the war's ending triggers. The life of seeming-solid, unbudgeable dullness is itself beginning to break down and with it the novel's realism.

Part two, which immediately follows, begins by describing Lolly's newly acknowledged sense of apparently unmotivated anxiety.

> At these times she was subject to a peculiar kind of daydreaming, so vivid as to be almost a hallucination: that she was in the country, at dusk, and alone, and strangely at peace .... while her body sat before the first fires and was cosy with Henry and Caroline, her mind walked by lonely sea-bords, in marshes and fens, or came at nightfall to the edge of a wood. She never imagined herself in these places by daylight. She never thought of them as being in any way beautiful. It was not beauty at all that she wanted, or, depressed though she was, she would have bought a ticket to somewhere or other upon the Metropolitan railway and gone out to see the recumbent autumnal graces of the country-side. Her mind was groping after something that eluded her experience, a something that was shadowy and menacing, and yet in some way congenial; a something that lurked in waste places, that was hinted at by the sound of water gurgling through deep channels and by the voices of birds of

ill-omen. Loneliness, dreariness, aptness for arousing a
sense of fear, a kind of ungodly hallowdness – these were the
things that called her thoughts away from the comfortable
fireside. (p. 76-7)

It has been most delicately prepared for, this deep yearning for a life
that will transgress against the stolid normality of her London existence, and although its manner of expression may owe something to
the promptings of "The Farmer's Bride" and even *Lady into Fox*,
the deliberate literariness of the cadences – "or came at nightfall to
the edge of a wood" – belongs to Lolly's inner life, fed as it has been
on reading and a necessarily incomplete imagining of the witch-like
"ungodly hallowdness" that is out there, beyond the confines of her
brother's house. And so Townsend Warner begins to reach beyond
the limiting, yet apparently immovable solidity of realism which is
the mode of the first part of the novel, and which has accompanied
an unquestioning endorsement of permanent social arrangements
that belong to the pre-war world. Now, at the war's conclusion, this
realism begins to be undermined.

It is therefore crucial that at this moment the nature of Henry's
reactionary politics, together with his capitalist sense of value, is
insinuated into the novel. Lolly has spent extravagantly on some
lilies.

> 'Where do these come from?' Caroline had asked, knowing
> well that nothing so costly in appearance could come from her
> florist.
> 'From Africa,' Laura had answered, pressing the firm, wet
> stalks into her hand.
> 'Oh well, I daresay they are quite common flowers there,'
> said Caroline to herself, trying to gloss over the slight awk-
> wardness of accepting a trifle so needlessly splendid.
> Henry had also asked where they came from.
> 'From Anthos, I believe,' said Caroline.
> 'Ah!' said Henry, and roused the coins in his trouser pocket.
> *(p. 80)*

The involuntary, comic gesture is to be read as a betrayal of Henry's
sexual excitement at such carefree spending, together with his more
conscious warning to money to be on its guard. And just after this
he and Caroline are indeed imaged as Lolly's guardians and warders
both. "Much better that Lolly should not be worried about money
matters. She was safe in their hands. They could look after Lolly.

Henry was like a wall, and Caroline's breasts were like towers." (pp. 80-1). Comically grotesque these images may be, but they also imply a deeply de-humanised quality about the husband and wife. A little later and Lolly becomes aware that "Henry and Caroline, whom she saw every day, were half hidden under their accumulations – accumulations of prosperity, authority, daily experience. They were carpeted with experience." (p. 89)

Lolly's new awareness of lives suffocated by possession coincides with and is to be explained by her increased openness to imaginative possibilities. She, too, is a haunted woman, although unlike Isbel Loment she is haunted not by nostalgia for the unavailing past but by what lies beyond the constrictions of the present. She buys a small guide book to the Chilterns and in the privacy of her own room reads "a list of all the towns and villages, shortly described in alphabetical order. Lamb's End had three hundred inhabitants and a perpendicular font. At Walpole St Dennis was the country seat of the Bartlett family, faced with stucco and situated upon an eminence. The almshouses at Semple, built in 1703 by Bethia Hood, had a fine pair of wrought-iron gates. It was dark as she pressed her nose against the scrolls and rivets. Bats flickered in the little courtyard, and shadows moved across the yellow blinds." (p.87-8)

This is a key moment. The extraordinary movement from a guide-book description of the wrought-iron gates to Lolly's pressing her nose against them is given with no narrative interpolation, no reassuring, realistic explanation of how she might be imagining this. And it is because of this transformative stepping-across from one mode of existence to another that Lolly knows she has woken "from a twenty-years slumber" to see Henry and Caroline as half-hidden by accumulations, children of wealth in a warm nursery. The displacement of the novel's realistic mode necessarily coincides with Lolly's awakening visions of the limitations of her London life and of her corresponding ability to envisage a life beyond it. Vision is the opposite of daily seeing. She will now be able to translate to her new life as witch, choosing to live in a small, not-especially friendly village, and rejecting Henry's anxious wish that she should return to London, because, as he explains, he has invested her money in an enterprise that has turned bad. "'Unfortunately, owing to this Government and all this socialist talk the soundest investments have been badly hit.'" Lolly asks him to explain why he invested her money in "something that doesn't pay" and Henry tells her that the stocks "'will rise again the moment we have a Conservative Government, and that, thank heaven, must come soon. But you see at present it is out of the question for you to think of leaving us.'" (pp. 103-4)

Townsend Warner has taken care to tell us that this conversation takes place in the winter of 1921. At that time Lloyd George was prime minister of a coalition government which was rapidly losing credibility. 1921 was also a year of strikes. As we shall see in Chapter 5, "all this socialist talk" was a great deal more challenging than Henry pretends. By the time *Lolly Willowes* was published the first Labour government had been elected. Admittedly it was a minority one and it did not last for long; but its defeat and even the defeat of the General Strike in 1926 could not be taken to mean that capitalism was free to resume its untroubled progress. On the countrary, it was possible to imagine a very different kind of future. And this is one reason why *Lolly Willowes* is so radical a novel. Lolly's own transformative imagination, her ability to become different, is surely not to be thought of as spectacularly individual, let alone an escapist fantasy. Her life as a witch at Great Mop is an imaginative expression of freedom from those restraints that go with the deadening capitalist accumulations of Henry and Caroline's existence. Lolly frees herself from their "realistic" belief that how they live is how people *must* live, where "must" carries a double charge: meaning that which is both inevitable and morally imperative.

Lolly's imagination is strongly feminist. At the end of a novel which has by now virtually transcended realist constraints, she has a meeting with the Devil in which she tells him that women are like sticks of dynamite which can with perfect safety be used to poke the fire. "'They know they're dynamite, they long for the concussion that may justify them. Some may get religion, then they're all right, I expect. But for the others, for so many, what can there be but witchcraft? That strikes them real. Even if other people still find them quite safe and usual, and go on poking with them, they know in their hearts how dangerous, how incalculable, how extraordinary they are." (p. 237) "That strikes them real." Not *as* real. The refusal of simile insists on the transformative power of what can be imagined. In other words, although Lolly's mode of expression is predominantly feminist, it allows for a radical vision that isn't exclusive to woman as witch or as fox. The vision is a shareable one, even though it took a remarkable woman novelist to articulate it.

In this sense *Lolly Willowes* contrasts very interestingly with *Mrs Dalloway*. Clarissa Dalloway's imagination is often a form of retreat, or a lament for the defeat of transformative hopes.

> Like a nun withdrawing, or a child exploring a tower, she went upstairs, paused at the window, came to the bathroom. There was the green linoleum and a tap dripping. There was an emptiness about the heart of life; an attic room. Women must put off their rich apparel. At mid-day they must disrobe. She pierced the pincushion and laid her feathered yellow hat on the bed. The sheets were clean, tight stretched in a broad white band from side to side. Narrower and narrower would her bed be.[52]

Such a passage implies much about the limitations of Clarissa Dalloway's life, in particular perhaps her less than full or fulfilled sexuality. But "the emptiness about the heart of life", which I take to be Mrs Dalloway's own thought, generalises from a pathology Woolf has sharply individualised but which at the same time has to be thought of as middle-class. In *Lolly Willowes* Townsend Warner offers a more radical sense of what the imagination can nourish. In *Mrs Dalloway* Woolf is quite properly concerned with the un-radical containments of Clarissa Dalloway's consciousness. Yet Townsend Warner's novel has received far less critical attention than *Mrs Dalloway* – it isn't even always in print. And such commentators as it has attracted have failed to see that its formal radicalism is *intrinsically* political. The novel moves through a succession of deftly presented narrative stages which are also historical, social moments: from pre-war England via the war itself to the post-war period and on into the near future. As it does so realism loosens its apparently "natural" and unyielding grip and the fantastic and visionary increasingly take control. And as they do, so the sense of capital's four-square bricky presence – its claim to be the "real" world – is first disputed and then replaced by liberated and liberating glimpses of alternative possibilities, other ways of living. At war's end the breakdown of Lolly Willowes subtly shadows a larger, more absolute breakdown. Power shifts. Those who took for granted their claim to power are made to look absurd and powerless to prevent if not oppose the empowering of those whom they had previously despised and whose lives they had manipulated for their own ends. Townsend Warner's decision to join the communist party in the early 1930s does not present a new departure, still less a change of heart. If we read *Lolly Willowes* aright it becomes difficult to imagine that she could have done anything else.

## Notes to Chapter 3

1. There are, it goes without saying, many studies of this change. A good "coffee table" account is offered by Alan Jenkins, *The Twenties,* Book Club Associates, London, 1974. And during the decade a growing number of books by women argued the feminist case. Of these, few were more important than Dora Russell's *Hypatia,* 1925, in which Russell remarks at one point that for working women "the principle of feminine equality is as natural as drawing breath – they are neither oppressed by tradition nor worn by rebellion." D. Russell: *Hypatia: or Women and Knowledge,* London, Kegan Paul, Trench and Trubner, 1925, p. 7 For dress, see James Laver, *Taste and Fashion,* London, Harrap, 1937, and Georgina Howell, *Vogue: Six Decades of Fashion,* London, Book Club Associates, 1979, esp pp. 1-100.
2. Alison Light, *Forever England: Femininity, Literature and Conservatism Between the Wars,* London, Routledge & Kegan Paul, 1991, p. 10.
3. Much work has been done by the journals *History Workshop* and *Past and Present* in recovering this history. See also Sybil Oldfield (ed): *This Working-Day World, Women's Lives and Cultures in Britain, 1914-1945,* London, Taylor and Francis, 1994.
4. Margaret Llewelyn Davies, *Life As We Have Known It: By Co-operative Working Women* with a new intro. by Anna Davin, London, Virago, 1977, pp. xxi and xxxxi.
5. For this see Val Warner (ed) *Charlotte Mew: Collected Poems and Prose* Manchester, Carcanet, 1981, p. xii.
5a. The Dymock poets, which included Lascelles Abercrombie, Wilfred Gibson, Rupert Brooke, John Drinkwater, Robert Frost and Edward Thomas, came together in a remote corner of Gloucestershire in the spring and summer of 1914. Although the grouping does not signify a self-conscious "school" of poetry, the members were all interested in bringing back into poetry a kind of grittily attentive realism, both in subject matter and in use of demotic speech.
6. See Warner, p. xii, Mew became extremely depressed after the death of her remaining sister, Anne, in 1927.
7. All quotations come from the Penguin text, David Garnett, *Lady into Fox and A Man in the Zoo,* Harmondsworth, 1980, pp. 20-1. Future quotations will be followed by page reference to the Penguin edition.
8. Although the original edition of *A Voyage to Arcturus* sold slowly, the novel has been reprinted at least six times and has never lacked for distinguished, and ardent, advocates.
9. For this see the Introduction to the Canongate edition of *The Haunted Woman* by John Pick, Edinburgh, 1987, pp. vii-viii.
10. Pick, p. vii. All quotations are from this edition and will be followed by page references to it.
11. For this see Charles Carrington, *Rudyard Kipling,* Harmondsworth, Penguin,

1970, pp. 432-4. For discussion about the "heart of England" see my *Modern English Poetry: From Hardy to Hughes,* London, Batsford, 1986, pp. 50-56.

12. Douglas Goldring, *The Merchant of Souls,* London, Jarrolds, 1926. Quotations are from this edition and will be followed by page references to it.

13. The William Hickey gossip column is of especial importance in this context.

14. F.R. Leavis, *D.H. Lawrence, Novelist,* Harmondsworth, Penguin, 1964, p. 277-8. Lawrence's poem *Purple Anenomes,* (1921) satirises "two disenfranchised women," and Graham Martin has suggested to me that the novella, *The Ladybird* (1923) "tackles the theme of aesthetic idealisation of sexuality as the peculiarly modern 'dead end,' one reason for proposing 'the feral' instead." This is so, but in *The Fox* Lawrence's animus against his female protagonists feels more unguarded and hence instructive.

15. Leavis, p. 72.

16. Graham Holderness, *D.H. Lawrence: History, Ideology and Fiction,* London, Gill and Macmillan, Dublin, 1982. p. 172. The Lawrence quotation comes from the Penguin edition of *Three Novellas: The Fox, The Ladybird, The Captain's Doll,* Harmondsworth, 1969, p. 151. All future quotations are from this edition and will be followed by page references to it.

17. Holderness, op. cit. p. 167. He refers to key passages in the tale to be found at pps. 103 and 148. These bear out his reading.

18. Holderness, p. 174.

19. Holderness, p. 171.

20. Paul Fussell, *Abroad: British Literary Travelling Between the Wars,* London, O.U.P., 1980, p. 16.

21. There are several accounts of the relationship and flight to Paris of Vita Sackville-West and Violet Trefusis. Probably the most reliable as well as the least sensational is that provided by Nigel Nicolson in *Portrait of a Marriage,* London, Weidenfeld and Nicolson, 1973.

22. Quoted by Anne Chisholm in *Nancy Cunard,* London, Sidgwick and Jackson, 1979, p. 46.

23. Chisholm, pp. 36-8.

24. Chisholm, p. 49.

25. For this see Henry Pelling, *A History of British Trade Unionism,* op. cit. pp. 163-5.

26. Chisholm, p. 59.

27. Chisholm, p. 96 and (esp) pp. 102-126 passim.

28. Fussell, *Abroad,* p. 16.

29. In his society novel of the 1920s, *The Green Hat,* Michael Arlen comes closer to understanding Nancy when he has his narrator say of the character based on her that "you felt she had outlawed herself from somewhere, but where was that somewhere? You felt she was tremendously indifferent whether she was outlawed or not." Quoted by Chisholm, pp. 69-70. This catches something of Nancy's independent spirit, her refusal to accede to her mother's increasingly importunate demands that she should model her behaviour on "respectable" standards.

30. I am grateful to Marion Shaw for this information. She suggests that Holtby went to South Africa to cope with her feelings after Vera Brittain's marriage. However, what concerns me is Holtby's ready involvement in radical politics.

31. Alison Thomas, *Portraits of Women: Gwen John and her Forgotten Contemporaries,* Oxford, Polity Press, 1995. For Gwen John see Susan Chitty's 1982 monograph and Cecily Langdale and David Fraser Jenkins, *Gwen John: An Interior Life,* London, Phaidon Press & Barbican Gallery, 1985 – this is a well-illustrated catalogue to a major exhibition of Gwen John's work.

32. Nina Hamnett, *Laughing Torso,* London, Virago, 1984, pp. 118 &123. This wonderfully louche work was first published in 1932.

33. *Quartet* was first published under the title *Postures* in 1928. My quotations are

107

taken from the Penguin text, Harmondsworth, 1973, and page references are identified after each quotation.

34. Carole Angier, *Jean Rhys: Her Life and Work,* London, Penguin, 1992, p. 126.
35. Angier p. 126, For the relationship between Rhys and Ford see Angier pp. 129-219 passim. Angier, like most biographers of writers, wants to find "originals" for Rhys's characters, thereby reducing her originality and the force of her imagination.
36. Evelyn Gibbs graduated from the Royal College in 1928 and was awarded the College's Rome Scholarship. For further details see Pauline Lucas, *Evelyn Gibbs, 1905-1991,* Nottingham, Angel Row Gallery, 1993. This is the catalogue for a major exhibition of Gibbs' work. See also Katy Deepwell, *Ten Decades: Careers of Ten Women Artists, 1897-1906,* Norwich Gallery, 1992, the catalogue for an exhibition which included examples of Gibbs' work and a brief, not always accurate, account of her life. Sadly, Nan Youngman died as I was writing this book. I do not therefore know what has happened to the painting "Le Depart".
37. Quoted by Eileen Agar, *A Look at My Life,* London, Methuen, 1988, p. 87. Agar's discovery of Paris included meetings with many famous artists and writers working there. As a result she became recognised as one of the leading surrealist painters of her time, which almost certainly would not have happened had she stayed in England.
38. For more on this see Katy Deepwell. See also Katherine Hale's autobiography, *A Slender Reputation,* London, Frederick Warne, 1994 pp. 139-142. Although Hale's first visit to Paris in the mid-20s was a short one she at once decided she wanted to live there permanently.
39. V. Woolf, *A Room of One's Own,* London, Penguin, p. 107.
40. For this see Augustus John, *Chiaroscuro: Fragments of Autobiography,* London, Cape, 1954, p. 72.
41. See Maroula Joannou, "'Nothing is Impracticable for a Single, Middle-Aged Woman with an Income of her Own': The Spinster in Women's Fiction of the 1920s"; in Sybil Oldfield (ed), *This Working-Day World,* op. cit. p. 176.
42. Katherine Mansfield, *The Garden Party and Other Stories,* London, Constable, 1922, pp. 125-6. All future page references, which follow quotations, are to this edition.
43. Alison Light: *Forever England,* op. cit. p. 46.
44. Alison Light provides a most persuasive account of how Compton-Burnett's early years fed into her fiction; she is especially good on the concealment of origins, the class-based shame and embarrassment of the family's circumstances, of not being sure where they stood in relation to others. See Light pp. 24-31.
45. *Brothers and Sisters* was first published in 1929. My text is the one reprinted by Alison and Busby in 1984. All future references, which will follow quotations, are to this edition.
46. Alison Light, p. 24.
47. Robert Liddell, "Notes on Ivy Compton-Burnett" *Twentieth Century Literature, Ivy Compton-Burnett Issue,* guest ed. Charles Beerkhart, vol. 25. no 2, (Summer 1977), p. 135.
48. Alison Light, p. 233.
49. Dating Elizabeth Daryush's poems is very difficult but it is probable that the sonnet was written either at the end of the 1920s or sometime early in the 1930s. *The Collected Poems* makes no attempt at dating. Manchester, Carcanet, 1978, p. 57.
50. Sylvia Townsend-Warner, *Lolly Willowes.* The novel was first published by Chatto & Windus in 1926. My text is the Women's Press Reprint of 1978, p. 6. All future quotations are from this text and will be followed by page reference.

51. In their amiable *The Long Weekend: A Social History of Britain 1918-1939,* London, Faber & Faber, 1941, Robert Graves and Alan Hodge claim that between 1917, when it first appeared, and 1919, when it was finally put down, the 'flu pandemic "killed twenty seven million people throughout the world." p. 22.

51. V. Woolf, *Mrs Dalloway,* London, The Hogarth Press, 1925. p. 48.

CHAPTER FOUR

# DRUGS, DRINK, DANCE
# and THE DEVIL'S MUSIC

Sometime in 1922 Kathleen Hale was invited by Philip Heseltine to a beer party. She was to find that beer wasn't the only attraction on offer.

> [Heseltine] presented his guests with tiny parcels wrapped in lavatory paper. Since everybody swallowed the contents under draughts of ale, so did I, not knowing that the parcels contained hashish. One by one the guests fell blissfully asleep on the floor, and Philip took me, all bland acquiescence, to bed with him, unaware of being under the influence of the drug. However, the 'fate worse than death' was to pass me by on this occasion. I spent the night innocently in Philip's tender embrace, while I endured horrendous nightmares about colossal and malign elephants. Next morning I awoke in considerable alarm. Still under the influence of hashish, I was convinced that I had become an object of utter ridicule with a monstrous body and eyes that had totally disappeared behind puffed eyelids. My class at the infants' school began at nine o'clock, and for a teacher to arrive in this condition would be disastrous. Philip insisted on seeing me to my bus and by the time I got there, the results of the drug had – mercifully – worn off, and I was composed. I have never been tempted to repeat the experiment.[1]

As intimated in the previous chapter, Kathleen Hale was one of those young women from middle-class circumstance who in increasing numbers were beginning after the war to find freedom through art. She had trained initially at Reading University's art department, which she entered in 1915, and then went on to London, much to the horror of her widowed mother, who had planned that her daughter should return home to Derbyshire and enrol for a course in shorthand and typing. "'I am *not* going home again,' I replied. 'I am not going to type. I am going to be an artist. You can send a policeman to fetch me, but I shall come back to London again and again.' She gave up."[2] In London Hale attended Jacob Epstein's Sunday tea-parties and began to frequent the Café Royal. She inevitably met Augustus John, became his secretary, and once, "out of curiosity, allowed him to seduce me. The sex barrier down, this aberration only added a certain warmth to our friendship."[3]

Like *Laughing Torso*, Hale's autobiography *A Slender Reputation* (1994) is both wonderfully funny and a most instructive account of life among certain of the young in the post-war years. The fact that Kathleen Hale is looking back from her nineties no doubt allows her to add a spice of relish to her deadpan tales; yet her enjoyment of life in the twenties, as a young, liberated woman, isn't to be questioned. And on an occasion when I was privileged to listen to Elisabeth Vellacott and Nan Youngman reminisce about their days as art students and then as young artists in the twenties, it became clear that they had shared Hale's sense of exultant delight in freedoms achieved and joyously celebrated. A photograph of Nan, taken in 1924 while she was an art student at the Slade, shows her sitting cross-legged on a patch of grass outside college buildings. She wears trousers, strums a ukelele; and a cigarette dangles casually from her lips.[4]

Trousers, ukelele, cigarette: iconic symbols of freedom. If you played a ukelele you made your own music – "jazz" or dance music, as like as not. Trousers however told a different tale. "The first women to wear trousers and dungarees wore them because they went with the job – dirty, hard jobs that women were taking over from the soldiers .... Working clothes weren't considered part of fashion at all."[5] Thus Georgina Howell, writing of women in wartime. But as she goes on to say, after the war some women at least refused to adapt to dress that signified a return to domestic circumstance. For a woman to wear trousers was to show that she was serious about work that didn't confine her to the house. It also testified to a refusal to accept conventional images of womanhood. In *Goodbye to All That* Robert Graves recalls the comedy of his marriage in January 1918 to Nancy Nicholson. Furious at her discovery that the marriage service required her to vow obedience to her husband, Nancy left the wedding reception "and changed back into her land-girl's costume of breeches and smock."[6]

As to smoking in public. Although women began to do it in the immediate post-war years, it was still considered daring and scarcely respectable. The cigarettes had to be "Egyptian and Turkish, not Virginian." (Presumably because the more expensive the cigarette the less likely the smoker to be mistaken for a prostitute.) "It was considered all right to smoke in the restaurant car of a train, but vulgar on the top of a bus. Some women smoked in restaurants, and a waiter in one knocked a cigarette out of a lady's mouth."[7] In 1922 *Vogue* carried a sketch for a flowerpot hat by Helen Dryden in which the model has a fox fur draped over her shoulders and holds in her left hand a long, elegant cigarette-holder with smouldering cigarette.[8] On the table in front of her stands a coffee cup, although a cocktail glass could probably have been substituted without arousing unacceptable hostility.

Women smoking and women drinking were, then, tolerated, even if such habits weren't always approved. Drug-taking was a different matter. Yet as Kathleen Hale's account of her night with Heseltine indicates, drugs were not only around in the 1920s, they were comparatively easy to come by. There are studiously casual allusions to drug taking in Aldous Huxley's early novels. In literature, if not in life, drugs were associated with decadence: they signify the arid hedonism of the Bright Young Things or the deeper decadence of a society living out its final days. Hence, the appearance of cocaine in the Earl of Halsbury's *1944*.

This very peculiar prophecy of doom was published in 1926 and as far as I can tell made scarcely a ripple before it sank into invisibility. There were few if any reviews and I have come across no mention of it in discussions of the decade, either then or later. Yet it is not without interest. Intended as a dreadful warning of future war and of how that would depend on air power, *1944* supposes that a secret alliance has been made between Germany and Russia and that at an agreed signal the two nations, bent on world domination, will use incendiary and gas bombs to reduce that rest of the world to rubble. The bombing starts, only a few escape, and as a couple of them, a young man and his fiancée, make their way across a ruined England, they stumble on a house-party in Somerset. The party is in high spirits – literally. Their plan is to "'Eat, drink and be merry. To-morrow we die, and all that sort of thing.'" The young man asks them what they'll do when they've run out of everything, and the head of the party says:

> 'But we shan't have run out of everything. See that gold pot there in the middle of the table? We shan't run out of that.

That's las' thing to run out of."
'What is it?'
'Thing my father won in local dog-show, and at the present
moment it's full of snow.'
'Snow?'
'Yes, snow. Coco-Cocaine. If y'eat enough of that, y'won't
want to eat any more.'[9]

Halsbury was projecting onto 1944 what he knew of the 1920s, and
by the time he sat down to write his novel the use of drugs by the
younger generation had become a much canvassed topic. The
implied drug dependency of the hero of *The Vortex* was the major
cause of the shocked reception of Noel Coward's play, first staged at
the Everyman Theatre in Hampstead in 1924, from where it transferred to the West End. According to Sheridan Morley, *The Daily
Mail* fulminated against what it called "This dustbin of a play," and
Sir Gerald du Maurier, in the course of a lengthy attack on the
immorality of modern drama, singled out *The Vortex* for especial
condemnation. Hannan Swaffer called it "the most decadent play of
our time," and another commentator remarked that "the fault, dear
Noel, lies not in our Ma's but in ourselves that we are slaves to
dope."[10]

None of these criticisms makes much sense. *The Vortex* may be
about decadence but it certainly doesn't celebrate it. On the contrary, it is tediously determined to demonstrate the brittle insufficiencies of those who live for pleasure: theirs are the days of cock-
tails, cigarettes, and casual affairs, all of which are accompanied by,
and in a way identified through, the mania for dance-music. The
stage direction for the opening of Act II, which is set in a country
house "about forty miles from London," runs in part as follows:

> The gramophone is going, and there is a continual buzz of
> conversation .... There must be a feeling of hectic amusement
> and noise, and the air black with cigarette smoke and
> superlatives. During the first part of the scene everyone must
> appear to be talking at once, but the actual lines spoken while
> dancing must be timed to reach the audience as the speakers
> pass near the footlights.[11]

This is a dance of death, so we are made to feel, the actors engaged
in a ritual that will be echoed in different ways throughout the
decade. Hence, the car races of *Vile Bodies*, where frenzied, purposeless living leads to the inevitable crash and to death. Hence,

too, John Armstrong's painting "The Dance of Nothing," in which harlequins with wooden swords and uplifted, vacant faces, move in an endless, meaningless circle. In Coward's play, drink and drugs speed the characters on their way to damnation, although the only drug-taker is Nicky, whose mother, an ageing beauty, tries to deny the passing of the years by involving herself in affairs with men half her age. Her drunken, shameless exhibitionism is, so it is suggested, somehow responsible for Nicky's habit. At one point his friend Helen tries to tell him he must stop.

> Helen: You fool! You unutterable little fool!.
> Nicky: Don't be dramatic, dear.
> Helen: I thought you had more common sense; I credited you with more intelligence than that.
> Nicky: If you persist in being absurd.
> Helen (suddenly with intense feeling): Nicky, don't resist me, don't fight me, I'm your friend, I wouldn't have said a word if I weren't. You've got to stop it; you haven't got very far yet, there's still time – for God's sake listen to reason .... Throw it away....
> Nicky: You needn't be frightened, Helen, I only take the tiniest bit, once in a blue moon!
> Helen: If anything goes wrong, you'll take a lot – throw it away.
> Nicky: What could go wrong?
> Helen: Never mind, throw it away![12]

"It" is a small box in which Nicky presumably keeps cocaine, although the kind of drug he takes is never mentioned. Near the end of the play, when he and his mother confront one another in an unintendedly hilarious bedroom scene during which they try to be terribly truthful with one another, she hurls his box from her window. But this may not be the end of the matter. For he has just told her that "it's the fault of circumstances and civilisation – civilisation makes rottenness so much easier – we're utterly rotten – both of us – .... How can we help ourselves? We swirl about in a vortex of beastliness"[13]

Audiences in 1924 would have been quick to link Nicky and Florence's "set" to that "rottenness" which, although it could hardly be thought to amount to civilisation, might nevertheless symbolise aspects of post-war society which between them could be labelled decadent. And they would have connected the set to a number of drug scandals which had made newspaper headlines in the years between 1918 and 1923, when *The Vortex* was written.

These have been well documented by Marek Kohn in *Dope Girls: The Birth of the British Drug Underground*. Two cases in particular stand out. Late in 1918, after attending a Victory Ball held at the Albert Hall, the proceeds of which were to go to Nation's Fund for Nurses, a young comedy actress Billie Carleton was found dead in her hotel room. The probable cause of her death was a cocktail of drugs – including opium and cocaine – and drink. But public interest focused less on the inquest than on the subsequent trial of those accused of drug peddling. They included Reggie De Veulle, who was hinted to have made a living as a male prostitute, and a Chinese woman, Ada Lau Ping, sentenced to five months hard labour and described by the sentencing magistrate, Frederick Mead as "the priestess at these unholy rites." (It was Mead who would ten years later condemn as obscene the Warren's Gallery exhibition of D. H. Lawrence's paintings). By "unholy rites" Mead meant an opium party which had been described in court and at which, the court heard, people "had undressed and changed into nightclothes; pyjamas for the men and chiffon nightdresses for the women."[14]

Kohn points out that following the Carleton scandal there came the all-too predictable scare stories of a widespread drug menace. *The Daily Express* ran a short series on the issue and *The Daily Mail* quoted "an expert" as saying that "Men do not as a rule take to drugs unless there is a hereditary influence, but women are temperamentally attracted." Cocaine was especially associated with sexual "looseness", that is with untrammelled femininity and the effeminate; and it's possible that Coward means to hint at Nicky's "hereditary influence" and true sexual orientation in giving him his cocaine habit. In the course of the play Nicky loses his girlfriend to his mother's latest young man, but *The Vortex* repeatedly suggests that Nicky is being merely conventional in pretending to love Bunty. The police found a "little gold box ... half full of cocaine" on Billie Carlton's bedside table. When Nicky finally reveals to his mother his drug habit, he takes "a small gold box from his pocket."[15] (*The Daily Express's* "Special Correspondent" was invited to a "dope party" by a man "who lisped like a woman ... and reeked overpoweringly of perfume.") And in David Garnett's 1919 novel, *Dope Darling*, the hero, Roy Plowman, is saved from battlefield injuries and for love by a virtuous woman, Beatrice Chase, while Roy's sister, Claire, who is a nightclub singer and free with her sexual favours, dies of cocaine addiction.[16]

Just over three years after the Billie Carleton scandal a young woman called Freda Kempton collapsed and died from the effects of cocaine mixed with water. Kempton was a nightclub dancer who took to cocaine in order "to stay appealing and lively through a long night." Unlike Carleton, however, it seems that Kempton intended to kill herself. She had apparently written the beginnings of a note which ran "Mother, forgive me. The whole world was against me. I really meant no harm and ..." The inquest found that she had committed suicide while temporarily insane. (Of course.) Dance and drugs were now linked as twin signs of modern decadence. *The Daily Express* sent a special correspondent into a dancing den set in a "forbidding neighbourhood not far from Marble Arch," decorated "on the incoherent Futurist lines usual in such places," and featuring a band which played foxtrots, and "undersized aliens, blue about the chin and greasy." There were also numbers of young girls, thin and underdressed. Our correspondent soon realises that "This crowd had been carefully admitted."[17]

Sex, drugs, dance music. Signs of the times, elements in the vortex of beastliness. Not surprisingly, perhaps, the censors gave a hard time of it to two films which attempted to deal with these matters. (I can only suppose that *The Vortex* wasn't subject to the Lord Chamberlain's blue pencil because it "exposed" decadence rather than celebrating it.) The Birmingham film director Jack Graham-Cutts made a film to which he gave the title *Cocaine,* and which he described as a pioneer work of film journalism. The film, completed in six weeks was released in May, 1922. Kohn has a fascinating account of *Cocaine,* prints of which still exist, and of the censorship row it caused. It was banned in London, but played in other cities such as Cardiff and Manchester, because these had no night-clubs or "dancedope dens", and as a result, so Cardiff's Chief Constable argued, "the facilities for the drug traffic were so limited as to be non-existent." Two years later, however, the American film, *Human Wreckage*, was refused a certificate, even though it was "the brainchild of Florence Reid, the widow of the Hollywood star Wally Reid, a morphine addict who died in 1923." The opponents of decadence were now on full alert. And they were bound to be worried about the vast popularity of film and cinema-going. (In Henry Green's *Living,* 1929, his working-class characters go to see a film nearly every night, and although this may be something of an exaggeration of reality, film was undoubtedly extraordinarily popular, especially as a working-class form of entertainment.)[18] Censorship was now an issue.

## II

There were victories and defeats, depending whose side you were on. *Ulysses* was barred from entering Britain but Marie Stopes was allowed to keep her birth control clinic. On the other hand, she lost a libel action she brought against a writer who suggested that in selling contraceptives to working women Stopes was engaged in profiteering. Yet the clinic made no profit and all the proceeds from the ten editions of *Married Love* went into paying for its upkeep.[19] In 1921 an attempt to legislate against lesbianism was opposed by legal law lords on the grounds that not talking about it would very likely cause its disappearance. Lord Desart thought it a mistake "to tell the whole world that there is such an offence," while Lord Birkenhead was of the opinion that out of every thousand women "999 have never heard whispers of these practices. Among all these ... the taint of this noxious and horrible suspicion is to be imparted?"[20]

The new freedom of women undoubtedly carried with it the threat of such taint. Hence, I suspect, Lady Cunard's unease about her daughter's friendship with Sybil Hart-Davis. Hence, too, Lawrence's dislike of the close relationship between March and Banford in *The Fox* and, perhaps, the forced moment when March looks at Henry and

> wished she could stay with him. She wished she had married him already, and it was all over. For oh, she felt suddenly so safe with him. She felt so strangely safe and peaceful in his presence. If only she could sleep in his shelter, and not with Jill. In her dim, tender state, it was agony to have to go with Jill and sleep with her. She wanted the boy to save her. *(p. 141)*

Although March later writes to Henry to tell him that she and Jill have a life together and that "I love Jill, and she makes me feel safe and sane," (p143) we have to understand this as a fear of launching herself into the unknown life the boy offers her of which, we are also to understand, he will make a success for them both.

Henry's unequivocal maleness is a redemptive force. At the time he was writing *The Fox*, Lawrence was also writing *Fantasia of the*

118

*Unconscious*. Here, in the course of talking about "a successful sex union," he asserts that "The great thing is to keep the sexes pure. And by pure we don't mean an ideal sterile innocence and similarity between boy and girl. We mean pure maleness in a man, pure femaleness in a woman.... Women and men are dynamically different, in everything."[21] The fear that post-war men and women might *not* be dynamically different almost certainly accounts for Douglas Goldring's remark in *The Merchant of Souls* that young men nowadays are too effeminate; and a similar fear prompts the insistence that drugs and sexual perversion go together and that only women and womenly men become addicted to cocaine.

Lawrence was all for sexual freedom, but it had to be "normative." In the *Fantasia* he remarks that "The blood-consciousness is the first and last knowledge of the living soul: the depths .... And blood-consciousness cannot operate purely until the soul has put off all its manifold degrees and forms of upper consciousness." This is the plea for instinctual behaviour as opposed to "The scientific fact of sex" on the one hand, and, on the other, what he calls "the dear-darling-love smarm: the spiritual love." Between them, these two alternatives lead to a sterile, rational world of "understanding", which Lawrence insists has poisoned the mass of humanity. The recovery or fresh discovery of health requires us to expel this poison.[22]

I have no idea how widely read the *Fantasia* was. We know that Auden came across it either while he was an undergraduate at Oxford or very soon afterwards; and he seems to have approved of much that Lawrence was saying. This at first looks odd. How could he have sympathised with Lawrence's belligerency about pure maleness? But I suspect that Auden did what others must have done who had either read the *Fantasia* or felt that they knew Lawrence's argument: he took from it what he wanted. And what he and the others most wanted was to believe, as Auden himself said in a notebook entry for 1929, that "'Be good and you will be happy,' is a dangerous inversion. 'Be happy and you will be good' is the truth."[23] For Lawrence's belief in the intimate connection between liberation that results from "the sex relation" and overall health, moral, marital, and physical, was widely shared during the 1920s. This is how Lawrence put it in the *Fantasia*: "There is a threefold result. First, the flash of pure sensation and of real electricity. Then there is the birth of an entirely new state of blood in each partner. And then there is the liberation."[24]

Liberation was what others were after. They included Homer Lane, the American psychologist who worked in London after the war, and for whom "complete freedom of behaviour – full self-expression – must lead inevitably to goodness." In 1925 Lane was threatened with deportation following allegations that he had been sexually involved with a woman patient, and after pictures of an "indelicate" nature had been found in his consulting room together with "French preventatives". Lane left for France, caught typhoid, and in September 1925 died in Nice. Among his patients was John Layard, who instructed the young Auden in teachings derived from Lane. According to Layard, "'God' really means our physical desires, the inner law of our own nature," and the Devil is then "the conscious control of those desires – something we should avoid at all costs." Sin is disobedience to the god of our desires.[25] Behind Layard stands not merely Lane but the German psychologist, Georg Groddeck, whose belief in the psychosomatic nature of illness both connects back to Lawrence, of whom he was probably unaware, and behind him to that group of pre-war liberationist anti-psychiatrists who lived and worked at Ascona and whose influence Lawrence himself had come under through Frieda. (Before meeting Lawrence, Frieda had been sexually involved with one of the leaders of the group, Otto Gross, for whom she even contemplated leaving her marriage.) "Gross's doctrine was that the senses are our agents of Paradise, and they are frustrated by the anxieties of conscience and the nightmares of guilt aroused by society."[26] For Groddeck, all sickness is traceable to the deepest elements in human personality: constipation indicates the sufferer to be a miser by nature, hoarseness is caused by the attempt to prevent something conscious or unconscious being said aloud.[27]

It is no part of my present purpose to investigate or try to narrate the work of those various psychologists practising and pronouncing during the 1920s for whom connections between "self-expression" – for want of a better word – and "happiness" – for want of another – spelt true "liberation" – for want of a third. The point is simply that their positions could be used to strengthen the case of those coming to maturity in the post-war years who wanted to find arguments for rejecting and discrediting the moral and social views of an older generation which had sanctioned the war. The young could claim not only to have right on their side: they had the permission of "scientific" evidence. Restraint makes you unhappy, makes you ill, may even be said to have led to the terrible sickness of the years 1914-18. And so for the young, perhaps especially for young women, there was a new jauntiness about their declarations of sexual freedom. Kathleen Hale recalls meeting in 1922 Yvonne Kapp, "who had just run away from home aged nineteen and married, despite her parents' veto, Edmund 'Peter' Kapp, a superb caricaturist thirteen years her senior." Kapp would further appall her parents by publishing at her own expense a first novel, *Nobody Asked You*, because it was too obscene for orthodox publishing houses to take. Inevitably it was a huge success. And shortly afterwards Hale herself wrote to tell her mother that she had met a man she cared for, "but as he strongly disbelieved in marriage, we intended to live together."[28]

Living together could be a great deal more difficult if you were involved in more complicated liaisons, which is how the Bloomsbury coterie seemed by and large to conduct its affairs. Virginia, Leonard and Vita, Vita, Harold and his various young men, Vanessa, Clive, Duncan (and Maynard), Strachey, Partridge and Carrington (and Brenan). And beyond Bloomsbury there were Robert Graves and Nancy and Laura Riding (and Phibbs) and Winifred Holtby and Vera Brittan and *her* husband. Not all of these people were happy. It may well be nearer the mark to say that most of them were for most of the time wretchedly unhappy; but their refusal to accommodate themselves to conventional marriages does indicate an element in the 1920s which cannot be ignored: liberation as sexual rebellion.

One inevitable expression of this was the campness that went with a rejection of masculinity, of all those values and virtues which had been extolled both before and during the war. Lawrence and Goldring might fear the waning of "pure maleness", but for others that was not so much loss as gain. In an acute essay written to coincide with the emergence of James Joyce's works from copyright in 1992, Declan Kiberd speaks of Leonard Bloom as "the androgynous anti-hero of *Ulysses*" and the carrier of Joyce's utopian hopes. Although Kiberd does not say so, it seems reasonable to assume that Lawrence's furious rejection of Joyce's epic, his claim that it did dirt on life, was in part prompted by his recognition that Bloom wasn't an endorsement of the cocksure man Lawrence looked for. As Kiberd astutely notes, in Joyce's book "the very ordinariness of the modern Ulysses, Mr Leopold Bloom, becomes a standing reproach to the myth of ancient military heroism." He adds that although

Poldy and his wife may disagree on many things, "they share a principled aversion to war, violence and licensed coercion." In *Ulysses* Joyce wonderfully characterises the "brutish empire" as a compendium of "beer, beef, business, bibles, bulldogs, battleships, buggery and bishops." And Bloom, while he is no more in favour of sexual preditariness than he is of imperial conquest, is opposed to the self-imposed celibacy of Christ. "Jesus was a bachelor and never lived with a woman," Joyce remarked to Frank Budgen. "Surely living with a woman is one of the most difficult things a man has to do, and he never did it."[29]

Joyce's candid acknowledgement of Bloom's being a whole man who is also content to be a nobody includes acceptance of his conventionally improbable hero as an entirely probable one in actuality. Bloom as everyman acknowledges and takes for granted aspects of sexuality in an uncensorious manner which puts him at the opposite side of the world from Eliot's Tiresias. In the *Waste Land* Tiresias emerges as the prurient, disgusted voyeur of the animal-like sexual couplings which such critics as F.R. Leavis and Cleanth Brooks took to characterise relationships in the modern world: mechanical, sterile, joyless. More recently, however, commentators have suggested that Tiresias offers not so much an objective viewpoint on post-war city life as a betraying insight into Eliot's own predicament. I have no wish to add to what is surely Tiresias-like in its intrusive speculation about Eliot's life. On the other hand, I do not see how anyone can read his great poem without feeling that, for all the poet himself is meant to be invisible, a strong charge of what it may be most tactful to call sexual anxiety makes itself felt throughout. And I most certainly think that in the early post-war years, the fusing, confusing and refusing of gender distinctions (and roles) make for challenges that are as worrying to some as they are liberating for others. Here, then, it may be helpful to make mention of *Orlando*.

John Mepham suggests that Virginia Woolf's biography is "a deliberately superficial book," in that for once Woolf was able to lay aside the responsibility of being "a difficult author," of facing "the usual problems" of her concerns for the modern novel. He seems to assume that this must be so because Woolf wholly relished the experience of writing *Orlando* – she confided in her diary that while she worked on it she was "in the thick of the greatest rapture known to me" – and did not agonise over what she was doing. But it is at least possible that this rapture was connected to the liberating of her imagination, which the subject not only allowed but positively required. As Mepham says:

> its comic treatment of gender, and Orlando's experience of switching from male to female, highlights the conventionality, the artificiality, of social assumptions about men and women and what they are capable of. The book celebrates the richness of Orlando's personality which, containing as it does elements and capacities normally seen as the best of both masculine and feminine, thoroughly reveals the absurdity of these social categories. It rejects the idea that a person has a fixed gender, and is limited in what they can desire and enjoy to the standard, permitted forms of pleasure. Treating such subversive themes through fantasy allows them to be aired without too much anxiety, and allows moral and cultural norms and prohibitions to be transgressed in an unthreatening way.[30]

*Orlando* was published in 1928, the year in which Radclyffe Hall's lesbian novel *The Well of Loneliness* was banned. *In The Long Weekend: A Social History of Britain, 1918–1939,* Graves and Hodge report that public opinion was roused against Hall's novel by James Douglas, who wrote in *The Daily Express* that "I would rather give a healthy boy or girl a phial of prussic acid than this book."[31] That Woolf chose to treat subversive themes through fantasy may well have been because she sensed a new, nipping wind in the air. My feeling is that after the defeat of the General Strike in 1926 the old order began to re-group, that surly authority once more fancied its chances. You have only to compare the refusals of the law lords in 1921 to make lesbianism illegal with the successful prosecution of so innocent as well as inept a novel as *The Well of Loneliness* to feel that something nasty has happened, that reaction is once more in the ascendant.

It may be for this reason, as much because of increasing ill-health, that Ronald Firbank published his last novel in 1926. *Concerning The Eccentricities of Cardinal Pirelli* is perhaps the campest of his novels, although I don't share the view that it is particularly well written. There is a slovenliness about some of the prose which Beardsley, who is obviously a model for Firbank, would never have permitted himself. As here, for example. "While in retreat it was his fancy, while supping, to pursue some standard work of devotion ..." And much of the novel reads as a kind of routine "naughtiness." The Primate casts an eye over a sleeping boy folded in dainty sleep .... Witching as Eros, in his loose-flowing alb ...

'– And lead us not into temptation,' the Primate murmured, stooping to gaze on him.

Age of bloom and fleeting folly: Don Apple-cheeks!

'....How would you like my Velasqueth, boy? ...' His Eminence's hand framed an airy caress...

There was a spell of singing silence, while the dove-grey mystic lighting waxed and waned.

Aroused by it as much as by the Primate's hand, the boy started up with a scream of terror.

'Ouch, sir!'

'Olé boy?'[32]

Perhaps the same nipping air keeps from Ivy Compton-Burnett's later novels those snatches of dialogue which occur in *Pastors and Masters* where, to take an example, Theresa Fletcher, an aged vicar's wife, says to her middle-aged friend, Emily Herrick, that she supposes that "'[William] wants to marry you, doesn't he?' 'As much as he can want to marry anyone. Anyone who is a woman. And that is not very much.' 'Oh dear! These dons and people!' said Theresa."[33] *Pastors and Masters* was published in 1925.

An odd passage in *The Long Weekend* recalls that

> In post-war university circles, where Oscar Wilde was considered both a great poet and a martyr to the spirit of intolerance, homosexuality no longer seemed a sign of continued adolescence. Shakespeare, Caesar, Socrates, and Michelangelo were quoted in justification of the male practice; Sappho, Christina of Sweden, and the painter, Rosa Bonheur, of the female .... So long as one acted consistently in accordance with one's personal hypothesis, and was not ashamed of what one did, all was well. The homosexuals spent a great deal of their time preaching the aesthetic virtues of the habit, and made more and more converts .... The Lesbians were more quiet about their aberrations at first; but, if pressed, they justified themselves more practically than the men by pointing out that there were not enough men to go round in a monogamous system....
>
> When anti-French feeling in 1922 had caused a revulsion in favour of the poor downtrodden Germans, the more openly practised homosexuality of Berlin seemed brave and honest: in certain Berlin dancing halls, it was pointed out, women danced only with women and men with men. Germany land of the free! The Lesbians took heart and followed suit, first in Chelsea and St. John's Wood and then in less exotic suburbs of London.[34]

Quite why lesbians should be favoured with an upper-class initial letter I do not know. Perhaps the authors feel in awe of them? But the now stiff, now would-be relaxed tone of the passage reminds us that although Graves and Hodge had lived through the twenties, they were writing from the perspective of the very early 1940s, after a decade in which increased contempt had been directed against "pansy" intellectuals, often from the very people, on the left, who might have been expected to adopt a less reactionary stance. But then in the '30s, perhaps understandably, those on the left could not connect pleasure and radicalism. As so often in the history of English radicalism, pleasure, including the pleasure of transgression, seemed hostile to the task of changing society. Pleasure was decadent. Orwell is very much a man of the 30s.

In the years following 1918, however, pleasure did not need to be defended. It was to be championed. There was pleasure to be found in the very act of transgressing against all those taboos which could, with varying degrees of justification, be linked to the structures of orthodoxy – were, indeed those structures – which had built that society the war had fatally weakened and which the young proposed now to demolish. They would dance on its grave. As I have already noted, dancing was at the centre of the new world, the new pleasures. It was both fact and symbol of licence. That many dance halls failed to obtain drink licences didn't prevent them, together with café life, from becoming identified as places which tolerated as well as being the cause of transgressive behaviour. Kohn points out that early in the 1920s dance halls spread beyond the confines of the west end and out to "more plebeian" territory; he instances the Hammersmith Palais. (One of those "less exotic suburbs" of Graves and Hodge's account.)

> A new kind of woman sprang to life in contemporary imagination and iconography. She was a Futurist creature, starkly painted in stylised geometries of black, white and scarlet; glossy and sharp. Or she was a gay wanton; barebacked, stockinged, brazen and glamorous with her cocktail or cigarette holder.

Police began to raid clubs as a matter of routine. They were on the look-out for illegal drinking, for drug trafficking, for prostitution. In 1920, Dalton's Club, next to the Alhambra in Leicester Square, was prosecuted for having as many as 292 "women of the unfortunate class" on its premises. That at least was what police sergeant

George Goddard claimed. Goddard proudly told the court that he was so well disguised in top hat and tails that even his colleagues failed to recognise him as he made notes on his shirt cuff.[35]

The film *Cocaine* features one such club where, according to *The Daily Express*

> Sleek young men and thinly clothed girls (many of them the 'real thing') jazz and shimmy and fox-trot under the influence of late hours and excitement, nigger-music and cocktails, drugs and the devil.[36]

"Nigger music." That phrase or its equivalents is to be found in much writing of the period, and always it carries the identical charge of sexual licence, of abandonment to the pre-civilised, the barbaric, the untamed. The fearful fascination of an earlier generation of European writers and artists with heart of darkness has now modulated into or become focused on what was commonly called "jungle music" – in a word, jazz.

### III

But the word contained multitudes of meanings. Historians of the music continue to disagree about its origins and etymology, even about its correct spelling. Two matters however are beyond dispute, at all events among white historians, those "scholars *manqué*" who in Larkin's wonderfully witty lines "nod around unnoticed/ wrapped up in personnels like old plaids". They are that jazz is essentially city music and and that it has always had connections with sexual licence. Jazz first became known among white cognoscenti because it was the music of New Orleans brothels; as it spread out and northwards and then across to Europe in the 1910s it quickly became associated with dance-halls and the more *outré* cafés and café society of the time. Jazz was music to dance to and the dances it produced were themselves ones that suggested, even mimed, sexual abandonment. Moreover, the arrival of "nigger music" in Europe at about the time when the great war began, in a sense made legitimate young men and women dancing to it before the killing started. This was the orgy of sexual licence before the orgy of death.

When in the twenties people spoke of jazz music they very rarely had in mind the real thing. In his autobiography, *Half My Days and Nights: A Memoir of the 1920s and 30s,* Hubert Nicholson recalls as a young man in Hull hearing a friend of his play him gramophone records of "hot jazz."

> I ... had never heard anything like the terrific strident, hard, highly organised machine jazz of Red Nichols and His Five Pennies, Miff Mole's Molers, Venuti's Blue Four, Rollini's Goofus Washboards, to say nothing of the negro bands. Even the titles of the new music were different from Say it with a ukulele .... Hot jazz was a thing apart, and after I had my ear attuned to it I could never again care two hoots for "sweet society" playing or the commercial product of ordinary English bands.[37]

The gramophone record was crucial in bringing this new music to English ears because for the most part that was the only way jazz could be heard. There were very occasional tours by American bands and soloists – until the Musicians' Union put a stop to them – but they only took in major cities. As for the home-grown product, we need do no more than recall that Manchester and Cardiff chose not to ban *Cocaine* on the grounds that their cities lacked any night-clubs in order to realise how few opportunities there were for the development of jazz in England before the 30s. And although many of the "sweet society" orchestras began to introduce jazz numbers into their repertoires, these were at best tame imitations of the originals.

The society orchestras were to be found in London. They held residencies at "exclusive" hotels or they might be the major attractions at night-clubs or restaurants where there was a dance-floor; although they sometimes went out "on the road" for a brief tour of provincial cities, London remained their base. Those who lived elsewhere and who wanted to hear them or, more usually, dance to them, had to save up to make the trip to London, as Hubert Nicholson and his friends did with increased frequency, although as the twenties wore on they had the opportunity to listen to such orchestras on the BBC. For the BBC began to relay broadcasts live from the venues where, as Auden put it in "Consider this and in our time", those "constellated at reserved tables/Supplied with feelings by efficient bands" might be found.

That poem was written in March, 1930. Auden's mordant lines are directed at a social class he can legitimately identify as hollow, its predilection for strict-tempo music indicative of carefully apportioned feelings. Auden, as so often, points the way others would go in the 1930s, when for the radical left jazz acquired a reputation for being the music of the damned. George Thomson, for example, asserted that a working-class audience had been seduced from its true musical heritage of folk-music and Mozart by "jazz and other commercialised forms of music."[38] According to Adorno, who took a line that would be followed by the Frankfurt School, jazz was merely a form of repressive tolerance. In her seminal work, *The Jazz Revolution*, Kathy J. Ogren notes that Adorno's "analysis of the development of mass culture within advanced capitalist societies included an attack on jazz because it created the *illusion* rather than the reality of free creation and thus revealed its location in mass culture. Adorno complained that 'the authority of modern music is still apparent behind the liberty of the performed music' .... he regarded the use of popular songs in some jazz compositions as evidence indicating its commercialisation."[39] It could even be that lurking in Adorno's remarks is a hidden racism: a feeling that because jazz is "nigger music" it is basically uncivilised. This may be an unworthy thought but it is disheartening to realise that although Adorno and George Thompson travelled by different routes from the Nazis in order to reach their conclusion that jazz was decadent, both marxists were as vehemently censorious about it as any brownshirt could have wished. (And of course in the soviet bloc "jazz" continued to be proscribed music until the very end.)

In the 1920s, however, radicals would have rejected as solemn nonsense disapproval of jazz. Hostility to jazz came from those who were reactionary in social, sexual and political matters: jazz adherents were by contrast liberationist, democratic, of the city. Radicals were also quick to connect the cause of jazz to the cause of black advancement, and no matter how *ersatz* or trivially fashionable this might sometimes be, there is no mistaking the enthusiasm which greeted Josephine Baker's arrival in France, for example, even though the would-be praise of her as "a woman possessed, a savage intoxicated with tom-toms" was offering a hostage to fortune.[40] Those who opposed the music did so precisely because of the "savage" freedoms they feared it symbolised. Never mind that neither they nor jazz enthusiasts had much sense of the marvellous music coming out of New Orleans, Chicago and New York, "thrashing the astounded air" with its vitality: what mattered was that "jazz" meant above all transgressive energy. You could try to talk down that energy, as James Laver did in some verses of the period:

We've boyish busts and Eton crops,
We quiver to the saxophone.
Come, dance before the music stops,
And who can bear to be alone?
Come drink your gin, or sniff your 'snow',
Since Youth is brief, and Love has wings,
And time will tarnish, ere we know,
The brightness of the Bright Young Things.[41]

But "jazz" *was* a liberating force or the occasion for liberation. And dance, of course, was especially liberating.

There is no space here to more than mention how from the early years of the century modern dance had become self-consciously developed as an expression of erotic energy by Rudolph Laban and his group at Ascana.[42] Nor can I be certain how far knowledge of this had spread to England. But there seems no reason to doubt that it *was* known about and that it prompted a renewal of ancient fears of dance as bacchantic licence. This helped to make some imported dances – first the tango, then the foxtrot – appear as the epitome of dangerous abandon.[43] I have noted *The Daily Express's* identification of the foxtrot with a world of drugs and bought sex; Kathy Ogren quotes Virgil Thomson as singling out "the fox trot (sic) as a symbol of 'the disturbance that shook all of polite society when the lid of segregation was taken off of vice and the bordello irrupted into the drawing room.'"[44] The Foxtrot as the dance of the feral!

Ogren also quotes a far more sympathetic commentator of 1918, who fears that "Modern sophistication has inhibited many native instincts, and the mere fact that our conventional dignity forbids us to sway our bodies or tap our feet when we hear effective music has deprived us of unsuspected pleasures". She glosses this and similar comments as amounting to the conviction that "Experiencing jazz could release and rejuvenate buried emotions or instincts, thus liberating an inner, and perhaps more creative, person."[45]

But suppose jungle music liberated emotions that would have been better left buried? Ogren quotes a number of headlines which indicate a widespread hostility to jazz, or "jazz" as we had better call it. Among my favourites are "Ban Against Jazz Sought in Ireland," and "Welsh Invoke Curfew Laws As One Way To Stop Jazz."[46] Daft though these may seem, they testify to a deep-seated fear of the "buried life" to which "jazz" appealed. In *Sweeney Agonistes* Eliot makes use of what he clearly felt were jazz rhythms so that through them the characters may reveal or betray their own decadence, as for instance in Sweeney's syncopated speech:

> I knew a man once did a girl in
> Any man might do a girl in
> Any man has to, needs to, wants to
> Once in a lifetime, do a girl in.

Hoping to get some advice on how to write for the stage, Eliot had visited Arnold Bennett in September, 1924, and Bennett records in his *Journal* that the poet "wanted to write a drama of modern life (furnished flat sort of people) in a rhythmical prose 'perhaps with certain things in it accentuated by drum-beats.'"[47] The drum-beat is of course the very essence of "jungle music."

Eliot might not have known much about jazz but he was aware, as how could he not be, of the great extent to which modern music had become available as a form of entertainment: music to dance by. He and his first wife often went dancing. Long before the BBC began its outside broadcasts the gramophone had made music "mechanical." And this could be connected to a routine and therefore debased sexuality, as in the case of the typist in *The Waste Land* who "smoothes her hair with automatic hand,/And puts a record on the gramophone." The table gramophone allowed for impromptu dances in the house; the widely-marketed portable version made possible music for dancing at picnics and open-air gatherings. Georgina Howell quotes Barbara Cartland as recalling that "Friday-to-Monday guests in the country would start dancing to the gramophone as soon as they arrived." (As indeed happens in *The Vortex*.)[48] For those who could not afford gramophones there was always the guitar or, more popularly, the ukulele, which sold in thousands, along with the "chord tutors" which enabled amateurs to master the large number of basic, three-chord tunes that were written with the instrument in mind, or at least in the title.

This chapter has been about freedoms associated in the 1920s with what were often the socially stigmatised phenomena of drink, drugs, sex and jazz. That such freedoms were often ends in themselves I would not deny, nor that they were likely to be tokenistic, nor that they could be adopted as elements in behaviour patterns intended to signal a disillusionment with the post-war world. It is entirely *a propos* that when in *The Vortex* Nicky has reached the crisis of self-knowledge which is meant to intimate a wider sense of

130

despair, the stage direction reads: "He goes to the piano and begins to play jazz."

But it is also *a propos* that Anne Chisholm should describe Nancy Cunard's relationship with the black jazz musician, Henry Crowther, as the most crucial in her life. "In Henry Crowther she found ... a cause, a symbol, a weapon, a victim .... Through Crowther she became ... a woman who chose, deliberately, to cross the boundaries of convention, class and race in pursuit of a cause .... In 1928 Nancy blundered into, and for the next few years floundered around in, one of the most intractable and serious of human problems: the sexual, social and political attractions and antagonisms of whites and blacks."[49] I am not about to defend Nancy Cunard's decision to turn a relationship into a cause, although as far as I can tell she did more damage to herself than to Crowther in the years they were together, and between them they did after all produce the massive and important anthology, *Negro,* as well as work from the Hours Press which Nancy funded and which included Beckett's first publication, *Whoroscope,* as well as a collection of contemporary songs compiled by Crowther, the majority on political and social themes. (For example, Walter Lowenfels' "rallying cry about Sacco and Vanzetti.")[50]

And this is the point. For at least some of its white aficionados, jazz was to be linked to radical political causes. "Jazz" therefore came to mean among other things an expression of radical politics. During the 1920s, throughout the U.K., marches of the unemployed were a regular feature of radical protest. Such marches were often led by bands in which kazoos and snare drums predominated. Both then and when they re-appeared during the miners' strike of 1984-5 these bands were called "jazz bands."

*****

A last point. I am aware that this chapter may well look to be special pleading. Why should not the material and names here adduced indicate that between those who played at radicalism – the Bright Young Things – and those for whom radical thought and activity were altogether more vital the gap often became blurred and even closed? I do indeed think this is so; but I am also certain that at key points the gap is wide and clearly defined. And these points will be identified in the following chapters.

# Notes To Chapter 4

1. Kathleen Hale *A Slender Reputation: An Autobiography,* London, Frederick Warne, 1994, p. 127.
2. Ibid p. 52.
3. Ibid p. 91.
4. The photograph of Nan Youngman is to be found in Katy Deepwell's *Ten Decades* op. cit. (See the entry on Youngman: the catalogue is unpaginated).
5. Georgina Howell: *In Vogue: Six Decades of Fashion,* London, Vogue Publications, p. 4.
6. Robert Graves *Goodbye to All That,* London, Cape, 1929, pp. 336-7.
7. *In Vogue* p. 4.
8. See Howells p. 42. On p. 3 she reproduces a photograph of the musical comedy actress, Molly Ramsden, "brazenly smoking a cigarette." The photograph is undated, although it appears to belong to the period 1916-20 and Ramsden may be in the pose of the fallen or loose woman.
9. The Earl of Halsbury, *1944,* London, Thornton Butterworth, 1926, p. 224.
10. *Noel Coward: Plays: One* introduced by Sheridan Morley, London, Methuen, 1991, p xi.
11. Ibid, p. 129.
12. Ibid, pp. 142-3.
13. Ibid p. 169.
14. Marek Kohn, *Dope Girls: The Birth of the Drugs Underground,* London, Lawrence and Wishart, 1992, see pp. 80-104. It is noteworthy that at the ball itself Lady Diana Manners, who had for some time been adicted to opium, or at least morphine, appeared as Britannia. See p. 32-3 and 82.
15. Ibid p. 55 and Coward, *Plays: One* p. 172.
16. Ibid pp. 56 and 106-7. Kohn makes the fascinating point that soldiers at the western front often became dependent on opium – or morphine – because it was so widely used as a pain killer. Moreover, Lady Diana Manners recalls that "a tube of quarter-grains [of morphine] was always sent in our war parcels of brand-handkerchiefs, pencils and pocket classics". Kohn adds that such practices were actively enouraged by the Mayfair chemists, Savory and More, who put an advertisement in *The Times* for cases containing gelatine sheets impregnated with morphine and cocaine, 'useful presents for friends at the front.'" p. 33.
17. Ibid, pp 128-9.
18. Ibid, pp 134-140. The popularity of film as a medium led Bermondsey Borough Council to set up small educational film units which operated throughout the Borough from 1923 onwards and which propagandized for improved health. The population was enabled to see films about the Health Department's concern for everything from "the testing of drains to the treatment of teeth." The films were taken round by van and shown from street to street. For more on this see Elizabeth Lebas, "When Every Street Became a Cinema: The Film Work of Bermondsey Borough Council, 1923-1953." *History Workshop Journal,* No. 39, Spring, 1995, pp. 42-66. But for most people film was entertainment and as such, according to L.C.B. Seaman, was regularly denounced by headmasters on speech days. See his *Post-Victorian Britain 1902-1951*, London, Methuen, 1966, p. 161.
19. Graves and Hodge, *The Long Weekend* op. cit. p106.
20. Quoted by Katrina Rolley, "The Treatment of Homosexuality and *The Well of Loneliness"* in Paul Hyland and Neil Sammels (eds), *Writing and Censorship in Britain,* London, Routledge, 1992, p 220.
21. D.H. Lawrence, *Psychoanalysis and the Unconscious and Fantasia of the*

*Unconscious*, New York, Compass Books, 1960, p 215. The *Fantasia* was first published in 1922.

22. Ibid. pp. 202 and 148.
23. *The English Auden*, Ed. Mendelson (ed) London, Faber, 1977, p. 300.
24. *Fantasia of the Unconscious* p. 214.
25. For all this see Humphrey Carpenter, *W.H. Auden: A Biography,* London, Allen and Unwin, 1981, pp. 86-89.
26. For this see Martin Green, *Mountain of Truth: The Counterculture Begins: Ascona, 1900–1920* London, University Press of New England, 1986. Esp. pp. 29-45. Gross wished to replace patriarchy by matriarchy – very un-Lawrentian, that – and argued that the expulsion of women from religion by Jews, Greeks and Moslems was the world's first White Terror. Lawrence would have rejected some of this – as well, I imagine, as pointing out that Gross knows precious little of Greek mythology if he imagines women are expelled from the pantheon of Greek gods – but he would have approved his assertion that eroticism possessed a philosophical and metaphysical value that transcended personal jealousy. Freud, who had at one time felt very warmly towards Gross, decided in 1909 that he was a dangerous heretic – but by then Gross had decided Frieda had defeated Freud by "defeating all the fathers", most importantly his own. See Green p. 31. It should also be mentioned here that in post-revolutionary Russia sexual freedom was considered intrinsic to the making of the new stateless state. Neurosis was, after all, a product of decadent, capitalist societies, with their prohibitions and taboos. Sex ought to be as "easily available and as refreshing as drinking a glass of water," as one Russian revolutionary put it.
27. Carpenter, *W.H. Auden* p. 88.
28. *A Slender Reputation* pp. 125 and 161.
29. For all this see Declan Kiberd, "Bloom the Liberator" in *The Times Literary Supplement* Jan. 3rd 1992, pp. 3-6.
30. John Mepham, *Virginia Woolf: A Literary Life* London, MacMillan, 1991, pp. 127-8.
31. Graves and Hodge, *The Long Weekend* p. 241.
32. R. Firbank, *Valmouth, Prancing Nigger, Concerning the Eccentricities of Cardinelli Pirelli* Harmondsworth, Penguin, 1961, p. 257. The original edition of *Eccentricities* was published in 1926 by Grant Richards.
33. I. Compton-Burnett, *Pastors and Masters* London, Gollancz, 1952 reprint, p. 48.
34. The Long Weekend pp. 101-2.
35. *Dope Girls* p. 122. At the end of the 1920s Goddard was himself found guilty of accepting heavy bribes from clubland.
36. Ibid p. 135. For more on dance halls and cafés where dancing was permitted see *A Slender Reputation* – Kathleen Hale loved to go dancing and tried out most of the venues – and Hugh David *The Fitzrovians: A Portrait of Bohemian Society, 1900-1955*, London, Michael Joseph, 1988. esp. chs. 7 and 8.
37. Hubert Nicholson, *Half My Days and Nights: A Memoir of the 1920s and 30s*, London, Autolycus Publications, 1993, p. 64. The book was first published by Heinemann in 1941. I have puzzled over Nicholson's phrase "machine jazz." He may mean music especially recorded for the gramophone, or he may have in mind jazz as precise, speedy, efficient (in Auden's sense of the "efficient bands"): music of the new machine age. In which case it is worth noting a remark of Robert Musil's in the second part of his great novel *The Man Without Qualities,* that during the early years of the 20th century people were beginning to discover the songs of the workshops, "the rivetting hammers and the factory sirens .... What does one still want with the Apollo Belvedere, when one has the new lines of the turbo-dynamo." Of course, Musil's ironic prose doesn't suggest an uncritical obeisance to such "songs," unlike, say, Mondriaan's famous *Broadway Boogie-Woogie* (1942-3) with its dazzle of grid-lined colours suggesting some-

thing of the syncopation of much jazz music.

38. As far as I know Thomson first made this charge in an unpublished lecture of the mid 1930s, but regularly returned to it. See my review essay on realism and radicalism in *Socialist History* no. 5, Summer 1994, pp 43-50.

39. Kathy J. Ogren, *The Jazz Revolution: Twenties America and the Meaning of Jazz* New York, O.U.P., 1989, p. 155.

40. *In Vogue* p. 51.

41. Quoted by John Montgomery, *The Twenties*, London, Allen and Unwin, 1957

42. This is the subject of a fascinating chapter in *The Mountain of Truth* see esp. pp. 83-115.

43. I suspect there is a book to be written about the number of women, often in disturbed emotional states and/or difficult marriages, who turned to dance as a way of trying to "unlock" their inner selves and who were not infrequently driven further into madness by the experience. I think, for example, of James Joyce's daughter, of Zelda Fitzgerald, of Vivienne Eliot.

44. *The Jazz Revolution* p. 155. There is some doubt as to the origins of the term "foxtrot". According to A.H. Franks the dance was born in 1914. "Possibly the most convincing story of its origin is that a comedian named Harry Fox, who worked in the Ziegfield Follies, introduced in 1913 a number of trotting steps accompanied by rag-time music into his act, and that this strange kind of movement became known as Fox's trot. On the roof garden of the New Amsterdam Theatre a well-known dancer and dancing master, Oscar Duryea, was engaged to lead the pony-ballet girls through the audience, using trotting steps to an accompaniment of lively 4/4 music. This proved to be a popular innovation, and the patrons were invited to join the procession ... every evening... when Harry Fox was playing. This constant trotting motion, however, proved quite tiring, with the result that a less strenuous variation was interpolated, consisting of a few walking-steps." Franks also notes that other historians of twentieth century dance, while agreeing that the foxtrot orginates in America and probably in 1913/14, claim that it is the "direct offspring of the One Step and the Rag." See *Social Dance: A Short History*, London, Routledge & Kegan Paul, 1963, pp. 183-4. Marshall and Jean Stearns, however, suggest that the foxtrot may have been created by Vernon and Irene Castle as a variation on such pre-war American popular dances as The Turkey Trot, Grizzly Bear, Monkey Glide, Chicken Scratch, Bunny Hug, Kangaroo Dip, Possom Trot, Frog Hop and Scratchin' the Gravel. But according to them, the foxtrot was different from all other dances in being performed to the blues. W.C. Handy is quoted as saying that "Jim Europe, head of the local Clef Club, was the Castles' musical director. The Castle Walk and One-Step were fast numbers. During breath-taking intermissions, Jim would sit at the piano and play slowly the Memphis Blues. He did this so often that the Castles became intrigued by its rhythm, and Jim asked why they didn't originate a slow dance adaptable to it. The Castles liked the idea and a new dance was introduced...." The Stearns also quote Irene Castle's words: "It was Jim Europe ... who suggested the foxtrot to us, and for all I know he invented it." See *Jazz Dance: The Story of Vernacular American Dance*, with new foreword and afterword by Brenda Bufalino, New York, Da Capo Press, 1994, pp. 95-98. What is clear is that the foxtrot becomes singled out as a specifically jazz dance and one which, unlike say the black bottom or charleston, is danced to slow music. Given that it is also danced by couples in close body contact it can then become a symbol of sexually abandoned behaviour. In this context, the foxtrot in *Façade* (1922) "Old Sir Faulk," is a missed opportunity in that its aimless surrealism doesn't exploit the possibilities identified with the dance. On the other hand, by deciding to incorporate the foxtrot into her work, Edith Sitwell is choosing to cock another snook at respectable opinion. "Old Sir Faulk" is there to shock.

45. Ogren, p. 146. I thought of this when I saw the wonderfully funny TV shot of various bits of the monarchy trying to sway in time to music played in London for Nelson Mandela, music to which the great man himself responded with ease.
46. Ibd p. 140. It is worth noting that in Patrick Hamilton's *Craven House* two of the inmates see a film about a young girl keen on jazz who is going to the devil. (ch. 3, ch I ii).
47. For this see my *Arnold Bennett: A Study of His Fiction*, London, Methuen, 1974, p. 223. Bennett not long afterwards wrote a story "The Woman Who Stole Everything," which features a muscular man "with hairy hands, arms and chest," who is called Sweeney Todd. Ape-like Sweeney.
48. *In Vogue* p. 50.
49. Anne Chisholm, *Nancy Cunard* op. cit. pp. 118-9.
50. Ibid, p. 154. Nancy Cunard apparently first had the idea for an anthology of "Negro history, politics and art" soon after meeting Crowther. See *Nancy Cunard* p. 153 and pp. 207-222.

## CHAPTER FIVE

# THE ROUGH BEAST
## BETWEEN VISION and PROPHECY

In 1919 Yeats produced his famous vision of the Savage God, "The Second Coming."[1] The poem's origins are complex and owe much to The poet's schematising of history into gyres, two-thousand year epochs, the latest of which was, he believed, rapidly approaching a violent end. It is therefore important to note that Yeats began the poem "in direct response to the Great War". An early draft of the opening reads: "The gyres grow wider and more wide/The hawk can no more hear the falconer/The Germans to Russia to the place."[2] But although Yeats was at first beset by fears of the chaos war brought with it, these were soon replaced by his preoccupation with the threat of socialism, which he saw as spreading like a modern plague across the Western world. Yeats' widow remarked that he was deeply apprehensive of "the socialist revolutions in Russia, Germany and Italy during and after World War1"[3]; and much nearer to home he knew that the leaders of the 1916 Easter Rising in Dublin, Connolly and Pearse, were both Marxists, and that their actions had been prompted by their certainty of the need for the blood sacrifice.

"The blood-dimmed tide is loosed, and everywhere/The ceremony of innocence is drowned." That plangent claim, poised between vision and prophecy, has its source in a note to an earlier draft of the poem: "The Germany of Marx has led to Russian Communism/There everyday some innocent has died."[4] We know that at the time Yeats was working on "The Second Coming" he was also re-reading *The Prelude;* and he marked as of especial importance lines where Wordsworth speaks of his despair at the turn towards violence taken by the French Revolution. Wordsworth's brooding over "The indecision on their part whose aim/Seemed best, and the straight-forward path of those/Who in attack or in defence were strong/Through their impiety" finds a close echo in Yeats' "The best lack all conviction while the worst/Are full of passionate intensity"; and Wordsworth's Burkein rejection of violence has its counterpart in Yeats' "every day some innocent has died."[5]

In a characteristically sophisticated reading of "The Second Coming," Stan Smith notes of the lines "Things fall apart; the centre cannot hold;/Mere anarchy is loosed upon the world," that

> 'Mere anarchy' is an abstraction which hovers between cosmology and politics. It becomes more tangible as the emotive 'blood-dimmed tide.' The two processes are revealed to be a single one in the repetitions of 'is loosed upon', which converts a metaphor of political control (the feudal, aristocratic grasp of the falconer) into the impersonal image of the loosened flood waters, culminating in that powerful 'drowned'. The passive voice, here and throughout, gives the impression of a process in which human agency is no more than a hapless instrument of impersonal, cosmic forces...[6]

To this I would add that when Yeats comes to describe the savage god itself, moving its "slow thighs" across the sands of the desert which in its level sterility seems the beast's natural habitat, he imagines that it "Slouches towards Bethlehem to be born." And here human agency is not only more than a hapless instrument but is surely working-class? The plebs slouch. Yeats' fear is that history now shapes and is shaped by "the roof-levelling wind" of democratic energies which will actively threaten and destroy a culture, a civilisation, where "all's accustomed, ceremonious". (The phrase comes from "A Prayer for My Daughter," which follows "The Second Coming" in the volume *Michael Robartes and the Dancer*.)

"The Second Coming" was finished in June, 1919. Stan Smith thinks that the cruellest April of Eliot's *The Waste Land* may also be that of 1919. "After the Armistice in November, 1918, revolution swept through the armies and working classes of the defeated nations, sweeping away the *anciens regimes* overnight. In the spring of 1919, a second wave of Bolshevik-style soviets sprang up throughout Germany and the former Austro-Hungarian Empire. In early 1919 the tide had turned in the Civil War which followed the Russian Revolution .... The first Bavarian Revolution had begun in November 1918. On April 4 1919, a second revolution, proclaiming direct allegiance to the newly instituted Third International, erupted on the streets of Munich ..."[7]

Who are those hooded hordes swarming
Over endless plains, stumbling in cracked earth
Ringed by the flat horizon only
What is the city over the mountains
Cracks and reforms and bursts in the violet air
Falling towers
Jerusalem Athens Alexandria
Vienna London

In these lines from *The Waste Land* questioning modulates into a note of appalled, knowing fascination. As with Yeats, so here: we are poised between vision and prophecy. But whereas Yeats' lines evoke a world history – as, given his belief in the gyres, they have to do – history in Eliot's poem moves from the sandy wastes of a middle-eastern flat horizon through successive cities until the rough beast finally slouches into London.

London 1919? London 1920? It scarcely matters. In either year there was plenty to alert Eliot to the course history seemed to be taking. That he did not like what he saw is made plain in a letter he wrote to Richard Aldington in April, 1921. "Having only contempt for every existing political party, and profound hatred for democracy, I feel the blackest gloom. Whatever happens will be another step toward the destruction of Europe. The whole of contemporary politics etc. oppresses me with a continuous physical horror like the feeling of a growing madness in one's brain." We now know that Eliot's mental state at the time was decidedly precarious. Nevertheless, his loathing of "contemporary politics" deserves to be taken seriously if only because it alerts us to ways in which the immediate post-war years seemed to threaten – or of course promise – colossal political changes in the Western World. Stan Smith has rightly noted that many of those changes either had occurred or were occurring in the Spring of 1919; but as the Irish "troubles" show, such occurrences were not confined to the European mainland. Nor were they limited to 1919 and 1920. And though with the benefit of hindsight we can say that from 1921 the violent energies of post-war radical politics began to dwindle, people living in England during the early post-war years were far more likely to feel themselves in a nation where things were falling apart.

There were, for example, the army mutinies of early 1919. 10,000 soldiers mutinied in January 6 at Folkstone, 2,000 at Dover, and 60,000 at various other camps: on that and the following three days lorry-loads of angry mutineers descended on Whitehall. There were riots at Kinmel Park where the Red Flag was raised (in the ensuing violence five men were killed and twenty-one seriously wounded), barracks at Witley were burned down, and at Epsom, where the police station was stormed, the Station Sergeant was killed.[9] The same year there were strikes aplenty, the most serious being that by the miners; and in Clyde and Belfast engineers struck. The strike on the Clyde was part of a growing socialist militancy which clearly marks industrial Scotland off as more politically radical than either England or Wales, as the setting up of Glasgow Soviets and Churchill's dispatching tanks to the city also show.[10]

In 1920 there were further strikes, as there would be in the years following. John Stevenson has noted that "Strikes among engineers, railway men, cotton workers, Yorkshire miners, foundry workers and the police, to name the most prominent, gave the post-war years a character quite different from the rest of the inter-war years."[21] I remarked in an earlier chapter that one of the most significant instances of industrial militancy of 1920 involved action taken by London dockers. The Government decided to help the Poles in their war against Soviet Russia, which by and large meant sending them munitions. Dockers refused to load the munitions and prevented the boat intended to carry arms from sailing. In his account of this episode Henry Pelling concludes that while there is no certainty that the dockers' action forced the government to change its mind, there is also no doubt that Lloyd George did stop sending aid to Poland. Then, in October, came "The Battle of Downing Street" in which, according to the *Daily Mirror,* "Wild scenes were witnessed in Whitehall and Downing Street yesterday during a demonstration by 10,000 unemployed, headed by the mayors of the fifteen London boroughs where there is a Labour majority. Baton charges were frequent, and at one time mounted police cleared Whitehall at the gallop." Over 50 people were injured.

Strikes and marches don't of themselves amount to the arrival of the rough beast. Yet the mood of those years seemed to testify to the certainty of further change. The spectre that Marx in 1848 had said was haunting Europe might now be about to burst from its tomb. In August 1920 the Communist Party of Great Britain was formed with 10,000 members mostly drawn from three radical groups: the dissolved British Socialist Party, Sylvia Pankhurst's east-end Workers' Socialist Federation, and part of the Socialist Labour Party.[12] Left-wing newspapers were rapidly increasing

140

their readership. Cole and Postgate put the circulation of *The Daily Herald* at between 200,000 and 300,000, and although by comparison both *The Communist* and *The Labour Leader* were small beer (neither exceeded 60,000), there was a quite new sense of militancy, of tangible radicalism, which could be traced to recent events in Russia and with which these newspapers and journals plainly sympathised. Strikes, lock-outs and hunger marches of an increasing number of the unemployed were visible manifestations of unrest. Such visibility was sharpened by the regularity with which newspapers carried photographs of marches, by Labour Party posters which emphasised the poverty of many women and, particularly, men who had fought in the war, and by *Punch* cartoons. In one of these, a government minister recoils in horror from the threatening genie he has inadvertently conjured up by polishing a miner's lamp. The caption runs: "I am the Slave of the Lamp. I think you summoned me." "Yes, I know: but I didn't think you'd be so ugly." (*Punch*, October 20, 1920). Earlier that year, on April 7, the same magazine had carried a cartoon of a giant striker posed as Oliver Twist and asking for more from the cowering figure of Lloyd George. Behind his back the miner conceals a large club labelled *Strike Threats*. Unemployed marchers habitually formed fours, began "to hold up shopping thoroughfares and frighten rich women and their chauffeurs, to lock up and scare some of the worst sort of Boards of Guardians .... the bulk of those who threw their energies into their protection were communists. In the autumn of 1921 the Party founded the 'National Unemployed Workers Committee Movement'; and the pressure was soon greatly increased."[13]

The suggestion of a workers' army – on route the marchers would sometimes whistle "Colonel Bogie" – has to be set against the fact that those on marches as often carried the union jack as the Red Flag and that, as Cole and Postgate admit, the marchers were, for all the apprehensions Arnold Bennett gives to Mrs Prohack, remarkably unthreatening. They wrecked no buildings, seized no food. Even so, people living in the immediate post-war years can hardly be blamed for imagining that what had happened and was happening elsewhere in Europe might happen here. *The Times* reported on 6 November, 1920, that

> The Socialist Sunday School, or rather the Proletarian School Movement, is particularly strong in Glasgow and the indus-

trial districts of the Clyde. Its teaching is openly revolutionary, and while one may doubt whether the average child, even
of Communist parents, understands the wild rubbish of the
songs, the texts, and the addresses which make up the
lessons, the general effect of the propaganda may be traced in
the noisy insolence and general lack of discipline among
many of the boys and girls who roam the streets.

Those who roam now may slouch later.

Or they may rouse themselves to overthrow a system that offers
them nothing. It will be recalled that in *The Black Curtain*,
Goldring's 1920 novel, the aged Lord Midhurst reads to Philip
from a book written in 1848 which, he says, "contains an interesting prophecy, by an inspired but embittered hunchback named
James Finton Lalor." Lalor was a leading Fenian who argued passionately for the restoration of the land to the people; but what
Midhurst concentrates on is Lalor's claim that if people once
began to wage war for the land, such a war "would propagate itself
throughout Europe .... the principle I propound goes to the foun-
dations of Europe, and sooner or later will cause Europe to out
rise. Mankind will yet be masters of the earth." Having quoted
these words, Midhurst tells Philip that if a new prophet is to
appear "in the course of the present world catastrophe, [he] will be
recognised by the masses."[14]

Midhurst's words might be taken to anticipate Mussolini, Stalin,
Hitler. They more usefully remind us that in 1920 there were grand
advances in trade union membership. Union strength increased
with the absorption of several small craft-unions into the General
Workers' Union, the National Union of General and Municipal
Workers, and the Amalgamated Engineering Union. Early the following year the powerful Transport Union came into existence.
This was the moment when the Labour Party issued the following
manifesto:

> We of the Labour Party ... recognise, in the present world cat-
> astrophe, if not the death, in Europe, of civilisation itself, at
> any rate the culmination and collapse of a distinctive indus-
> trial civilisation, which the workers will not seek to recon-
> struct .... The industrialist system of capitalist production ...
> with the monstrous inequality of circumstances which it pro-
> duces and the degradation and brutalization, both moral and
> spiritual, resulting there from, may we hope, indeed have
> received a death-blow ....[15]

Even if the death-blow had not yet been delivered, there were reasons to suppose that it soon would be or that external forces – Marxist Leninism – would forge the weapon to be wielded by British labour. By 1921 Lenin was known to be advising strike leaders to accept the need for political as well as industrial action and to join the Marxists of the British Socialist Party and then the newly-formed Communist party in adherence to the Third International.[16] Lenin's British sympathisers included, quite apart from the London dockers and the industrial workers of Clydeside, a number of leading intellectuals, Bertrand Russell among them.

In 1920 Russell published *The Practise and Theory of Bolshevism*. It was based on a trip to Russia which lasted from May 11th to June 16th of that year, during which Russell toured factories and industrial plants and met and talked at some length with Lenin. Russell is certain of two things: first, that "The Russian Revolution is one of the great heroic events of world history." It is, he says, of more importance than the French Revolution, because "it does more to change the daily life and structure of society: it also does more to change men's beliefs." Second, "By far the most important aspect of the Russian Revolution is an attempt to realize Socialism. I believe that Socialism is necessary to the world, and believe that the heroism of Russia has fired men's hopes in a way which was essential to the realization of Socialism in the future."[17]

Yet although Russell believes that "The existing capitalist system is doomed, its injustice is so glaring that only ignorance and tradition could lead wage-earners to tolerate it," he does not believe Bolshevic socialism will prove a world-wide success.[18] More particularly, he gives it no chance of working in England. Nor does he want it to. He is prepared to concede that the hopes which inspire Communism are as admirable as those instilled by the Sermon on the Mount: "but they are held as fanatically, and are likely to do as much harm. Cruelty lurks in our instincts and fanaticism is a camouflage for cruelty. Fanatics are seldom genuinely humane, and those who sincerely dread cruelty will be slow to adopt a fanatical creed." Supposing a Communist Party were able to acquire power in England, Russell says, it would be able to show itself more tolerant than any government can hope to be in Russia. Yet this is a matter of degree. "A great part of the despotism which characterizes the Bolsheviks belongs to the essence of their social philosophy, and would have to be reproduced, even in a milder form, wherever that philosophy became dominant."[19]

The most interesting part of Russell's book comes with the report of his discussion with Lenin and deserves to be quoted at some length. Russell begins by asking Lenin how far he recognizes "the peculiarity of English economic and political conditions." Lenin admits that there is little chance of revolution in England now and that this is because workers are not sufficiently disgusted with Parliamentary Government. But he hopes that, should a Labour Government come into existence, revolution would soon follow.

> He thinks that, if Mr Henderson, for instance, were to become Prime Minister, nothing of importance would be done; organized Labour would then, so he hopes and believes, turn to revolution. On this ground, he wishes his supporters in this country to do everything in their power to secure a Labour majority in Parliament; he does not advocate abstention from Parliamentary contests, but participation with a view to making Parliament obviously contemptible. The reasons which make attempts at violent revolution seem to most of us both improbable and undesirable in this country carry no weight with him, and seem to him mere *bourgeois* prejudices. When I suggested that whatever is possible in England can be achieved without bloodshed, he waved aside the suggestion as fantastic. I got little impression of knowledge or psychological imagination as regards Great Britain...
>
> He does not seem to know that the attitude of British Labour has done a great deal to make a first-class war against Russia impossible [Russell presumably has in mind the Labour Party's endorsement of the dockers' refusal to load arms for Poland], since it has confined the Government to what could be done in a hole-and-corner way, and denied without too blatant mendacity.
>
> He thoroughly enjoys the attacks of Lord Northcliffe, to whom he wishes to send a medal for Bolshevik propaganda. Accusations of spoliation, he remarked, may shock the *bourgeois,* but have an opposite effect upon the proletarian.[20]

Russell is probably wrong to speak of "Great Britain" (this is almost the only time in his book when the term occurs), since he is thinking exclusively of England. But a year later he would have found ample justification for his belief that Lenin did not understand the English desire to avoid confrontation. 1921 was the year of "Black Friday", when a promised triple alliance of miners, railwaymen and transport workers failed to materialise. The conditions for confrontation could hardly have been more exact. At the end of March the government returned the mines to the private ownership from which they had been taken during the war years. The owners immediately announced a cut in wages. The miners refused the terms and were locked out. The other members of the alliance at first promised to strike in sympathy and then, at the last moment, backed away As explanation for their action they cited an incautious speech by the miners' secretary, Frank Hodges, which had seemed to suggest that the miners would accept a compromise over wages without a National Wages Board to which the government had committed itself. Yet most commentators, both then and later, agree that the other two unions had little stomach for a fight. *The Daily Herald* editorialised the defeat as "the heaviest ... that has befallen the Labour movement within the memory of man. It is no use trying to minimize it. It is no use pretending that it is other than it is. We on this paper said throughout that if the organized workers would stand together they would win. They have not stood together and they have reaped the reward."[21]

Henry Pelling notes that after "Black Friday" and the defeat of the Triple Alliance, and given the trade depression and the consequent diminishment of trade union membership, "industrial unrest tended to die down in the immediately succeeding years."[22] Yet in the general election of November 1922 the number of Labour MPs increased to 142 from the 59 who had been returned in 1918. And Labour's share of the popular vote (4.2 millions) put them second behind the conservatives' 5½ millions. Moreover, two communists won seats.[23] The Labour advances undoubtedly owed something to the imprisonment from September 1 until October 12, 1921, of George Lansbury, together with twenty-nine other members of Poplar's Council, for refusing to levy the LCC rate. The reason for this act of defiance was as simple as it was morally compelling. Twenty-five per cent of Poplar's workers were unemployed. They required outdoor relief which simply couldn't be met from the rates. (The rich borough of Hampstead had only 400 registered unemployed.) Lansbury told his councillors that "When the law is wrong, break it, and thereby create a classless society." As a result of Lansbury's action a bill was passed spreading the cost of relief more equitably over London's boroughs. But Lansbury was a christian socialist whose pacifism had cost him his seat in the 1918 "Khaki election". He was in no sense a red-blooded revolutionary.

Those who formed the first Labour administration were as much given to gradualism as any Leninist could have wished. This was partly because the Labour Government was a minority one. When Baldwin decided to go to the country in November, 1923, he lost his overall majority in the commons. Even so, with 258 members returned the conservatives were still the largest single party. The Labour party now had 191 members, the Liberals 158. Asquith announced his readiness to support a Labour administration. Mindful perhaps of this, Ramsay MacDonald put together a government whose ministers were, as Charles Mowat notes, "anything but revolutionary," although MacDonald's own natural tendencies were anyway gradualist and during the period before the election he had been careful to avoid any commitment to left-wing parliamentarians or to radical policies.[24]

Yet the coming to power of the Labour Party caused great alarm. In *Last Changes, Last Chances* the by then veteran journalist H.W. Nevinson recalls how he felt as he looked down from the press gallery while the new government ministers took their seats in the house of commons. Nevinson, a friend of MacDonald's, suggests that there were plenty of reasons for the Labour Party to refuse to form a government, "the strongest being the problem of the unemployed. For if the Party that stood for the working people could not come to the relief of their most urgent need, and alleviate the most terrible apprehension that can haunt men, women and children, what reliance upon a Labour Government could working people place." But when the commons met for the first time after MacDonald's decision to form a government

> I felt the sense of inferiority that I always feel in the presence of men who have confronted poverty and themselves toiled at the hard business of ordinary life. Two of those Ministers had worked in cotton mills; one had been born to weaving in Yorkshire; one had been an iron moulder; another had driven locomotives; three had worked in coal mines; one, a feminine figure, eloquent and wise, for whom there was hardly any room on the crowded Bench, had been a shop assistant. Most of the great branches of our productive work were represented; nearly all except shipping and agriculture. Before such people I felt ashamed, as I long had felt, of the littleness of my literary education and of the easy-going, sheltered life which I could not have enjoyed but for my birth in a fairly well-to-do family.

To his astonishment, however, or so he says, Nevinson discovered that friends and acquaintances did not share his attitude. "For the

146

first week or so I heard open expressions of fear, horror and disgust." There were also prophecies of "national calamity and the collapse of our Imperial grandeur,"[25] but these soon died down, temporarily at least. Even MacDonald's official recognition of the Soviet republics as the legitimate government of Russia caused little stir. Nevinson adds that "The resolutions passed at Labour Conferences (as in London in June of the previous year) proved to [MacDonald] that the majority of his supporters regarded Marxism or Communism as a disruptive force unsuited to the nature of a country which still refused to reject democracy as an obsolete and putrefying corpse."[26]

MacDonald's government lasted for a few months. Then, on October 9, 1924, parliament was dissolved. MPs went back to the hustings, and on October 25th came the publication of the infamous "Zinoviev letter," perfectly timed to do the maximum damage before polling day on the 29th. Writing in 1928, Nevinson could not be sure whether the letter was genuine or a forgery, but he claims not to have been surprised by it. "Everyone, however slightly acquainted with the Marxist doctrine, knew that the Soviets felt bound to instigate a general revolution – a 'planetary revolution' – and that our country would be their first objective as being their strongest obstacle."[27] Maybe so, but what is extraordinary is MacDonald's apparent belief that the letter would do him and his party no harm. In fact, it wrecked his election chances, although Mowat, at least, does not think the Labour party would in any case have won. "Baldwin's plea for a 'sane, commonsense Government' was winning votes long before the Zinoviev bombshell."[28]

Still, bombshell it was. *The Times* said as much. "Soviet Plot. Red Propaganda in Britain. Revolution urged by Zinoviev. Foreign Office 'Bombshell'". The letter, purporting to have been signed by Zinoviev, President of the Presidium of the Communist International in Moscow, and by "McManus", a British member of the Presidium and "Kusenin", its secretary, was addressed to the British Communist Party, and marked "Very Secret." The gist of the letter was a call to violent revolution. It is indispensable, the letter said, "to stir up the masses of the British proletariat, to bring into movement the army of unemployed proletarians..." The leaders of the Labour Party would be no help, because they "may easily be found in the leading strings of the *bourgeoisie*."

"An extraordinary concoction," Mowat calls the letter, though he adds that it could be used as a stick with which to beat the government. Official recognition of the Soviet republics could now be seen "as the harbinger of revolution in Great Britain." And MacDonald's reluctance to realise the damage the letter was doing, his tardy response to the fact that the press accompanied its leaking of the letter with one which came from the Foreign Office protesting at the "interference in Britain's affairs from outside," thus making the Zinoviev letter seem genuine – all this meant that the conservative press could accuse the prime minister of having something to hide.[29]

Whether the letter was in fact genuine or a forgery is of less importance than the effect it produced. Even if Mowat is right in maintaining that Baldwin would anyway have won the election, there is no doubt that the Zinoviev letter revealed a depth of fear about the possibility of revolution that was in no sense matched by an excited response to the call to arms. "Armed warfare must be preceded by a struggle against the inclinations to compromise which are embedded among the majority of British workmen, against the ideas of evolution and peaceful extermination of capitalism." Thus Zinoviev. On October 29th, the inclinations to compromise were so marked, the rough beast so little in evidence, that the conservatives won 415 seats, Labour 152 and the Liberals 42. As for the popular vote: the conservatives polled 7.4 million and the Labour Party 5.5 million.

And yet 5.5 million was an increase over the 4.3 million vote which had brought Labour to power in 1924. Radicalism was still a growing force, although fears of revolutionary violence must have played some part in preventing its more rapid expansion, and this despite the large numbers of unemployed, the widespread poverty, and the evidence of social injustice all across England in the mid-twenties. It was this which turned Frank Cousins into a socialist. A young lorry driver in the 1920s, Cousins was sitting one day in a transport café when a couple on the tramp came in with their baby. Cousins was struck by their pinched looks, their threadbare clothes. But what most moved and upset him was the sight of the woman carefully folding a sheet of old newspaper to use as the baby's nappy. From that moment, he said, he became committed to socialism. The famous Labour Party poster, first issued in 1920, "Yesterday – The Trenches" showing a soldier ready to go over the top, "TO-DAY—UNEMPLOYED", in which a young man and woman with baby trudge through a wet, desolate industrial landscape, did no more than tell a terrible truth about the fate of mil-

148

lions of people in post-war Britain. 11.2% of the population were without work in 1923, although the figures were higher in the North, at 12.2%, and in Scotland, 13.5[30] Unemployed men, many of whom had fought and been injured in the war, had to put up with bad housing, inadequate food, and the pittance of dole money. "Nobody," as Cousins said, "should have to live like that."

It might then be thought that the General Strike was inevitable. The only surprise was that it took so long to arrive. But according to this view the far greater surprise would have to be the ease with which it was broken and the humiliating defeat of organised labour which accompanied its collapse. Reasons can be found for this. Unlike the unions, the government had been making plans for coping with a general strike since July 1925, and was therefore better prepared when it was called on May 4 1926. Its immediate cause was the mine-owners' insistence on longer hours and lower wages but more general and deeply-felt grievances lay behind the almost complete stoppage of work in all industries. The strike really was general. The BBC, still a private company and by 1926 with an estimated audience of 2½ million, offered the freedom of the airways to the government to put across its point of view,[31] for with printers on strike few newspapers were able to get onto the streets. (Those who refused to produce *The Daily Mail* – "for King and Country" – did at least temporary damage to the government cause.) And as is well known, undergraduates, for whom the strike was the opportunity for a jolly lark, volunteered to drive buses, trains, trams, and to shift goods from the docks, although they soon found this work far too heavy for them. Yet the sudden order to return to work issued by the Trades Union Council on May 12 must have amazed even the most optimistic of government supporters. Henry Pelling says that the order amounted to surrender.

He puts what gloss he can on this. The climb down was not a betrayal of rank and file. "Neither the leaders nor the great body of the strikers really intended that the strike should turn into a revolutionary outbreak; and consequently, in the face of a government determined to resist its pretensions, the General Council had no alternative but to give way sooner of later."[32] Mowat remarks that the strike brought out two things very clearly: "the enthusiasm for a common cause, and the genius for improvisation and organisation shown by local trade union groups." For the rank and file, he adds, "the strike was a triumph: for most of its national leaders a humiliation."[33] They achieved nothing. Baldwin made no concessions and when the miners finally went back to work later that year they had to do so on the owners' terms.

Nevinson felt that the strike demonstrated that England was not a divided nation. During its ten days' duration, he walked some 100 miles about the working districts of London gathering information for the *Baltimore Sun*, "and cheered only when the young Oxford blacklegs, as they started their tube trains for Golders Green, would cry: 'Any more for the nightingales?' and when, as the window of one of their 'buses was shattered, they pasted over the hole, 'Emergency exit only!' My faith in the unity of English blood was thus restored."[34]

A rather different view was taken by Hubert Nicholson, then working as a journalist in Hull. His branch of the union of journalists decided neither to blackleg nor to strike: instead, they went to the newspaper office "for strictly journalistic work," of which there was none, because there as elsewhere the printers had struck. Nicholson and his journalist friends stayed at their offices, "arguing, wondering whether the revolution had come." At one point he goes out for a stroll, "just as the mounted police made a savage baton-charge on a defenceless crowd." He sees undergraduate "scabs" brought in to drive "our tram cars, protected by wire-netting against half-bricks and fireworks which the crowd flung at them," and soon decides that he detests "these swanky blacklegs from Oxford and Cambridge, and only wished the missiles were more numerous and effective." Not much unity of English blood here.

Then, all too soon, the strike is over.

> It is an old story. The men were betrayed, sold out to the government whose bitter revenge is now ancient history. Yet still I recall the exalted feelings, the surge of hope reaching even a middle-class youngster in a provincial place, and leaving forever in his mind the great IF. What seemed possible was in fact possible. And how would the rest of my life have been lived IF the workers had marched on and taken power, and turned the old regime upside down.[35]

## II

Looking back to the General Strike it is easy enough to find explanations for its failure and to judge that failure inevitable. But for those living through the period 1919-1926 matters felt very different. If the General Strike turned out to be a severe anti-climax that could only be because people were prepared for, eagerly anticipating or dreading, some sort of climax. Hence the significance of "The Second Coming", poised as it is between vision and prophecy. The same holds true of *The Waste Land*. Other writings of the period are similarly poised, might even be said to have that as their defining characteristic. Edgell Rickword's "Luxury" is a case in point.

According to Rickword's biographer Charles Hobday, the poem was inspired by a visit Rickword paid to Paris in 1924. "A jeweller's shop window in the Place de la Paix" provided the stimulus for "a Baudelarian vision with revolutionary undertones."[36] But the shop window has gone from the poem we have; and its "stony city" could be any modern metropolis.

> The long, sleek cars rasp softly on the kerb
> and chattering women rise from cushioned nests,
> flamingo-tall, whose coral legs disturb
> the mirror-surface where creation rests.
>
> Aconite, Opium, Mandragora, Girl!
> Essential phials exquisite array!
> Poisons whose frail, consumptive fervours whirl
> The stony city to a fierce decay.
>
> The churches' sun-dried clay crumbles at last,
> the courts of Justice wither like a stink
> and honourable statues melt as fast
> as greasy garbage down a kitchen sink.
>
> Commercial palaces, hotels de luxe
> and Banks in white, immutable ravines,
> life's skeleton unfleshed by cynic rooks,
> remain to warn the traveller what it means.
>
> The shady universe, once haunt of play,
> in leafless winter bares its way of stone;
> the paths we shared, the mounds on which we lay
> were ruled by Time and lifted by old bone.
>
> Time has no pity for this world of graves
> nor for its dead decked out in feathery shrouds.
> The ghoul must perish with the flesh he craves
> when stars' hoarse bells of doom toll in the clouds.

Rickword was an ardent admirer of Donne, and the poem's last line echoes Donne's famous warning to his congregation not to send to know for whom the bell tolls: "It tolls for thee." Yet this, coupled with the insistence that Time is about to close down the playgrounds of the west, is less revolutionary than fatalistic. There is a sense of imminent collapse at work in the poem, a thinly-veiled relishing of ruins of empire. Churches and courts of justice, those symbols of accustomed social orderliness, are on the verge of a destruction brought on by old age ("at last"). Even the gorgeous women turn out to be visions of death-in-life: their expensive dresses "feathery shrouds," their expensive perfumes drugs to kill by excess: ("whirl" hints at the dance of death, and with "consumptive fervours" together with "fierce decay," suggests also a frenzy of sexual abandonment, even perversion). But while the sense of distaste amounting almost to disgust for the "stony city" is unmistakable, especially in the image of the honourable statues which "melt as fast/ as greasy garbage down a kitchen sink," and although there is bound to be a feeling that "'tis well an old age is out," the poem doesn't say that it is "time to begin a new." Later in the 1920s Rickword would move more radically leftward, a move which would in the early 30s lead him into the Communist Party. But "Luxury" is a pre-Revolutionary poem.

It certainly doesn't imagine the rough beast's intervention in political affairs. It may therefore be contrasted with an even more remarkable poem, Ivor Gurney's "Sonnet – September 1922."

> Fierce indignation is best understood by those
> Who have time or no fear, or a hope in its real good.
> One loses it with a filed soul or in sentimental mood.
> Anger is gone with sunset, or flows as flows
> The water in easy mill-runs; the earth that ploughs
> Forgets protestation in its turning, the rood
> Prepares, considers, fulfils; and the poppy's blood
> Makes old the old changing of the headland's brows.
>
> But the toad under the harrow toadiness
> Is known to forget, and even the butterfly
> Has doubts of wisdom when that clanking thing goes by
> And's not distressed. A twisted thing keeps still –
> That thing easier twisted than a grocer's bill –
> And no history of November keeps the guy.

If the date that forms part of the title is correct – and I have no reason to disbelieve it – the poem must have been written at the very moment when Gurney's mental instability was becoming so severe that it would require his removal to an asylum.[37] This being so it might be thought that the poem's packed phrases make little sense. Yet meaning is to be unpacked from them. The title alone indicates that the sonnet offers to report on both the poet and his nation at a time of crisis common to them both. The opening phrase is surely indebted to Swift's well-known epitaph and aptly so: the social injustices visited on the Irish against which Swift had raged are echoed in the injustices visited on the unemployed – many of them former soldiers – against which Gurney had previously spoken in "Strange Hells" (a poem mentioned in Chapter 2) and to which he would return. (In "A Wish", for example, with its hope "for the children of West Ham/Wooden-frame houses square, with some-sort stuff/Crammed in to keep the wind away that's rough".) But, he says, fierce indignation can be understood best — and I assume kept burning — by those who have time on their side, who aren't fearful of the consequences of showing their indignation, are, we may infer, not vulnerable to dismissal from work, imprisonment, or other forms of official disfavour, and who live in hopes that their indignation can accomplish something. It is easy to lose such indignation through personal failings (Gurney was repeatedly harassed by thoughts of sin – see, for example, "Quiet Fireshine," where he speaks of "a soul too sick for dreams"), or by falling prey to that traditional English vice of sentimentality – by which I think he means collapsing anger into pity.

That Gurney was capable of deep, sustained anger against the social order we know from that sonnet he sent Marion Scott from the Front and which had so disturbed her because of its threat to "cut the cancer" he saw threatening England's life. Gurney, as I have suggested, had learned or come to socialism in the trenches, and a probable reason why "Sonnet – September 1922" is a more radical poem than "Luxury" may be traced back to the fact that whereas Gurney was a line soldier Rickword served as an officer in the Artists' Rifles, a regiment which was, as Hobday remarks, "a predominantly middle-class body."[38] Gurney's immediate companions were other line soldiers, and the ranker's genial contempt for officers comes through in his poem "The Silent One," where an officer with "the politest voice – a finicking accent" says to him, "'Do you think you might crawl through there there's a hole,'" and he "as politely replied – / 'I'm afraid not, Sir.'" But in the sonnet anger fades with the going down of the sun as though what happens is in the natural course of events. The plough becomes an image of history as change: uprooting the past, driving over the numberless dead (and living), expecting the cut worm to forgive it. Sacrifice now seems inevitable. The rood is the rood cross, and thus the blood sacrifice – no doubt of soldiers in the first instance, but not *only* of soldiers. It is whatever happens to happen: an inevitability that "Prepares, considers, fulfils." As Robert Graves says of his "one story," it nothing promises that is not performed. And in what had by 1922 become an almost familiar metonym, the poppy can be imaged as the blood of countless dead endlessly altering the look of the land.

But then, in the sestet, the sonnet takes a new turn. The first eight lines had seemed to sustain an account of anger as inevitably passing into resignation: the world is a place of suffering, always. Now, by vivid exploitation of a cliché, the toad under the harrow becomes capable of forgetting its "toadiness": that is, its creeping subservience, its dank servility. It may truly rise to become a rough beast. The butterfly I take it to be an image of those who live for the moment. Gurney may have at the back of his mind Galuppi's contemptuous remark of the Venetians as "butterflies [who] dread extinction" – he loved Browning's poetry although it is possible he is thinking of Yeats's "wisdom is a butterfly". This is a variation on Rickword's flamingo-tall women. Yet even the butterfly may doubt the account of history as an endless destroyer which seeks no justification for itself, and which as war machine or image of impersonal power – "that clanking thing" – wrecks the lives of ordinary people. And so the "twisted" thing, an example of human beings whose lives have been distorted by economic or other circumstances over which they have little seeming control, can be used as a spill of paper to start a huge conflagration. For I read the last line to mean that even if those who opposed injustice are expunged from official history they are still there – they still keep – and are now ready for action.

My interpretation is to some extent speculative. Yet opaque though the poem in some ways is, "Sonnet – September 1922" protests at a very deep level the account of contemporary history and therefore social circumstance as unavoidable. I don't, in other words, see the last line as a fatalistic statement to the effect that all protest is useless, although I *can* see that it may accept that conflagration – as a symbol of violent uprising – destroys many who cause it. I do not know whether Gurney might have had in mind the slaughter in Asia Minor, which reached its peak in the summer of

1922, and for which the British Government, along with its allies, refused to accept any blame even though they were all eminently blameworthy; nor do I know whether he felt especial outrage at the complacent budget passed by the coalition government in Spring 1922, in which public expenditure dropped for the first time since the war to below £1,000 millions and there was even talk of abolishing the Ministry of Labour and Employment Exchanges (at a time of acute unemployment). Nor do I know whether the Irish Civil War preyed on his mind. It is probably wrong to look to any one instance to explain the poem's power, its use of the language of pastoral to deny the reading of history so often associated with pastoral, as cyclic and therefore by implication inevitable. But "Sonnet – September 1922" is certainly not to be explained away as a symptom of Gurney's own distressed mental condition.

It is, however, a sad irony that in November of that year toadiness came to the rescue of the conservatives. As a result of the general election, called when the coalition finally collapsed, and after Bonar Law had campaigned on a platform of "tranquillity and freedom from adventures and commitments both at home and abroad", a conservative goverment was returned to power.[39] This is the election to which Henry Green must be referring in his first novel, *Blindness* published in 1926, some at least of which was written while he was still at Eton. In the early pages of this alert and discreetly symbolist novel, the schoolboy narrator recalls in his journal how he and some friends passed "A Labour and Socialist meeting" on their way back to school and decided to set up their own.

> They had their spokesman, an old labourer, very tub-thumpy....
> Looking round in the middle of it I saw that all the Conservative men and women were formed up behind us, which was touching. All this time messages were coming from the fellows on the outside that the people there were talking lovingly of murder (on us), and matters did look very nasty at one time, but it worked off. The police men came at the end with an inspector and marched us off, I shaking every man's hand that I could see.[40]

This feels to be the report of actual experience and is worth quoting because Green plainly wishes to reveal something of the protected life of his butterfly protagonist, John Haye, who is soon to be blinded when a small boy throws a stone at the first-class carriage window from which Haye studies the landscape as he travels home for the holidays. This symbolic act, the casual violence of which is surely meant to hint at the vulnerability of those who have been accustomed to think of their class as protecting them from harm – children of wealth in their warm nursery – leads to a further symbolic consequence. Haye is unable to inherit his ancestral home and estate. His mother realises that "he would never marry now, she would have no grandchildren. The place would be sold, the name would die." (p. 387)

Yet Haye himself has never wanted to become a landowner. He has already heard about the entirely unprecedented opposition of the villagers to his mother's rule of law: in a parish vote over a trivial issue she has been defeated, "because she had closed the public pathway at the bottom of the garden, a path which no one had used for nine years, and the gates were ugly and in the way. It had spoilt the drive, that wretched path. 'The first time, John, that the village has not followed my lead. It is so discouraging.' Oh, it had been tragic." (p. 398) As for John himself, "The life of the century was in the towns, he had meant to go there to write books..." (p. 399) And at the novel's end he does indeed go to London, taking his mother with him.

The scene where mother and son sit among their packed cases, waiting to leave their old home for the last time, is strongly reminiscent of the closing scene of *The Cherry Orchard*. Mrs Haye is like Madame Ranevsky, and Firs' part is taken over by the Haye's decrepit man-servant, William. "Poor old thing, he was quite upset. It was rather terrible," Mrs Haye thinks, as she glances at the doddery old man (p. 489). It is therefore of some interest to discover that *The Cherry Orchard* had its first successful staging in England during 1925, initially at Oxford, where of course Green then was, and later at the Lyric, Hammersmith. It then transferred to the West End. Arnold Bennett, an intense admirer of Chekhov, saw the production on more than one occasion. He told Beaverbrook that his first visit had provided "one of the greatest theatrical evenings of my life," and noted in his *Journals* that seeing the play again he had been still more struck by its "power and beauty."[41] *The Cherry Orchard* was a play calculated to appeal to many in the mid-1920s, for whom a foreboding sense of power and authority passing from its "natural" owners was bound to be strong, as it was for Bennett himself. Others might well read into contemporary affairs a hidden but soon-to-be-known fatal weakness, a deadly inanition, of those accustomed to be thought of and to regard themselves as the nation's leaders. In this sense, if in no other, it is possible to make connections between *Blindness,* the staging of Chekhov's play, and Galsworthy's *Old English.*

It is also relevant to bring into consideration here L.H. Myers' *The 'Clio',* published in 1925. In Myers' novel, a hugely expensive and elegant steam yacht carries a party of the rich and fashionable to South America. David Craig and Michael Egan see *The 'Clio'* in terms of a European and specifically white insecurity about the threat of "heart of darkness", in which fears of the collapse of empire are mingled with yearnings for "the wilderness and splendour of hot-blooded animal life that belongs there."[42] They rightly draw attention to this element in the novel, which in its turn throws some light on the fears of jazz and "nigger-dance" discussed in the previous chapter; but as they themselves point out, at a moment of danger, when the ship rams its bows into a bank of the Amazon, the party at once begins to fear imminent disaster, even though there is no reason to suppose that disaster is in the offing. Myers skilfully builds up a sense of the party's collective paranoia, their unnamed, unnameable fear that for all their elegance, riches, for all that they may seem to be "the fine flower of civilisation," as the ship's doctor thinks of them, they are about to be overwhelmed by dangers they cannot comprehend. But nothing happens. "The objective danger has been nil. What has happened has been a collapse of morale in face of untamed, alien life."[43]

Bennett builds up a very similar sense of unease, foreboding and fear of disaster in his novel *Accident,* although with one significant difference to which I shall draw attention when I come to discuss it in more detail. Here, I want merely to suggest that *The 'Clio'* too is poised somewhere between vision and prophecy, and to note that untamed, alien life doesn't have to be located in the jungles of South America. Well before the war London had been stigmatised as a heart of darkness; and if, as John Haye realises, the life of the century is to be found in the towns, that may be because, as he also senses, it is there that new life, new energies, exist, waiting perhaps to overwhelm the faded, by now parodic life of the country which his mother tries to maintain. When Mrs Haye reads, which is rarely, she reads about hunting. "This book was interestin', she had never known that the Bolton had distemper in '08 and mange in '09, a most awkward time for them, and the bitch pack had been practically annihilated." (*Blindness,* p 478). It is not just hounds who are threatened with annihilation.

In several fictional works of the period, conflict, even violent conflict, is a key feature and crucial to the works' meaning. That this should be so rather gives the lie to Ken Worpole's claim that "The two major traumas that dominate the 20th century novel of working-class life are, not the strike, not the factory accident, but early and unwanted pregnancy and hasty marriage, or the back-street abortion."[44] This may hold true of many novels but certainly not of key ones written in the opening decades of the century. On the other hand, Gustav Klaus is probably right to say that as far as the earliest of these novels are concerned, a naturalist concentration on suffering and brutalisation "corresponds to the objective situation and subjective experience of the working class, which is one of juridical attacks against its organization and of eroding real wages."[45] He has in mind Robert Tressell's classic *The Ragged-Trousered Philanthropists* and Bart Kennedy's *Slavery: Pictures from the Depths* (1905), whose title plainly suggests its debt to Jack London's *People of the Abyss*, (1903); but his remark could as well be applied to two novels published in the 1920s, Ethel Carnie's *This Slavery* (1925) and Leslie Welsh's *The Underworld.*

Welsh's novel first appeared in 1920, five years before Carnie's. Yet most commentators, myself included, think that Carnie's novel must have been written earlier, very probably sometime before the onset of the war. My information about her comes from the biographical sketch provided by Edmund and Ruth Frow. Carnie, (1886-1962), began her working life at the age of nine as a part-timer in a Lancashire cotton mill. Her first published work was a collection of poems, presumably in the tradition of Edwin Waugh, *Rhymes from the Factory*, (1907), and she thereafter became a "prolific writer of poems and journalism, novels and children's stories." All her best novels, including *Miss Nobody* (1913), *General Belinda* (1920) and *This Slavery,* have at their centre tough, independent-minded women. Of them all, the last named is the most radical, which may be why it was not published until 1925.[46] I agree with Klaus that *This Slavery* is remarkable for its "description of agonising poverty and its pressure on working men and women," although I am less convinced by his claim that "its revolutionary ardour foreshadows the post-war works and indicates how much it owes to the 1911-14 unrest when industrial conflicts were spreading, and the deployment of troops against strikers, as related in the novel, was no unusual feature."[47] This was undoubtedly what made the novel so timely in 1925. Yet the attention Carnie pays to the outbreak of a strike in the cotton industry is to a large extent wasted. The latter part of her novel is taken up with a conventional love story which ends in tragedy when Hester, the heroine, is hit and killed by a stray bullet as she urges the soldiers not to become the class enemies of their striking brothers and sisters.

*This Slavery* remains an impressive achievement, but its energies are for the most part directed towards a defeatist vision where suffering seems endless and injustice a fact of life that no amount of protest can surmount. Hester tries to raise herself above working-class status through marriage to a wealthy business man. The marriage fails when, after the death of her son, her husband throws her out because he considers her to be a spy working for the strikers against his business interests. Hester now rediscovers her class roots and this may be said to lead directly to her death. The problem is not with that, nor even with what may be thought of as an interesting re-fashioning of the main plot of Elizabeth Gaskell's *North and South*. It is rather that by paying so much attention to Hester, Carnie loses sight of the representative nature of the issues her novel ought to be addressing. She apparently reacted very strongly against this criticism when it was made by a reviewer in *The Sunday Worker*. The love-interest was, she said, "an elemental part of human life."[48] But this misses the point, which is that Hester's death directs attention away from the strike itself.

Yet against this it has to be said that *This Slavery* does imply that class conflict may be violent, that those upholding law and order may find themselves opposing their own best interests, and that the law is likely to be used as an instrument of class justice and as such directed against working-class people. In the 1920s these considerations were rapidly assuming the status of inevitable truths. They are certainly woven into the fabric of Leslie Welsh's *The Underworld* (1920), a first novel which proved so successful that within a matter of months it had sold 50,000 copies. As a result, the novel remained in print throughout the decade. (Its relative obscurity nowadays is probably due to its being overtaken by *The Ragged Trousered Philanthropists* with which, despite its being set in a Scottish mining community, it has much in common.) *The Underworld* is more directly relevant to a proper account of Scottish socialist writing and Welsh himself, (1880-1954), who was an active trade unionist and an MP for Coatbridge from 1922-1931 and then for Bothwell, 1935-1945, is best seen as an important contributor to Labour History.[49]

Like *This Slavery, The Underworld* ends with the death of the central character. Such a death, in a mining accident during which Robert has been trying to help his companions, is both plausible and tragic, but it is also in a measure defeatist. The very last paragraph of the novel runs as follows:

> But pain and tragedy forever seem to have no limit to their hunger; and in the clear spring air above the place where the bodies of her boys lay, Mrs. Sinclair's heart was again the food upon which the tragedy of life fed. All the years of her existence were bound up in the production of coal, and the spirit of her dead husband and of her sons call to-day to the world of men – men who have wives, men who have mothers, men who have sweethearts and sisters and daughters, stand firm together; and preserve your women folk from these tragedies, if you would justify your manhood in the world of men.[50]

The message may seem clear enough: something must be done. But what and how? As David Smith remarks, Welsh's next novel, *The Morlocks*, 1924, which deals with the failure of a revolutionary uprising in Britain, makes clear his "complete rejection of violence."[51] This is in line with Welsh's combination of Fabianism and Christian Socialism. It is also in opposition to a number of fictions which at this time were contemplating the likelihood, even the inevitability, of such violence. Among the first of these is Edward Shanks' *The People of the Ruins.*

Published in the same year as *The Underworld,* Shanks' novel glumly looks forward to Europe, and most particularly England, a century after it has been taken over and wrecked by communist revolution. All traces of decent civilisation have disappeared. As the title suggests, the people of the novel live among the ruins of the past. *The People of the Ruins* is poor stuff.[52] I mention it only because we need to note that as a professional writer Shanks cannily chooses a subject which, in suggesting the inevitability of violent revolutionary change at some time in the not far-distant future, plays on public fears and expectations. His novel is of additional interest because it is cited in a much better one, *Revolution,* by J.D. Beresford, which was published the following year.

Like Shanks, Beresford was a professional writer who by 1921 had a string of novels to his credit. According to Hugh Walpole, Beresford was "read very little but *strongly* liked by his following,"[53] and in *The Georgian Literary Scene* Swinnerton provides a sympathetic account of a novelist who, he says, "has always been a reader of philosophy, has always been interested in current ideas. His books have tended more and more to present those ideas.... 'What is happening to the world?' he says .... and he inclines his ear for an answer."[54] *Revolution* is, it seems safe to say, written to the moment and addresses itself to current interests and anxieties. It is however set in the immediate future – probably 1924 or 5. Its hero, Paul Leaming, is a young man who has returned from the great war in a shell-shocked state. We are to understand that his physical symptoms are partly caused by the psychological anguish of a war whose justice he has come increasingly to doubt. Paul's father assumes his son will join him in his city business, but Paul has no love of it. Nor does he feel any admiration for the older generation of merchant men and presumably profiteers. (Shades of Charlie Prohack.) Moreover, although Paul says he has no interest in politics, he is disgusted by his father's strong adherence to conservative values. He is therefore fascinated by the figure of Isaac Perry, an idealistic christian socialist and union leader who is threatening a general strike.

The first movement of the novel is taken up with the days before the strike. Paul's father reads in *The Daily Telegraph* that the Labour Party has split: older members refuse to associate with the Perry manifesto, which calls for strike action, younger ones back it. Mr Leaming and his business associates agree there is small chance of the strike happening. "'The British workman may be greedy, but he's no fool,'" a stockbroker remarks.[55] Paul decides to go down to the docks in order to talk to working men. There he meets a man called Price who had served under him in Egypt. Price tells him that he and other soldiers thought

> we were coming back to a wonderful fine place after it was all over. We believed it was going to be different, sort of Utopia, short hours, and good pay, and everybody pals with everybody else. I don't quite know where we got that idea from, but a lot of us had it.... Anyway, when we did come home we didn't get what we expected, not by a good bit. Things were worse than they'd ever been, with wages and prices chasin' each other all the time, and prices always a lap ahead.

Price inevitably mentions the profiteers, and when Paul asks him whether he thinks Perry's programme will improve matters, Price answers "'Oh!' oo cares .... The point is as us working-men realise as we've got to stick together.'" And he then adds: "'May be it'll be like the *Herald* says that we'll have to work longer hours and work a lot harder while we're at it. But we'll be workin' for ourselves, and not to keep a lot of blarsted millionaires and their fancy women in champagne and diamonds.'"(pp. 43-4).

Paul is impressed by Price's words, impressed, too, by what he feels is the inevitability of the "the general ideal of what was currently spoken of as democracy" (p. 46); he refuses to share his father's rejoicing at the government's trickery in apparently giving in to the unions' demands while in fact preparing to do exactly the opposite. Beresford is presumably drawing on Lloyd George's tactics here, which quite remarkably anticipate those Baldwin would use in 1926.[56] Paul in fact has now begun to realise that he must oppose his father, and after he has refused to consider joining a special armed force of "loyalists" – called up by the government "' to diddle the strikers when they come out,'" as his father gleefully explains – his sister tells him that he is not the Paul of old. "'You'd never have dared to [oppose him] in the old days,'" she says. To which Paul replies, "'I seem to see things more clearly than I used to.'" He now knows that he has got rid of "the moral cowardice that had once made him afraid to contradict his father." (pp. 55-8)

The next movement of the novel follows the beginning of the general strike. Discussions between the government and unions have broken down, and the government immediately moves to ban the left's newspaper, *The Daily Herald*. Perry arrives to talk to men who have gathered outside the newspaper's office, and Paul, who is in the crowd, is deeply affected by the man's almost saintly qualities. "It would have been more fitting if the hurrahs had been changed to hosannahs!" (p. 80). This is awkward, yet out of it Beresford makes a compelling move. Perry is shot and killed and as a result the strike turns to revolutionary violence. It is never clear whether the assassination of the union leader was accidental or intended, nor whether the government used the killing as a means to prompt violence which would then justify their own use of force. Mowat says that in 1926 there seems to have been some effort "by the more militant spirits in the government to produce the revolution they talked of in order to crush it decisively. Special constables were recruited in large numbers, so that their number increased from 98,000 before the strike to 226,000 at the end. In addition, the government on May 8 called for enlistments in a Civil Constabulary

162

reserve, which soon numbered 18,000".[57] Here as elsewhere in *Revolution,* Beresford is remarkably prescient.

Nor is it evasive of him to leave the issue of provocation in doubt. By the time Paul and his father hear of Perry's death they have abandoned strike-bound London for Mr Leaming's cottage in the country, there being no point in remaining in The City. In the country news is impossible to come by. Beresford is writing before the advent of the BBC which in 1926 was, as I have already noted, used to give exclusive announcements of the government's views and which suppressed all other views – even the so-moderate offer of intervention by the Archbishop of Canterbury.[58] Beresford very intelligently suggests how cut-off each community will be and more importantly *feel* itself to be in the event of a general strike and possible consequent violence; and I am sure he was tapping into a widely-shared disquiet about this. As Yeats wrote in "Meditations in Time of Civil War," We are closed in, and the key is turned/On our uncertainty."

But in the village new forces arise. Jem Oliver, a country labourer, has formed a group of potentially violent men, a kind of country militia. Then Lord Fynemore arrives from London. Lord of the parish and yeoman face up to each other. Paul suggests that the village form itself into a soviet (p. 140) in order to pool resources and surrender private property. He feels great sadness for Fynemore and his kind. "They had added a new beauty, even a new ideal to the world, but they no longer served the purpose of the life-force .... Paul loved them with a tender, protecting love. He desired passionately to save them from the terror." (p. 137) But as he tells Fynemore and his father, this will depend on their readiness to recognise that "'These men [meaning Oliver and his supporters] are the men we're going to work with, and unless we can learn to understand them and feel affection for them, there'll be no hope of peace." (p. 141)

He calls a meeting at the village school. There, his father refuses to listen to Jem Oliver, and Oliver, whom Paul now sees to be "stupid" and a "yokel," shoots and kills Mr Leaming. Paul feels no anger, only "an immense pity." Later, Oliver orders the execution of a local farmer who has refused to turn his land over to co-operative use. Later still, as the village struggles to work as a soviet, Paul gathers "from the somewhat irregular news" which reaches them that following the violent overthrow of the old government, "the Labour government had never firmly established itself. The railways ran uncertainly, industry was disorganised, and the Post Office service was quite unreliable." (p. 204) In addition – and this feels more plausible – foreign countries refuse to trade with the new government.

At this point Lord Fynemore's son turns up in the village and Paul realises that he is part of a counter-revolutionary force intent on overthrowing the government and restoring "law and order." Significantly called Winston, the son makes it clear that among other things he has come to arrest and execute Jem Oliver. Oliver succeeds in killing him but is then himself mown down by soldiers accompanying Winston Fynemore. Paul is disheartened. The cause of peaceful revolution, of a changed society, is now ruined. "'The men you're trying to set up again in Westminster, with a sentimentally restored monarchy to help them out, were discredited long ago'" he says. (p. 218) Discredited or no, by the novel's end Fynemore's daughter confirms that "'All the people, our lot, have come back, and they're worse than ever they've been – decadent, mad for amusement and excitement of every kind.'" But, she adds, "'I think they feel the present state of things isn't going to last long and they're trying to make the most of it – dancing on the edge of the pit. They simply don't care for anything or anybody, Paul.'" (pp. 247-8)

It is probably a mistake for Beresford to end his novel with the daughter's musings. "It seemed to her that all human life was but a little candle burning in the great dark house of the world, a trembling light of aspiration and endeavour that would presently be quenched by the coming of the dawn." This isn't to say that her mysticism, which feels very close to Paul's own brand of Tolstoyan Christian socialism, shouldn't be accommodated. But placing it right at the end of the novel dissipates the issues which *Revolution* has so interestingly and intelligently raised. It's as though they now don't matter. People will fall into the pit and that's that. It is however crucial that her thoughts should be followed by Beresford noting that the novel was written "March – September, 1920." The novelist invites his readers to consider the likely course the new decade will take; they are also to consider the possibility, even probability, of events which did seem to come to their climatic realisation on May 4, 1926, only to collapse in tragi-farce nine days later. This, too, Beresford had anticipated.

It may be for this reason that *Revolution* has never been much written about by literary historians of the left. Most simply ignore it. Gustav Klaus compares it unfavourably with H.R. Barbor's *Against the Red Sky*, which was published a year later than Beresford's novel, in 1922. "A curiously detached intellectual experiment," he calls *Revolution,* which ends "significantly, with the counter-revolution in the saddle."[58] Well, yes, but Klaus's protest at Beresford's ending ignores the fact that Lord Fynemore's daughter hints at further imminent disasters for those who dance on the edge of the pit and that, as the events of 1926 were to prove, Beresford was essentially right in his imaginative analysis of the attempt to bring revolutionary change to Britain. It simply wasn't going to happen. Not that he is making confident prophecies. To repeat, as with many of the other works with which I am concerned in this chapter, *Revolution* is poised between vision and prophecy. But in that case – in any case – I do not see that Beresford's novel is to be disadvantageously compared to *Against the Red Sky*.

Those who have warmly applauded Barbor's novel approve of the way in which its hero who, in Klaus's words, is "disillusioned about the state of bourgeois culture and the gloomy prospects it holds for his kind, throws in his lot with the working class."[60] The novel begins with a young would-be writer called Richard Constable happening on a street fight in the centre of London. He joins in on the workers' side. Although he does not know it at the time, the fight is part of a full revolution which leads to the emergence of a workers' state with him as President of the Revolutionary Tribunal. Even those most sympathetic to the novel feel bound to comment on the unconvincing nature of Constable's effortless rise to the top of the revolutionary tree. (As he climbs he changes his name to John Smith and falls in love with a young Irish woman, where previously he had been entangled with a married countess.) His elevation is surely fatal in a novel which is intended to be about collective action? *Against the Red Sky* simply re-instates the romantic hero as "natural" leader, much as a number of would-be radical novels of the 1930s were to do, notably Simon Blumenfeld's *Jew Boy*. By comparison, Beresford's careful refusal of an heroic role to Paul Leaming, and Leaming's own agonized, uncertain response to the coming of revolution, feel at once more tactful and plausible. It dramatises those split feelings which typified middle-class response to the strike itself, feelings perfectly encapsulated by Winifred Holtby when she wrote to Vera Brittain from South Africa to say that "It seems as though the whole twentieth century society was organised in order to put the strikers in the wrong. They are in the wrong too. And yet I feel that if I were in England I should go to the T.U.C. and not the O.M.S. to offer my respectable services."[61] Had she done so she would have been in a significantly tiny minority. To the vast majority of the middle-class the strikers were very simply "in the wrong".

But this did not assuage fears of coming violence. If anything, it increased them. Hence, perhaps, H.G.Wells's *Men Like Gods,* a utopian fantasy about the world as it might be imagined to be in several centuries' time. The book was published in 1923 and I suspect contemporary readers were likely to be less impressed by the kind of peaceful anarchic communism Wells depicts, about which there is a strong whiff, of Bauhaus-cum-test-tube science, than the fact that we are told that the achievement of present – i.e. future – bliss cost five centuries of violence. (This includes the overturning of a proletarian dictatorship.) The book's real interest is in the character Rupert Catskill, very obviously based on Churchill, an earthling who tries to conquer the ideal world to which he has been introduced. That he should be so obviously set up as a hate-figure bears out Douglas Goldring's contention that from the start of the 1920s Churchill's own "hatred of 'Bolshevism' and dislike and distrust of the masses was unconcealed."[62] Hence, not only Rupert Catskill but, as we have seen, Winston Fynemore.

Churchill was prominent among those who welcomed the conflict that most others feared. Miles Malleson had gone some way to revealing these contrasting feelings in his play of 1925, significantly called *Conflict.* Malleson was a committed radical (His *D Company* and *Black 'ell* had years earlier been banned for their anti-war views, as was mentioned in Chapter 2, and he would go on to write a play about the Tolpuddle Martyrs, *Six Men of Dorset,* published by the Left Book Club in 1937.)[63] *Conflict* was written with I.L.P. drama groups specifically in mind. The play is set within the mansion of Lord Bellingdon who represents landed property and political reaction. The text ends with a stage direction: "Outside someone begins singing the 'Red Flag', which is taken up in chorus, and howled down. Someone begins singing 'God Save the King.' which is taken up in chorus. Cheers and howls and countercheers..."[64]

Then came the General Strike. Perhaps the revolution foretold by Shanks, Beresford, Barbor, Wells, Malleson and others had finally begun.

But of course it hadn't. The rough beast was still-born. With hindsight it seems silly even to suppose that anybody could have feared prolonged and violent conflict. Yet as the foregoing section was intended to suggest, such fears and hopes were both real and widely shared; and they progressively intensified in the years leading up to May, 1926. On May 4th of that year, with the strike into its second day, Arnold Bennett noted in his *Journal* that he had lunched at the Reform Club where he found "most people gloomy, but all uncompromising. General opinion that the fight would be short but violent. Bloodshed anticipated next week." A week later, with the strike called off and in a vastly relieved state of mind, he wrote, "I am still sticking to my point with everyone that the calling of the general strike is a political crime that must be paid for. Also that the general strike is revolutionary, that is, aimed at the authority of the Government." But by the following day he has decided that "the general strike now seems pitiful, foolish – a pathetic attempt of underdogs who hadn't a chance when the over-dogs really set themselves to win. Everybody, nearly, among the over-dogs seems to have joined in with grim enthusiasm to beat the strike." Finally, on the 13th, he writes: "Duff Taylor told great stories of his adventurous journeys on the Tube train driven by swagger youths in yellow gloves who nevertheless now and then overran the platforms with their trains, or pulled up too short."[65]

These entries are instructive, not only because they show how even so normally kindly and magnanimous a person as Bennett could be driven to vindictive panic by the strikers' action, but because they reveal how quickly panic in the face of threatening violence turns to comic anecdote once the threat has disappeared. There is something shamefaced about this, too; and with a steadying of his nerve and, therefore, readiness to confront such shamefacedness, Bennett in the autumn of the year began a novel intended to explore something of the strike's underlying causes. *Accident* is a broken-backed affair. I do not propose to comment on it at length,[66] but I do need to note that it very remarkably betrays Bennett's own uncertainties about the social and political pressures which not only produced the strike but, more especially, prompted his reactions to it. And as *The 'Clio'* will remind us, such reactions were common to those in similar circumstances.

The novel falls into two halves. In the first, Bennett carefully builds a sense of foreboding, of possible catastrophe, which is then thrown away in the trivial comedy of the second half. *Accident* opens with a wealthy business man, Alan Frith-Walter, climbing aboard a boat train. As the train leaves on its journey so, suddenly, a feeling of incipient disaster begins to grow. The first ominous incident occurs when the train stops "in the middle of a wide Kentish landscape": no-one knows why, or if they do, they aren't telling. Then, as mysteriously as it had stopped, the train starts again. Eventually it reaches Paris and now there are rumours of a major accident somewhere ahead. Frith-Walter transfers to the Rome express and, hurtling through the night, he catches sight of what he thinks is the scene of the accident, although he is told that bodies he has dimly made out lying beside the rails aren't sheeted human corpses but those of cattle, and that the accident – the same? another one? – is minor. The sense of paranoia, of not knowing who to trust, increases.

It is bound up with, may be caused by, Alan's own sense of unease about England. From the very first, as he boards the train, he thinks of the vast gap between the rich, such as himself, and the poor, like the cab-driver who has brought him to Victoria Station and the porters who have assisted him into his pullman. "Something wrong somewhere: something wrong! ... society was sick." (p. 5) As he waits for the train to depart he looks out of the window and wonders,"'Why are we going, and why are they helping us to go? ... And why do they not storm the trains and take our places by force? All have their cares, and I have not a care in the world .... But the world is my care.'" (p. 9) Alan studies his fellow passengers in their first-class carriage, that microcosm of class exclusiveness, privilege, privacy: "What a cargo of opulent beings, of whom it might be said that for them the sensual world did indeed exist! What a cargo of fleshly ideals and aspirings!" (p. 12) His dissatisfactions bite deeper and now he realises that he has been carrying them around for years; "but of late these notions [of contrasts in existence] had been growing clearer in outline, less vague, more insistent: the spirit of the age besieging, investing, the citadel of his conscience." (p. 53)[67] A little later and he is reproaching himself for his "superfluity of money" and for "squandering it on an inexcusable self-indulgence" (p. 73) when it could and should be offered for the public good. At this point he becomes aware that in the eyes of others he is inevitably identified with the "opulent cargo" he has studied with such dismissive scorn and from which he has felt himself apart. And then the express crashes.

And with the crash the sense of mounting disquiet, even of horror, is dispelled. The second, tedious half of the novel is concerned with Alan's role in patching up his son's marriage. Family comedy replaces the larger social issues and crisis which the first half of the novel had so impressively prepared us for. *Accident* is therefore a most instructive novel, because it so obviously testifies to the sense of anti-climax which followed the ending of the general strike. For Nevinson, as we have seen, anti-climax was also relief: his "faith in the unity of English blood" was restored by the jokiness of the undergraduates strike-breakers. "We take our troubles with a smile," he concludes. "We are artists at play, and jolly amateurs in disaster."[68] And in the letter to Vera Brittain from which I have already quoted, Winifred Holtby remarks how the strike will divide people's sympathies, her mother's included. "She loves a vague abstraction called England amazingly, and it makes her perpetually uncomfortable and miserable when something goes wrong. She can only comfort herself by extracting some flavour of nobility from a situation, like 'our brave boys', 'our gallant allies', 'my splendid daughter...'"[69]

The sudden end of the strike could therefore be presented as a triumph for the national spirit. It may have been in accord with this spirit that Alfred Noyes' *Sherwood,* which had been written in 1908, received its first performance in 1926. Yet as Stephen Knight sardonically remarks, the closing stanza of the famous poem celebrating Robin and his merry men has about it a dying fall:

> Robin! Robin! Robin! All his merry thieves
> Answer as the bugle-note shivers through the leaves,
> Calling as he used to call, faint and far away,
> In Sherwood, in Sherwood, about the break of day.

Where earlier in the poem the outlaws had been presented as "a fox-hunting pack or a group of privileged louts, educated bourgeoisie at play," they are now part of a dream "from which even the author must wake."[70]

This is the dream from which Alan Frith-Walter is temporarily woken by the fears of a crash ahead. But when the crash comes and turns out to be nothing much he can lapse back into that contentment which Nevinson and others suggest typifies a spirit of national unity. Such a suggestion, however, glosses over the brutal, triumphal vindictiveness shown by government and bosses to the defeated strikers, above all the miners. It also ignores the fact that while for some the events of May, 1926, seemed to show that taking sides was not after all required of them, for others it became the occasion that defined their movement towards radical commitment. One of them, at least, would come to diagnose the contentment of Alan Frith-Walter as "classic fatigue." And Auden, whose phrase that is, and who uses it to such telling effect in "Consider This and In Our Time," had chosen not to identify with other undergraduates at the time of the general strike. Instead, he worked for the strikers.

## Notes to Chapter 5

1. Yeats's famous remark about the Savage God has of course been much used as a tool to prise open different versions of Modernism. I use it merely to register his sense that in the opening years of the 20th century a new barbarism was making its presence felt. I am not here concerned with whether such barbarism has its roots in socialism, primitivism or Nietzsche, to name three of the more usually identified sources.

2. See Daniel Albright, (ed) *W.B.Yeats: the Poems*, London, Dent, 1990, p. 619. Albright has useful notes on the poem, pp. 619-22.

3. Quoted by Donald Torchiana, *W.B. Yeats and Georgian Ireland*, London, O.U.P., 1966, p. 214.

4. Quoted by Stan Smith in *The Origins of Modernism*, Hemel Hempstead, Harvester/Wheatsheaf, 1994, p. 152.

5. For Yeats's reading of Wordsworth, see Patrick J. Keane, "Burke, Wordsworth and the Genesis of 'The Second Coming'" in *The Bulletin of Research in Humanities*, New York, Spring, 1979.

6. *The Origins of Modernism*, p. 154.

7. Ibid. p. 149.

8. The letter is quoted by Donald Davie in *Poetry Nation Review*, vol. 17, no. 5, 1991, p. 24.

9. For this see G.D.H. Cole and Raymond Postgate, *The Common People*, London, Methuen, 1946, p. 546.

10. For Clyde/Glasgow see a number of pamphlets about the strike and Scotland in the *Our History* pamphlet series, especially *John Mclean*, The History Group of the Communist Party, London, King Street, Spring, 1976. In 1921, during the miners' strike of that year, Lloyd George remarked that "the populations of the Scottish mining villages are a savage folk."

11. John Stevenson, *British Society, 1914-1945*, Harmondsworth, Penguin, 1984, p. 197. Quite why the Yorkshire miners should be singled out for mention I don't know, unless it is that Stevenson is writing from Leeds.

12. *The Common People*, p. 554. According to T.A. Jackson, "sentiment in favour of the Bolsheviks, Revolution was so strong and widely diffused in the I.L.P. that it took all of MacDonald's genius as a wire-puller, and a manipulator of the Party-Machine to hold back a mass influx into the C.P. No historian will do justice to the subject-matter who fails to pay the proper 'tribute' to the superlative dexterity and ingenuity with which MacDonald aided by the astute and crafty old

style T.U. officials – and aided too by the muddled pacifist sentimentality predominant in the I.L.P. contrived to stave off what could have been a 'final horror.'" In the interests of being seen to do justice to Jackson I quote his view that Ramsay MacDonald succeeded in persuading those who wanted to become communists from becoming communists. See *Solo Trumpet: Some Memories of Socialist Agitation and Propaganda*, London, Lawrence and Wishart, 1953, p. 165.

13. Ibid. p. 561.
14. *The Black Curtain*, op. cit. pp. 150-152.
15. Quoted in *The Long Weekend*, op. cit. p. 151.
16. Henry Pelling, *A History of British Trade Unionism*, op. cit. p. 167.
17. Bertrand Russell, *The Practice and Theory of Bolshevism*, London, 1920, reprinted; 1954, p. 7.
18. Ibid. p. 19. Russell makes clear his detestation of western capitalism in its attempts to de-stabilise the Russian experiment. "There is no depth of cruelty, perfidy or brutality from which the present holders of power will shrink where they feel themselves threatened," he remarks, p. 10.
19. Ibid. pp. 18 and 20.
20. Ibid. 34-7.
21. See *The Common People* pp. 562-3.
22. *A History of British Trade Unionism*, p. 166.
23. Charles Loch Mowat, *Britain Between the Wars, 1918 -1940*, London, Methuen, 1968, (first published 1955) p. 145. The following year when the I..L.P. won a majority on Bermondsay's Council, "one of the first gestures of the Council was to replace the Union Jack on the flagstaff of the town hall with a flag for which the colour red was specifically chosen." For this see "'When every Street Was a Cinema," *History Workshop Journal*, no. 39, op. cit. p. 49. Yet this red dawn heralded no day of revolution: the Borough Council behaved as a responsible, popularly elected, local government body.
24. Ibid. pp. 171-2.
25. H.W. Nevinson, *Last Changes, Last Chances*, London, Nisbet & Co, 1928, pp. 304-5.
26. Ibid. p. 311 Nevinson's view is shared by a much more recent historian, Gordon Phillips, who notes that "A Labour ministry did not entail any national catastrophe. The government behaved like a government, handling day-to-day affairs with competence, running departments of state, paying its bills and treating with foreign powers like any of its predecessors." See G. Phillips, *The Rise of the Labour Party, 1893-1931*, London, Routledge, 1992, p. 37.
27. *Last Changes, Last Chances* p. 311.
28. *Britain Between the Wars*, p. 190.
29. For a full account of the letter and its impact see *Britain Between the Wars* pp. 188-192.
30. Ibid p. 275.
31. My source here is an unpublished talk by Leonard Miall, "This Was the BBC, 1929," given at Loughborough University, May 3rd, 1979. Cole and Postgate refer to Reith's "strong, one-sided intervention" in the strike, *The Common People,* p. 612. It is of interest that the first BBC radio play, broadcast in 1924, by Richard Hughes, was centred on a mining accident. Presumably it was felt that radio as a "dark" medium was well suited to deal with life in the dark. The miners are sympathetically portrayed, but they do not protest against their sufferingts: they are hapless victims, that is all.
32. *A History of British Trade Unionism* p. 177.
33. *Britain Between the Wars* p. 313.
34. *Last Changes, Last Chances* p. 321.
35. Hubert Nicholson, *Half My Days and Nights*, op. cit. pp. 79-80.

36. Charles Hobday, *Edgell Rickword: A Poet at War*, Manchester, Carcanet, 1989, p. 84.
37. There is a brief, harrowing account of this terrible moment in Gurney's life in Michael Hurd's biography, *The Ordeal of Ivor Gurney*, Oxford, O.U.P., 1978, see esp. pp. 145-155. I suspect Hurd's account will need to be greatly expanded and clarified in any future biography.
38. *Edgell Rickword*, p. 27.
39. *Britain Between the Wars*, p. 145.
40. Henry Green, *Nothing, Doting, Blindness*, London, Picador, 1979, p. 356.
41. James Hepburn (ed), *The Letters of Arnold Bennett*, 3 vols, Oxford, O.U.P., 1968, vol. 3, p. 243, and Newman Fowler (ed) *The Journals of Arnold Bennett 1921-1928* London, Cassell, 1933, p. 92.
42. In Stephen Knight and Michael Wilding (eds), *The Radical Reader*, Sydney, Wild and Woolley, 1977, pp. 26-8.
43. Ibid p. 27.
44. Ken Worpole, *Dockers and Detectives: Popular Reading, Popular Writing*, London, Verso, 1983 p. 23. I should make clear my admiration for Worpole's work and challenge only his, as I think, untenable assertion as it affects the 1920s and (possibly) 1930s.
45. H. Gustav Klaus (ed) *The Socialist Novel in Britain*, Brighton, Harvester, 1982, p. 94.
46. See "Ethel Carnie: Writer, Feminist and Socialist," in H. Gustav Klaus (ed) *The Rise of Socialist Fiction, 1880-1914*, Brighton, Harvester, 1987, pp. 251-266.
47. *The Socialist Novel in Britain*, p. 95.
48. Ibid pp. 96-7.
49. There is an account of him by Joyce Bellamy and John Saville in the 2nd volume of *Labour History*, 1974, pp. 399-401. There are also critical studies of Welsh by H. Gustav Klaus, "James C. Welsh: Major miner novelist," *Scottish Literary Journal*, XIII no. 2. 1986, pp. 65-86 and by David Smith, *Socialist Propaganda in the Twentieth Century British Novel*, London, MacMillan, 1978, pp. 41-4.
50. Leslie C. Welsh, *The Underworld*, Redhill, Love and Malcomson Ltd. 1920, p. 256.
51. David Smith, *Socialist Propaganda in the Twentieth Century British Novel*, p. 42.
52. In *Figures in the Foreground*, London, Hutchinson, 1963. Frank Swinnerton records Hugh Walpole saying that Shanks "knows nothing about the novel at all" an opinion which Swinnerton, normally a kind man, fully endorses. See pp. 98-9. Osbert Sitwell pillories Shanks in his pamphlet "On the Squirearchy: 'Who Killed Cock Robin? Or Jolly Squire and Shanks Mare'". For this see Douglas Goldring, *The Nineteen – Twenties*, op. cit. p. 103.
53. *Figures in the Foreground* p. 75.
54. Frank Swinnerton, *The Georgian Literary Scene*, London, Dent/Everyman, 1938, p. 221.
55. J. D. Beresford, *Revolution*, London, Collins, 1921, p. 38. All future quotations from the novel will be followed by page references to this edition.
56. For Baldwin's "studious vagueness" when confronted by the demands put to him by the T.U.C. leaders see especially *Britain Between the Wars* pp. 313-331. Lloyd George was also a master at pretending to offer much while conceding nothing, and Baldwin probably learned his tactics from him.
57. Ibid. p. 316.
58. Ibid. p. 320.
59. *The Socialist Novel in Britain* pp. 99-100.
60. Ibid. p. 99.
61. Vera Brittain and G. Handley-Page (eds) *Selected Letters of Winifred Holtby and Vera Brittain*, London, A. Brown and Sons, 1960, p. 124. The letter was written

on May 11th, 1926, by which time the strike had been called off, although Holtby wasn't to know this. Seigfried Sassoon's poem "The Case for Miners" similarly acknowledges divided feelings. The poem begins with him saying that "Something goes wrong with my synthetic brain/When I defend the Strikers and explain/My reasons for not blackguarding the Miners." But though he strives to hold his own with friends at the club they usually outgun him. The poem ends with his rehearsing their clichés: "That's how my port-flushed friends discuss the Strike./And that's the reason why I shout and splutter./And that's the reason why I'd almost like/To see them hawking matches in the gutter." *Collected Poems: 1908-1956,* London, 1961, p. 137. But the poet is, as he reveals, part-implicated in the cosy world of clubland and isn't at all sure that he can bear to give it up.

62. Goldring, *The Nineteen-Twenties,* p. 221. Goldring quotes a speech Churchill made in Rome in 1927, in which he praised Mussolini in the most fulsome terms and said, "If I had been an Italian I am sure that I should have been whole-heartedly with you from the start to finish in your triumphant struggle against the bestial appetites and passions of Leninism." He also lauded Mussolini for providing leadership which showed that "Hereafter no great nation will be unprovided with an ultimate means of protection against the cancerous growth of Bolshevism." p. 223. This throws an interesting forward light on the British government's non-interventionary policy in Spain in 1936. As for *Men like Gods* David Smith writes generously about the book (see *Socialist Propaganda* pp. 45-6), although I find myself largely in agreement with the more sceptical line taken by Michael Draper in his *H.G. Wells,* London, MacMillan, 1987, esp. p. 67.

63. The play was first performed at Wolverhampton, 1937, with a cast that included Lewis Casson and Sybil Thorndike.

64. For information about this see Andrew Davies, *Other Theatres: The Development of Alternative and Theatre in Britain,* London, Macmillan, 1989, pp. 99-100.

65. *The Journals of Arnold Bennett, 1921-1928,* pp. 132-135.

66. For an extended discussion of the novel see my *Arnold Bennett: A Study of His Fiction,* London, Methuen, 1974, pp. 213-222.

67. As I indicated in Chapter 3, "Citadel" is a word used to significant effect in Elizabeth Daryush's sonnet of the '30s, "Children of Wealth," who are imagined as thinking their privileged house is a citadel: i.e is safe from outside forces but also self-consciously a defence against them. The poem brilliantly plays on para-noid fears of "the gathering multitude" which Auden evokes in another key poem of the period, "A Summer Night."

68. *Last Changes, Last Chances,* p. 321.

69. *Selected Letters of Winifred Holtby and Vera Brittain,* p. 124.

70. Stephen Knight, *Robin Hood: A Complete Study of The English Outlaw,* Oxford, Blackwell, 1994, pp. 211-212. On my own shelves I have a children's *Robin Hood and his Merry Men,* by Sara Hawks Sterling, in which Robin is a good Anglican, a Royalist and a decently married man. (Though he and Marian have no chil-dren). This was published in London, by Coker, in 1928.

CHAPTER SIX

# POETRY, CIVILISATION,
# CULTURE and THE MASSES

According to a widely accepted view, English poetry after the war entered the doldrums. Those who ought to have formed the new generation of poets had died in France. As a result, the 20s was a decade when an older, discredited generation of poets still managed to dominate: among them, Squire, Herbert Palmer, Edward Shanks, and various of Edward Marsh's Georgians. There is some truth in this. In 1922 Marsh published an anthology of *Georgian Poetry 1920-1922* in the preface to which he rebutted the charge that his chosen poets offer "an insipid sameness". How can this be true, he asks, of an anthology which contains "the work of Messrs. Abercrombie, Davies, de la Mare, Graves, Lawrence, Nichols and Squire."[1] He has a point, though it is a small one. There are several good poems in his anthology and a few – including Lawrence's "Snake" – which are more than good. More remarkably, however, the anthology includes no war poems other than the entirely anodyne lyrics of Frank Prewett. As far as Marsh is concerned, the events of 1914-18 have become invisible, wiped from the record.

Five years later, Iolo A. Williams published *Poetry To-Day*. Here, to be sure, we can find an account of the poetry of war. "After Rupert Brooke's, Owen's was perhaps the most considerable talent lost to us by the war.... Happily, however, not all of the poets who first wrote as soldiers lost their lives; and among them were a number of men who have since continued their literary careers.... Among these may be mentioned such poets as Mr Siegfried Sassoon, Mr Robert Nichols, and Mr Robert Graves, each of whom is still writing with distinction." Williams provides quotations from all three (which in Nichols' case has the unintended effect of making it clear that he never wrote with distinction); and by way of concluding his survey of the poetry of to-day

175

he brings in the names of Edmund Blunden and Vita Sackville West, whose *The Land* apparently puts "her firmly among the few most important living poets."[2] And that is it. Nothing about Yeats other than his early verse. No mention of the dead Rosenberg and Edward Thomas, no word about such survivors as Gurney and Rickword. And not a whisper about *The Waste Land*.

*Poetry To-day* might more appropriately have been called *Poetry Yesterday*. Its absolute refusal to confront new poetry – unlike other commentators Williams does not even allow himself a sneer at Eliot – implies a determination to regard the best poetry as still existing within a "Georgian" tradition. This belief in an unbroken line, whether or not it has been traced to Williams, has seemed to subsequent commentators the prevailing orthodoxy of English poets and critics of the post-war years. Hence, the frequent citing of a remark Hardy was supposed to have made to Robert Graves and which has been used as evidence against Hardy and post-war English poetry. According to Graves, Hardy claimed that "*vers libre* would come to nothing in England," and added "all we can do is to write on the old themes in the old styles, but try to do a little better than those who went before us." I happen not to believe that Hardy said any such thing and have argued elsewhere my reasons for thinking that Graves was putting words into the older poet's mouth.[3] But this matters less than that literary historians have on the whole eagerly seized on the words as proof that post-war English poetry was marooned in brackish, shallow backwaters, where it remained until Auden brought with him the new "vigours of the sea."

Take, for example, Donald Davie's combative *Thomas Hardy and British Poetry*. Here Davie quotes with approval from the introduction to Sidney Bolt's anthology, *Poetry of the Twenties*, in which Bolt quotes Hardy's presumed remarks to Graves and adds "The implication that the old styles were linked to the old themes is clear, and whether or not they recognised the fact, the themes of these poets were too new to be accommodated by minor modifications of the style they inherited. As a result, the honesty which they had in common sometimes exposed the limitations of their verse."[4] It is not easy to know who Bolt is thinking of. Graves? Blunden? Sassoon? Nor is it easy to know what themes he has in mind. If he means that each of these poets made some attempt to come to terms with the conditions of the post-war world and failed, then I agree. But if he means that only poets willing to embrace *vers libre* were able to succeed, then I disagree.

Nevertheless, Bolt's thesis, heavily dependent as it is on Leavis's *New Bearings in English Poetry*, does point to an intriguing paradox. Those most insistent on making it new were also those most preoccupied with tradition, whereas those who like Graves wanted to say Goodye to All That were far more likely to be formally conventional. The radical impulse in poetry of the 1920s is, therefore a complex matter. I can well understand that English poets, no matter how they felt betrayed by the events of 1914-18, needed to be able to cling to some conventions, traditions, verities, which they felt or hoped might have survived the ravages of history: they felt, even if they couldn't openly argue for, a deep commitment to the survival of English poetic forms. Eliot and Pound, on the other hand, who felt no such need, had a very real commitment to an ideal of European civilisation for which they had chosen to leave their native America. This commitment will explain the urgency with which they set about shoring up what fragments they could against that civilisation's possible collapse.

## II

Fragmentariness seems indeed to be the condition of art in the 1920s. Dada, imagism, stream of consciousness, the shifting momentariness of cabaret acts, of cinema montage: these all testify to art as collage. Fragmentariness is mimetic, expressive of, and/or a critical response to a world gone smash. Here, then, the little magazine may look to be the ideal literary form of the moment. Little magazines are essentially collagist. They typically include reviews, poems, fictional and non-fictional prose, commentary, perhaps illustrations: and usually without any overall theme or pattern. Fragmentariness is their point, their *raison d'être*. And it is, of course, a fact that during the 1920s a large number of small magazines came into existence. Others, which had begun life earlier, were directed along new paths. Among them are *The Athenaeum* under Middleton Murry, *Time and Tide* and *The Fritillary* (two literary magazines for women about which there will be more to say later), *The Coterie* and then *New Coterie,* Edgell Rickword and Douglas Garman's *Calendar of Modern Letters*, and Wyndham Lewis's *The Enemy* and *The Tyro*. These last two were more unified than most if only because Lewis disliked fellow contributors as much as they

177

soon came to dislike him, with the result that he had to do most of the writing himself. All had in common their opposition to the older magazines which seemed for the most part to be run by John Squire and the Squirearchy, and of which *The London Mercury* was at once the most successful and despised. They also had in common an air of being provisional.

But it is possible to overdo the idea of fragmentariness. In his account of some of these journals, David Bennett argues that the editor as *bricoleur* endorses "an aesthetic of fragments or discontinuity."[5] This is to ignore the fact that nearly all the magazines had a coherent editorial policy, both for and more particularly against; and it was this that gave them their cutting edge, even their relish for attack. Editors and contributors were united in thinking that issues of vast significance were at stake, and although it might seem faintly absurd that small circulation magazines should wish to address such issues, it was precisely this that motivated them.

This was modernism. And the high seriousness of modernism, even in its English manifestation – which essentially means *The Calendar of Modern Letters* and just possibly Wyndham Lewis's one-man enterprises – took for granted, or at least for argument's sake, the opposition of small circle to mass society. In T. S. Eliot's case the opposition was that of a very small circle to mass democracy.

In 1922 Eliot began his own magazine, with money which had been put up by Lady Rothermere and with the guarantee of complete editorial independence. He could choose whichever contributors he wanted; the magazine's policy was equally for him to decide. As to its name, *The Criterion* was apparently suggested by his wife. *The Criterion* was, so Peter Ackroyd says, the name of a restaurant where she used to dine with her former lover, Charles Buckle. But the name very obviously suited its editor's purpose. Eliot wanted his quarterly, "to look simple and austere"; he made it his business "to employ the best critics, and not only those in England. He did not want the magazine to become lodged in an English provincial tradition, but saw it rather as a magazine for Europe." He therefore "took the opportunity which his editorship offered him of establishing relations with eminent men of letters throughout Europe – among them Valéry Larbaud, Ortega Y. Gasset and Ernst Robert Curtius."[6]

Eliot's ambition was plainly to make *The Criterion* an embodiment of cultural concerns which were also social and political con-

cerns. Above all, *The Criterion* was to testify to a cultural contin-
uum which survives as a platonic image of civilisation and can be
set against the wreckage of modern society. In a piece written some
years earlier, for *The Egoist,* Eliot had said that

> What we want is to disturb and alarm the public: to upset its
> dependence on Shakespeare, Nelson, Wellington and Sir Isaac
> Newton; to point out that at any moment the relation of a
> modern Englishman to Shakespeare may be discovered to be
> a modern Greek to Aeschylus .... That the forces of deteriora-
> tion are a large crawling mass, and that the forces of devel-
> opment half a dozen men ... for if our predecessors cannot
> teach us to write better than themselves they will surely
> teach us to write worse ...
> We must insist upon the importance of intelligent criti-
> cism.[7]

Those words of May, 1918, point up the social responsibility of art
and criticism. But by 1922 Eliot's rejection of the "large crawling
mass" – his version of the slouching beast – means that he regards
*The Criterion* as a way of saving civilisation for the fit few.
Admittedly its opening issue carried an essay by George Saintsbury
on "Dullness" and a short story by May Sinclair, neither of whom
can be readily imagined as belonging within Eliot's select circle; but
it also includes Valéry Larbaud on *Ulysses* as well as the text of *The
Waste Land.*

As everyone who comments on Eliot's poem inevitably points out,
the voices of its many prophets utter cries of lamentation over the
city's plight and/or over its need for salvation. Ted Hughes puts this
succinctly when he says that the starting point for the poem is "a new
kind of reality .... the whole metaphysical universe centred on God
had vanished from its place. It had evaporated with all its meanings.
This emptiness was Eliot's starting point." There had been fore-
shocks, Hughes says, but "the First World War left the truth bare. It
was as if only now, at this moment, mankind was finally born. For the
first time in his delusive history he had lost the supernatural world
.... In its place he had found merely a new terror: the meaningless."
Equally telling is Hughes' remark that the "descralized landscape"
which Eliot evokes had never been there before. "Eliot found it,
explored it, revealed it, gave it a name and a human voice. And almost
immediately, everybody recognised it as their own."

Here, it is relevant to note Forster's use of India to focus the
contemporary fear of nothingness: the reverberating echo in the

Marabar caves where, to the Western ear, "everything and nothing mean the same." But Forster finds in "old" India a coherence lacking in the colonised nation: "So long as his subjects are uneducated peasants," he writes in "The Mind of the Indian Native State", "a Prince is in a strong position from every point of view. They revere him with the old Indian loyalty, and a glimpse of his half-divine figure brings poetry into their lives. And he understands them even when he is indifferent or unjust, because like them he is rooted in the soil." (The essay, written in 1922, is included in *Abinger Harvest*.) Forster offers his English readers a glimpse of a sacralised, organic community, gone now from European society, yet whose appeal works as strongly on the liberal novelist as it does on the more conservative poet. It is evoked in the words from the Upanishads which end *The Waste Land,* and it will be strongly felt throughout *The Four Quartets.* It is a social vision developed during the 1920s and its allure, as we have seen in the example of *The Haunted Woman,* is to an "old" (i.e pre-war, pre-catastrophe) England to which Lawrence and F.R. Leavis will also appeal. The "organic" community becomes a key term or image to hold in opposition to the fragmented present.

But for Eliot, salvation does not lie in a social vision, not directly, anyway. As Lucy McDiarmid acutely notes, "the fragments of secular life [the poet] cannot arrange into an order; poetry he can."[9] This helps to explain Eliot's deep commitment to that tradition into which the individual talent is subsumed and which it then modifies. It occasions the key moment when he claims that existing works of art "form an ideal order among themselves," and that this is

> modified by the introduction of the new (the really new) work of art among them. The existing order is complete before the new work arrives; for order to persist after the supervention of novelty, the whole existing order must be, if ever so slightly, altered; and so the relations, proportions, values of each work of art towards the whole are readjusted; and this is conformity between the old and new.[10]

I am by no means the first to note that this is art as an imaginary museum. But although commentators have been severe on the concept, noting its readiness to divorce art from the historical process, we ought to recall that it was the historical process itself, the vast horror of the war, that gave such urgency to Eliot's project. Joyce was not the only modern writer for whom history was a nightmare. The desire to create a timeless world of cultural artefacts is at one with Eliot's desire to establish an ideal society of the civilised: a gathering at the chapel perilous.

This desire finds an echo in Forster's imagining that "We are to visualise the English novelists ... as seated together in a room, a circular room, a sort of British Museum reading-room, – all writing their novels simultaneously." So at least Forster wants to consider his chosen novelists in *Aspects of the English Novel*, his 1927 Clark Lectures; and he chooses this notion of simultaneity in order, he claims, to try to arrive at impartial judgement unclouded by "pseudo-scholarship," by which he seems to mean historical considerations. These would lay him open to the charge of special pleading, from which he plainly wishes to distance himself. So much so, indeed, that he early on announces that "No English novelist is as great as Tolstoy .... No English novelist has explored man's soul as deeply as Dostoevski. And no novelist anywhere has analysed the modern consciousness as successfully as Marcel Proust."[11] In his deceptively mild way Forster is here aligning himself with new critical forces which insistently took an internationalist perspective and refused to honour the tradition of exclusive concentration on the home-grown.

Although that tradition was comparatively recent it had, in the hands of the Squirearchy, become prevalent enough to require the withering attention of those who rightly regarded it as a betrayal of high standards. "Let the public ask itself why it has never heard of the poems of T. E. Hulme or Isaac Rosenberg, and why it has heard of the poems of Lady Precocia Pondoeuf and has seen a photograph of the nursery in which she wrote them," Eliot remarked in 1920. And he breathed a wish that "[we] come to look back upon reviewing as a barbarous habit of a half-civilised age."[12] His plea is not for an end to criticism but for the birth of responsible criticism. In a world gone smash the critic's responsibility is to salvage what he can for civilisation. Or as Pound put it in some famous words of 1928, the function of literature

> has to do with the clarity and vigour of "any and every" thought and opinion. It has to do with maintaining the very cleanliness of the tools, the health of the very matter of thought itself .... The individual cannot think and communicate his thought, the governor and legislator cannot act effectively, or frame his laws, without words, and the solid-

ity and validity of these words is the care of the damned and despised litterati. When their work goes rotten ... the whole machinery of social life and individual thought and order goes to pot.[13]

Eliot's poetic and critical enterprises have as shared concern the maintenance of this machinery. Hence, the many voices evoked in *The Waste Land,* whose function is less perhaps to act as judge or jury than to provide compelling evidence of Eliot's ability to summon what an earlier poet, Samuel Daniel, had called "the dead living" into counsel. The poem establishes the standards by which it is to be judged. And these are formal as well as contentual. Eliot's skills as a parodist have often enough been noticed, but his almost disdainful handling of a wide variety of metres has received less comment. Yet *The Waste Land* is a technical masterwork in the Renaissance sense of that word. Admittedly the poem that we have owes much of its coherence to Pound's editorial genius; but that is as it should be. The two writers have a common purpose, at least to the extent that Pound knew how to draw out and give most concentrated meaning to Eliot's preoccupation with poetry as impersonal: that is, as able to transcend individuality in order to become a defining voice for its moment. Its deliberately fragmentary, "disordered" state implies a coherence, an awareness of standards which transcend historical and social relativities.

Commentators have regularly made the mistake of confusing the definitive with the defining. As a result they have either blessed or cursed Eliot for claiming more than he ever did for the poem.[14] But whatever he chose to say about it, *The Waste Land* surely set new standards? That is why Alick West, in one of the earliest considered essays on the poem, is wrong to suggest that it "finally leaves us where we were." West intends by this remark to claim that Eliot never manages to transcend the individuality which his poem wishes to reject and that *The Waste Land* lapses into a despair that betrays its roots in a long-established social matrix where individuals want "to feel themselves part of some greater power than the insecurity in which they live; but since they do not want to change that world, the greater power reveals itself as the old conception of the bourgeois tradition, disintegrating but not changed otherwise."[15] For West, Eliot's poem is unintended proof of bourgeois individualism. He will also have had in mind the famous claim in "Tradition and the Individual Talent" that "Poetry is not a turning loose of emotion, but an escape from emotion; it is not the expression of personality, but an escape from personality." Eliot did not help his own argument by adding "But, of course, only those who have personality and emotions know what it means to escape from these things,"[16] because quite apart from appearing intolerably snobbish – ordinary people, we are to understand, are depersonalised zombies – the remark allowed, even encouraged, some commentators, including West, to infer that the "secret" meaning of the poem lay in Eliot's own psychological state at the time of writing. Perhaps he did mean to allow for such a meaning, or was anyway not averse from that being read into his remark. But it feels best to concentrate on the poet's desire to make his poem a truly radical utterance, an assemblage of voices which cry out of wells or thin air and between them, as Ted Hughes says, create an imaginative landscape that everybody can recognise as their own. That *The Waste Land* should have appeared in the same year as Edward Marsh's anthology of Georgian Poetry provides some measure of Eliot's achievement. It was *Marsh's* tradition, *his* England, that now looked unrecognisable. And it was *that* tradition which had hoped to leave people where they were.

III

Eliot set the standards. But it would be a mistake to think that his was a lone voice. One of the estimable features of journals of the period is how determinedly internationalist they typically were. Internationalism is indeed essential to much literary enterprise of the time, especially that of younger writers for whom it was a political matter – a rejection of the xenophobia of the older generation of the war-eager. It was also a way of taunting those elders who stood four-square behind a "native" Englishness. In an earlier chapter I mentioned Robert Bridges' decent attempt, first in his anthology *The Spirit of Man* and then in his post-war letter to the *Times,* to oppose this prevailing xenophobia. Younger writers were every bit as opposed to it, not merely because they saw it as politically questionable, but because the hideously smug patriotism which emerged after the war was engendered by the very forces which had gloried in that war. You did not have to be a communist sympathiser to regard the government-led-and-inspired hysterical reaction against the new Soviet Russia as grotesque, the blockade as barbarously cruel; and by the same token official insistence on the unchallenged might of the British Empire looked decidedly suspect. As Forster remarked of the 1924 British Empire Exhibition, "Millions will spend money there, hundreds will make money, and a few high-brows will make fun. I belong to the latter class." For all that the tone is light, Forster insists on the responsibility of being an intellectual. And although he would not have thought – or anyway said – that the small class with which he claimed allegiance had to save civilisation, he certainly thought – and said – that writers and intellectuals had a duty to oppose that Englishness which "is engaged in admiring [itself] and ignoring the rest of mankind."[17]

A mere glance at the new journals of the post-war period is enough to establish how determined they were not to ignore the writers of other countries. In *Figures in the Foreground* Frank Swinnerton recalls that at the outset of the twenties Middleton Murry urged him to write for *The Athenaeum,* of which Murry had become editor in 1919. Swinnerton didn't much like Murry, who certainly seems a peculiarly unlovable man; but he acknowledges that, quite apart from his praise for a number of continental European writers, Murry employed critics who "worked for the destruction of pre-war standards." And Murry, who included among his chosen reviewers Forster, Eliot and Virginia Woolf, himself wrote a piece about the Georgians, in which he identified as their chief fault that "There is nothing disturbing about them." He had in his sights the writings of Edward Marsh's chosen band, for whom the war might never have happened. England for the Marshians was still a place of rural contentment in which it was possible to repeatedly and unvaryingly "sympathise with animate and inanimate nature."[18]

In the year in which Murry claimed the editorial chair at *The Athenaeum,* a journal called *The Coterie* began its uncertain life. In its first manifestation it ran for a mere seven issues, until 1921. Then in 1925 it was re-born as *The New Coterie,* and in 1927, six issues later, finally perished. Like most magazines of the period, *The Coterie* and *New Coterie* were desperately short of funds.[19] But the journal was not frivolously undertaken. Despite its unfortunately arch title, it was serious, *avant-garde,* and internationalist. Among its contributors were Nancy Cunard, Liam O'Flaherty, H.D., Eliot, Aldous Huxley, Karel Kapek, Richard Aldington, Zadkine, André Derain, and Jean de Bosschére.[20] Osbert Sitwell and Herbert Read's *Art and Letters* also began life in 1919 and lasted even less time than *The Coterie*, whose editorial policy it broadly shared. Between them these magazines reveal an immediate post-war determination to undo the jingoistic fervour of the preceding years and to insist that culture, which knows no national boundaries, has to be safeguarded from the wreckage of war. Culture opposes the world of the waste land.

Above all, *The Coterie* and *Art and Letters* were opposed to the truly frightening postures adopted by Arther Quiller-Couch, Professor of English at Cambridge, and Walter Raleigh, who spoke for English studies at Oxford. During the war "Q" had given a series of lectures on "Patriotism in English Literature," in which he proved to his own satisfaction that German scholarship was "unfit to approach the beauties of English Literature." Raleigh meanwhile told his students that the "German University culture is mere evil," and that the deaths "of 100 Boche professors ... would be a benefit to the human race." In *The Social Mission of English Criticism* Chris Baldick, from whom I take these remarks, suggests that the cumulative effect of Quiller-Couch and Raleigh's attacks was to safeguard the English language as the world language. The appeal to English studies was to "national pride in the language as well as the literature." And this, Baldick argues, was the theme of a campaign which led to the famous Newbolt Report of 1921 on *The Teaching of English in England*. Baldick notes that "a poet who had so effectively popularised the identity of the national and school spirits was a likely candidate to oversee the kind of educational renovation which Lloyd George had in mind." Also in Newbolt's favour was his being president of the English Association, "which had been founded in 1906 'to promote the due recognition of English as an essential element in the national education.'" Newbolt's committee of 14 included no fewer than 9 members of the English association.[21]

In view of the committee's make-up and given its brief we could be excused for thinking that the nature of its report would be a foregone conclusion. Yet at least one member steered away from the deepest gulfs of xenophobia when, in his own polemic, *English for the English*, also published in 1921, he argued that "For school purposes, English literature means anything good to read extant in English. Whether it was originally written in Chinese, Hebrew, Greek, Latin, Italian, Spanish, French, German, Irish or Welsh, in the fifth century before Christ or the twentieth after, makes no difference." As Patrick Parrinder has commented, this is a good deal more enlightened than the pronouncements of more recent committees on the vexed question of English in schools.[22]

But the Newbolt Committee was less exercised by definitions of "English" literature than by the consideration that English studies could be used as a glue to stick the classes together. Behind its deliberations can be felt a very real anxiety, an uneasy sense that English society is breaking apart. In the previous chapter I argued that people living through the immediate post-war years had good reason to fear or of course welcome what seemed to be unmistakable signs of social upheaval. The long safe centuries had come to an end, the rough beast had roused itself, and, according to the Committee, the younger members of the working class regard education "mainly as something to equip them to fight their capitalist enemies." English studies must therefore look to recover ground lost since great literature and "common life" began to split asunder, a process which began in the middle ages and accelerated at the time of the industrial revolution.[23]

At this point the committee discovers a hope for the future: "since the time cannot be far distant when the poet, who 'follows wheresoever he can find an atmosphere of sensation in which to move his wings,' will invade this vast new territory, and so once more bring sanctification and joy into the sphere of common life."[24] Shelley's words are used to suggest that such a poet will come not *from* but *to* working-class life. The poet will invade *this* territory. The military metaphor inevitably implies a strategy for subduing the restless natives. And we should note that, as Baldick says, Sampson's *English for the English* has as part motive the need "to construct a world of Culture in which upheavals and disturbances can be dissolved."[25] From what has already emerged in this book, we can understand that such a need was bound to seem most urgent in 1921. It was even more of an urgent need in industrial Scotland, although as far as I know there is no Scottish equivalent to Sampson's treatise. Nor of course could there be. Scottish for the Scottish has a very different, subversive meaning, as does Welsh for the Welsh. "English for the English" on the other hand, can combine an ideal of national unity with a xenophobic dislike of foreign culture and a determination to celebrate what is supposed to be unique about Englishness. In other words, a deeply conservative political strategy is discoverable within and indeed prompts the committee's work and it is one which is bound to be opposed to and by the equally determined internationalism of those who founded and wrote for the little magazines and who typically saw the concern with Englishness as a discredited attempt to (re) impose a cultural political tradition which the war had both exposed as dangerous and broken up.

Yet we cannot dismiss all that Sampson and even the Newbolt committee's recommendations offer. There is, for example, a strong, Tawney-like conviction behind Sampson's assertion that "attempts to banish humanising elements from schools for the working class are vitally evil" and this is also implicit in the Committee's assertion that "literature is not just a temple for academic study, but one of the chief temples of the human spirit, in which all should worship." The very fervour of those words is reminiscent of the tone of Tawney's great essay of 1913, "An experiment in Democratic Education", with its scorn for a tradition "by which wealth protects learning and learning in turn admits wealth to its placid groves, [enabling] the upper classes to meet their inferiors! 'You see my good friends .... We govern you because we are wiser, because we have more knowledge, because we are *better educated* than you are.'"[26]

Out of the generous anger which prompted Tawney's words came the W.E.A. Out of Newbolt and Sampson came among other things a new passion to save the working-class from itself. Those enlisted or volunteering to invade the vast new territory sighted by the Newbolt Committee were armoured with distrust of working-class culture or anything that smacked of the "popular": the shudder of recoil regularly went with any mention of "jazz", for example. But in the 1920s those guardians were far more exercised by the degrading effect of cinema on working-class life. After Marie Lloyd's death in 1922, Eliot wrote an essay about her which mourns not merely her passing but the passing of a whole way of life. Her popularity, he says, represented something more than success: it was evidence "of the extent to which she represented and expressed that part of the English nation which has perhaps the greatest vitality and interest." She had a capacity "for expressing the soul of the people." In this, she was unique as her class was unique. "There is no such expressive figure for any other class. The middle classes have no such idol: the middle classes are morally corrupt." Unfortunately, a similar corruption now awaits the people.

> The working man who went to the music-hall and saw Marie
> Lloyd and joined in the chorus was himself performing part of

the act; he was engaged in that collaboration of the audience which is necessary in all art and most obviously in dramatic art. He will now go to the cinema, where his mind is lulled by continuous senseless music and continous action too rapid for the brain to act upon, and will receive, without giving, in that same listless apathy with which the middle and upper classes regard any entertainment of the nature of art. He will also have lost some interest in life.[27]

Five years later, in a preface to a new edition of *The Principles of Literary Criticism,* a book which had originally appeared in 1924, I. A. Richards argued it was now far too late to help the masses. Their cultural debasement had to be accepted. Mass civilisation was threatening to overwhelm minority culture. "It is perhaps premature to envisage a collapse of values, a transvaluation by which popular taste replaces trained discrimination. Yet commercialism has done strange things: we have not yet fathomed the more sinister potentialities of the cinema and the loudspeaker."[28] In both this work and *Practical Criticism*, which followed in 1929, Richards hopes to train his Cambridge undergraduates in habits of discriminative reading so that they can arrive at sure and certain judgements about the relative worth of whatever is put in front of them. They will then be able to resist the false allure of mass culture: of cinema, the newspapers, advertisements.

It is not necessary here to detail the ways in which Richards' confidence in his standards and values is based on assumptions that go uninspected; nor to spell out the political and social conservatism implicit in his belief that mass society – that convenient abstraction – is the helpless victim of mass media.[29] But Richards' enterprise has to be seen as belonging within a nexus of intellectual energy that is a distinguishing feature of the cultural life of the post-war years and in which the question of excellence is of prime concern. How is excellence to be known, how sustained, how encouraged? In a word, how is civilisation to be saved? These questions engaged writers whether they were within or, more usually, outside the academy; the split between "high standards" and the "metropolitan literary world" against which F.R. Leavis and his followers would later fulminate can hardly be said to exist in these years. By and large, young academics took their bearings from those living and working as free-lancers: from T.S. Eliot perhaps supremely, but also from others.

Among these, none was more important than Edgell Rickword. Rickword, who had been born in 1899, fought and was badly injured in the war. In 1919 he entered Oxford to read French, but after a year abandoned his studies for a life of literary journalism in London. This was a common enough practice at the time. Literary journalism was not difficult to come by, and although it didn't pay particularly well, living was cheap, accommodation usually available; and, as we have seen, post-war London held the promise of entertainment: of night clubs, dance-halls, and much else besides. But Rickword was also a poet. In 1921 his first collection appeared. *Behind The Eyes* includes a most beautiful love poem, "Intimacy," as well as four war poems and a witty fable of farewell to Oxford, "Complaint of a Tadpole Confined in a Jam-Jar."

> What reveries of far-off days
> these withered plaques of duck-weed raise!
>
> The creeping wretches, the crowded Pond,
> a Death-in-Life, no Culture, no Beyond;
>
> Light and No-Light in dull routine;
> Thought and No-thought two shades of green;
>
> the fair ideals all creatures need
> smothered beneath th'inferior weed,
>
> since highest Aspirations stop,
> for tadpoles, at the water-top!....
>
> Yet curious sensations range
> about the tail, and hint at change ...
>
> whilst in the valleys pipers play
> Over the hills and far away.

This poem has already developed a note that is uniquely Rickword's, a blend of lyric suavity and sardonic edginess. It neatly pins down those who live within Oxford's confines and for whom the outer world of "the crowded pond" means the mass civilisation of "no Culture". War had perhaps begun to radicalise Rickword. Oxford furthered the process. His biographer, Charles Hobday, notes that during his time there, brief though it was, Rickword "was brought into direct contact with the class struggle." He was among those who protested at the poor pay of striking Oxford busmen and he took part in an attempt to free a Ruskin student who had been arrested for trying to pull a blackleg driver from his bus. [30] It is important to note this, both because it knocks on the head the silly view, advanced by Clive James and others, that politics (by which they mean radical politics and which according to them Rickword came upon only in the early 30s when he joined the CPGB) ruined him for poetry, and also because his journal, *The Calendar of Modern Letters*, is not to be aligned with those, especially Leavis, who took much from it – including the title of his own *Scrutiny* – but whose politics became increasingly reactionary.[31]

With Douglas Garman, who had some money, Rickword set up *The Calendar of Modern Letters* in 1925. It led a hand-to-mouth existence and died two years later. Yet its influence was immense. Like the journals earlier mentioned which began life in 1919, *The Calendar* was avowedly internationalist. As well as including in its pages a number of important English writers, pre-eminently Lawrence, it published work by Pirandello, Liam O'Flaherty, Isaac Babel, Alexi Remizov, Hart Crane, John Crowe Ransom and Allen Tate. Just as important, its reviews and "scrutinies" were remarkable for their disciplined savaging of bad work. Besides, the *Calendar's* contributors were, in the words of Arnold Rattenbury, aware that what they attacked was "a largely moribund literature, and increasingly the issue was posed as to whether this was not because the whole of society producing it was moribund. The final number of the *Calendar* came to the conclusion that this was in fact the case, and the proper preoccupation of writers must now be social change. The questions had been literary, the answers political."[32] This may seem to make Rickword an upholder of minority culture. Unlike Pound, Eliot and Richards, however, Rickword's radicalism was of the left. When he next became an editor it would be of *Left Review*.

By the time the first issue of that journal appeared, in October 1934, Rickword's career as poet was as good as over. A second volume, *Invocations to Angels*, had been published in 1928, and there would be further work, including the celebrated "To The Wife of a Non-Interventionist Statesman"; but Rickword's poetic achievement belongs largely to the 1920s.[33] The poems that make up *Behind the Eyes* are usually well written, but with the exceptions of those mentioned above they are conditioned by a mannered world-weariness or of sensual lassitude in both rhythm and diction that may owe something to the French poets Rickword so admired, especially Baudelaire and Rimbaud, but which overall gives the work an enervate feeling. There are too many adjective-noun constructions, too many "limbs", "tresses," "bosoms", "maidens", too much reliance on "pale", "soft", and double-epithets such as "moon-cold" and "star-faint". There is altogether too much poetry. Where this is effectively deployed, as in "Regret for the Passing of the Entire Scheme of Things," the result is a kind of fastidious melancholy:

> Whilst now in dusky corners lovers kiss
> and goodmen smoke their pipes by tiny gates –
> these oldest griefs of summer seem less sad
>
> than drone of mowers on suburban lawns
> and girls' thin laughter, to the ears that hear
> the soft rain falling of the failing stars.

The exquisite note of this ennui is however ultimately debilitating.

The note recurs in *Invocations To Angels* as do other characteristic elements of Rickword's verse to which I have drawn attention; but the later volume has very considerable new strengths. There is for example, "Luxury," which has been discussed earlier. There is also a most powerful element of social satire. That this owes something to Eliot's 1920 poems is obvious – nowhere more so than in "Sir Orang Haut-Ton at Vespers," which even uses the octosyllabic quatrain Eliot had appropriated for his "Sweeney" poems. But the object of Rickword's satire is different. It is neither anti-Jewish, as in the hateful "Burbank with a Baedeker: Bleistein with a Cigar," nor anti-working-class, as in "Sweeney Among the Nightingales." The tone is rather one of bemusement at a world from which purpose seems to have leached away, leaving only the detritus of daily living: "as tram-lines on Bank Holidays/lure to that worn familiar sod/where the Ancestral Tripper plays/ in pungent groves the pagan god." Hobday notes that in an essay published in the *Calendar* in January 1926, Edwin Muir suggests that English poetry has for the first time become a poetry of town rather than of country and that such poetry testifies to "the peculiar set of impersonal feelings which all town bred people carry about with them, without guessing it, from their birth, the feelings which seem to make them part of the crowd and yet keep them outside it."[34] These feelings had been explored or at any rate attributed to French poets with whose work Rickword was familiar, above all Baudelaire, whose *Journeaux Intimes* he translated. The poet as *flâneur*, wanderer of the city streets, becomes a familiar type for 19th century French writers, and although it can be found in some minor poets of the 1890s, first importantly enters English poetry through the medium of Eliot's early poems, which also absorb and refine a tone Muir tries to pin down in the phrase "impersonal feelings," although it is in truth almost impossibly difficult adequately to define Eliot's subtle mixture of ironic detachment and the prurience which hints at involvement or at least fascination with what is offered for rejection.

I don't suggest that *Invocations to Angels* is dominated by this pose, these feelings; but something of what Rickword may be after can be gauged from the concluding stanza of "Race Day."

> Now man's great day is almost done,
> the colonels and the touts depart;
> still lingers, tiny on the Down,
> a huckster by his rifled cart.
> The crammed last bus, last Hope, is gone,
> and we, benighted, squeamish girls,
> coldly regard how, darkly blown,
> the crowd's foul pleasure-litter whirls.

The ironic echo of Kipling, the contraction of empire to the detritus of a race day's meeting, together with lower-case opening to lines (Rickword seems to have been the first to have made regular use of this device), combine to suggest utterance poised with knowing uncertainty between camp gesture and a more genuine inflection of distaste. And this tone, or something very like it, can also be found in a handful of remarkable poems which are not so much love poems as about lovelessness, given that they all turn on cynically self-regarding or self-aware sexual encounters. The best of these are probably "The Cascade", "Dream and Poetry", "Chronique Scandaleuse", and the title poem. Such poems may come from personal circumstance but they nevertheless subtly define a condition that belongs to the immediate post-war years.

In *A Survey of Modernist Poetry* Laura Riding and Robert Graves claim to identify this condition when they invoke Gertrude Stein's phrase "the lost generation" in order to say of it that "The present lost generation does not feel its lack of ideals as sinfulness, but rather as sophistication. It does not love itself, but it does not hate itself. It does not think much of life, but neither does it think much of death. It is a cynically common-sense generation ...." They impute this cynicism to the fact that "The disillusion of the War has been completed by the Peace, by the continuation of the old regime patched up with political Fascism, by the same atmosphere of suspense that prevailed from 1911 to the outbreak of war and [is] now again gathering round further nationalistic and civil wars."[35] A note of disillusion is certainly present in *Invocations to Angels*. It can be heard in the phrase "the jazz of death," from "The Epitaph" of the poem, "Poet to Punk"; and also sounds through "Strange Party," which uses the standard twenties trope of a dance – any dance – as a dance of death. The poem in its entirety runs:

> On that lawn's most secret shade
> joy-masked, your thoughts droop in their dance,
> as though your spirit, overweighed,
> tired of the saxophone's pert nonchalance;
>
> their arms gay gestures still intend,
> gently their voices lapse, and cold
> the cascades of the moon descend
> on shadowy dancers with false cheeks of gold.
>
> Discreetly mocking in the gloom
> these masqueraders bow and twirl,
> feigning to exorcise the doom
> that seals the fountains of your heart, queer girl.

The poem takes as epigraph a line of Verlaine's: *"votre âme est un paysage choisi."* Here, the chosen country combines echoes of a Watteau-like bal-masque with elements that belong to the twenties (and for that matter the thirties: Auden will use Rickword's *mise-en-scène* in his "Here on the Cropped Grass", where the poet hears "arising/From lanterned gardens sloping to the river/... saxophones".)

"Strange Party", as with a number of other poems in Rickword's second volume, can therefore be said to fall within the terms Riding and Graves provide as distinguishing the modernist poet, of "not commit[ting] himself whole-heartedly to any obvious conviction." Such poems feel to be waiting for the end, their langorousness indicative of spent emotion, drained energy. And this sense of impending doom is, as I have earlier suggested, most eloquently caught in "Luxury". An essential part of that poem's power is the power of disgust. But the disgust, while entirely proper, need not be merely negative. *Invocations To Angels* is not defined by sophisticated exhaustion and sardonic disenchantment. The volume's most ambitious poem, "The Happy New Year", inhabits markedly different territory. In what follows I can offer only a skeleton account of its achievement, but it is undoubtedly a very impressive work and one which deserves consideration in any discussion of the writing of the period.

That Rickword himself thought the masque of more than usual significance is to be inferred from the original title for the 1928 volume, which was *Invocations To Angels and The Happy New Year*. He worked on the masque between the spring and autumn of 1926. In other words, its composition spans the period of the General Strike. This is crucially important. So is the quotation from Jasper Heywood's version of Seneca's *Thyestes* with which "The Happy New Year" begins. *Thyestes* takes as subject the murder by an uncle of three young nephews and his serving them to the boys' father. This horrifying tale provides an apt allegory of the sacrifice of a generation in the Great War. And yet though there are moments in the masque which recall the war, I do not think these are integrated into the text as a whole. Lines such as the following, therefore, lend themselves to the overall atmosphere in which the action takes place, in a city much like London: "A fog-like poison drifts and whirls/such dreadful faces as the sun shone on/lying in fields, propped against walls, on beds/mottled with leaf-lights". It may well be that when Rickword began work on the masque he intended it to deal centrally with the effects of war on his generation. If so, it seems apparent that during the course of the writing something happened to make him change his mind or at all events re-direct his ideas and the meaning of "The Happy New Year."

To say this brings me to the most obvious influence of all on "The Happy New Year". Hobday quotes what he calls "a very curious paragraph" in the issue of *The Calendar of Modern Letters* for April, 1926, in which the writer, presumably Rickword, speaks of a poem which the editors have procured, and in which "the crops rot, the land becomes water-logged, and complete sterility ensues. This the author considers an adequate symbol of the contemporary consciousness .... literary references are intended to enrich the texture of the verse with imagery, for invention risks being vulgar, and, besides, the success of several very cultured poems has recently approved the innovation."[36] It may be, as Hobday suggests, that Rickword initially intended "The Happy New Year" to be a burlesque on *The Waste Land*. The masque has a city setting and a mythological sub-structure. In a prefatory note Rickword explains the action as spanning the course of a solar year, from the moment when the sun "falls through the celestial map (of the Ptolomaic system) from the zenith through the astronomical signs, Houses, to the no-where below the Arctic horizon." The sun then "retraces his steps and sequentially injects his vigour into the earthlings dwindling from his absence. The perigrination is observed with detachment expressed in an ironic commentary by the Sinisters who finally dissociate themselves."

The tone of this suggests that Rickword stands at some ironic distance from his own scheme. It may even suggest that he is not sure how seriously he wants his masque to be taken. If so, that can only be because he is distrustful of poetry's use of myth, regarding such use as a way foreclosing on the complexities of history – including the history of the present. In his opening speech, the Presenter provides a *mélange* of faded poetic styles or mannerisms, ways of speaking about the falling/failing sun:

> Rosy-slippered dawn
> goes tripping down the spangled lawns
> but drab reminders dun insolvent streets ... .
> where moribund the later sons of earth
> bask and chew up remainders of their days,
> contemning Sol's archaic ways
> whose heaped bonfire in the romantic style
> nurtures their candle-end of wit and wisdom.

Whether the sun is that of empire, of western civilisation, or of hope briefly aflare after the armistice is not to be known. Most likely it suggests all these things. But now in "the wall-eyed city" the Presenter announces that "Sol falls weakly through his ruined house,/a dead coal in a rusty grate".

Rickword was a member of the Labour Party. It doesn't follow that Sol's weak fall can be read as allegoric statement of MacDonald's first brief administration; but in "The Happy New Year" the Presenter speaks of those many whose hopes have foundered because "of vows rescinded, broken contracts," and of hordes who "renounce complaint in wan waters" or who "fall on pity's sword." The choice is between suicide or the death of self-regard. At which point, with wonderful inappropriateness, the Chorus intones "London has many merciful instruments." The Presenter then speaks of these "withered souls.../with bands of music wailing through the streets." And this is followed by the

195

direction *(Here the SINISTERS come on.).* Hunger marches, marches of the unemployed, of strikers: these are all implied in the "bands of music", as are street bands of former soldiers. This is London, 1926. The crowd that flowed over London Bridge in *The Waste Land* may well be recalled here, but with this difference: that whereas the dead souls of Eliot's poem belong to a desacralised city, Rickword's are the victims of social, political injustice. And as "Sinisters" they may be, or become, the emergent left's threat to those who see nothing to be done or needing to be done.

For in this London, "The sunny side of the road/crawls with the aged like a lousy seam." As a soldier himself, Rickword knew all about lice. Here, they are those relics of a discredited generation who, in a newly-risen sun (the defeat of the strike?) continue to bask in wealthy comfort. Their numbers include those literary coteries unwilling to confront the political-social issues of the present. So at least I read the Presenter's next lines, indicting "An embryo with dim reptilian brain/womb-bound in Wandsworth, and the female flocks/from dullest Kensington, and City ants,/and owl-wise Blooomsbury, [who] all send up a shout." They are joined by the "Dexters" who must surely be the Bright Young Things? For in their chorus they sing

> We do not crave eternity,
> love's bowl of quintessential pearl,
> since half an hour's propinquity
> exhausts the meaning of a curl,
> but hail one blessed Trinity,
> The Time, the Place and a Girl.

The Sinisters, however, although they briefly assent to the triumph of the sun newly re-risen, do so on different terms. "New blood begets new forms/for comedies or tragic shows,/new vigour to confront old storms." Rickword's use of masque should be seen in the light of his review in the *Calendar* of Enid Welsford's *The Court Masque* where, as Hobday points out, he speaks of the form as developing from "a rough, licentious ritual," and as having as its primary impulse the celebration, or inducement, of "fertility and felicity."[37] In "The Happy New Year," the Chorus's last lines are: "Like begets like, immortal in each kind;/through perishing units' union, death's defeat." Units may die, but in union lies ultimate victory. The failure of the strike was due to the collapse of the alliance of the unions and, as the strikers saw it, the caving-in of the union bosses to Baldwin's ambiguous promises. The choice of the masque form for "The Happy New Year" makes evident Rickword's radical intent to connect emergent and political social energies to new or at least revived cultural expressions.

Not that the masque ends on a note of triumph. After the Chorus's promise of death's ultimate defeat the Presenter makes a sombre concluding speech:

> I see others who walk the earth tonight, homeless
> throughout the city, pacing the void suburbs
> by unmade roads, raw gardens, blank-eyed lamps,
> cinders and tin-cans and blown evening papers,
> among refuse-pits and sewer-mouths,
> wandering fires and voices of the swamp;
> passing deliberately into the night
> through the infinite extension of this landscape.

This powerfully blends images of contentemporary London with an infernal Dantean landscape, where the poor who pass "deliberately into the night" may be seen as offering a future threat to those on the sunny side of the road. Hobday quotes from a review of Trotsky's pamphlet, *Where is Britain Going?* which appeared in the *Calendar* in July, 1926, in which the reviewer, whom Hobday thinks was probably Garman, poses the question as to whether "there exists a proletarian party to take advantage of the position" of contemporary social malaise. "The answer to it will decide whether England ... is to stay on the road of continually degenerating values, or to create a revolution as vital, potentially, as the inception of Christianity."[38] For Rickword "The Happy New Year" lies in the future and his masque offers an at once sardonic and deeply unsettling vision of contemporary society. The poor, the SINISTERS, are on the left, just as the DEXTERS, The Bright Young Things, are on the right (some of them were already praising Mussolini as the ideal leader); and the political implications of this opposition include the possibility of reclaiming London – the earthly city – for the masses. Threat is also promise. Eliot's mythic structure, and his use of the Upinishads to suggest redemptive powers, is exchanged for human empowerment. That such empowerment failed with the failure of the general strike does not mean it will not succeed at some time in the future. The SINISTERS, "passing deliberately into the night" are presumably going to plan for their return.

## V

Rickword's progressive movement to the political left happened over more than a decade. He did not join the CPGB until 1934. Ivor Gurney seems to have discovered his political radicalism in the army. I suggested in an earlier chapter that the collective experience of soldiers brought together in a war most of them came to hate as "the bosses' war" was almost certain to politicise them. Gurney's "To The Prussians of England" is unequivocal in its hatred of those in power and its speaking out for a democratic nation:

> Our silly dreams of peace you put aside
> And brotherhood of man, for you will see
> An armed mistress, braggart of the tide,
> Her children slaves, under your mastery.
> We'll have a word there too, and forge a knife,
> Will cut the cancer threatens England's life.[39]

Gurney's desire for a true internationalism – the "brotherhood of man" – is as intense as his detestation of braggart Britannia and of those who speak for her. In a letter to Marion Scott, dated 27 July 1917, he tells her that does not expect his volume of poems, *Severn and Somme*, will be especially well received:

> Where it will fail to attract is that there is none, or hardly any of the devotion of self-sacrifice, the splendid readiness for death that one finds in Grenfell, Brooke, Nichols, etc. That is partly because I am still sick of mind and body; partly for physical, partly for mental reasons. Also because, though I am ready if necessary to die for England, I do not see the necessity; it being only a hard and fast system which has sent so many of the flower of England's artists to risk of death, and a wrong materialistic system...."[40]

We may baulk at Gurney's conviction that as an artist he should have been spared the front line, but we need to recognise that he really was, as he knew himself to be, outstandingly talented; and that his protest against the "wrong materialistic system" – presumably he has in mind arms manufacturers and other profiteers – was made on behalf of those ordinary line soldiers with whom he shared the privations, misery and squalor of trench warfare. And we should further note that no other poet has written as well as Gurney about the daily drudgery of such warfare, or what he calls "the mechanic day-lore of modern war-making". (In the second of two poems which bear the title "First Time In.") Other important poems in this mode include "Laventie" and "Half Dead."

The experience of war, and especially his contact with other reluctant heroes, confirmed in Gurney a delight in idiom and dialect which inevitably had political implications because it equally confirmed in him a contempt for the class system which "took as naught" the value of the men alongside whom he fought. His relishing of the soldiers' talk goes with and occasions an intensely democratic regard for their "infinite lovely chatter."

In the 1880s, John Davidson had written a number of ballads about London street life, and Masefield had incorporated slang, including swear words, into his *Salt-Water Ballads* (1902-3). I suggested in Chapter 3 that Charlotte Mew may owe a debt to Masefield and the Dymock poets, who had made a habit of introducing demotic speech into some of their poems. Wilfred Gibson in particular took scenes from working life as subject for poetry, as in his volume of 1910, *Daily Bread*. Gibson even has a poem called "Red Fox" – it appeared in his 1912 volume, *Fires* – in which the male speaker uncovers his sexual jealousy of a rival who is, so he says, "A slinking dog-fox" and whom he plans to shoot, though in the end he acknowledges the other man's superiority. Gurney admired Gibson, even going to the extent of judging Gibson's *Friends* (1916), the work of a master.

But Gibson's handling of ordinary speech, frequently though it occurs in his work, is programmatic and stiff. Gurney by comparison doesn't always provide instances of the "chatter" he clearly relished, so that, for example, in the first of two poems which are called "First Time In" he contents himself with mentioning "roguish words by Welsh pit boys/... sung", but leaves us to guess what the words might have been. Nevertheless, the poems regularly praise the use of such words, such chatter. The result is that even where there is an awkwardness in the handling of speech, some moment of cherished "divine unliterate clearness" survives. (The context of that phrase will be explained a little later.) And so, listening to his Glosters, Gurney reports in "Billet" how

> one private took on himself a Company's heart to speak,
> 'I wish to bloody hell I was just going to Brewery – surely
> To work all day (in Stroud) and be free at tea-time allowed
> Resting when one wanted, a joke in season,

> To change clothes and take a girl to Horspool's turning
> Or drink at "Traveller's Rest" and find no cloud.'

"He spoke the heart of all of us," Gurney says.[41] This identification with ordinary soldiers, labourers, working men, is in no sense condescending or sentimental. That is why, after the war, when Gurney emerges as an indubitably great poet, he so often and so passionately speaks for those who, in the second "First Time In," he knows "were in after-war so surely hurt," those "disappointed men/Who looked for the golden Age to come friendly again." These are the men who returned home having seen

>                   ...a terror
> Of waste, endured horror, and were not fearer
> Before the barrages like Heaven's anger wanton known –
> Feared not and saw great earth spouts in terror thrown,
> But could not guess, but could not guess, alas!
> How England should take as common their vast endurance
> And let them be but boys having served time overseas."
> *(Mist on Meadows.)*

The tone of voice, that vibrant mingling of anger and sadness, nearly succeeds in disguising the clumsiness of the writing, or perhaps in persuading us that there are hardly words available to make manifest so much suffering, such ingratitude. But as is apparent from that poem, quoted elsewhere, Gurney could master this material.

"The heart burns – but has to keep out of face how heart burns," he says at the end of that poem. Why? Because he is forced into deferential role-playing, or because he sees himself as some one guarding in secret his detestation of an England which chooses to turn its back on the returned soldiers and on their dream of a golden age. He gave the title "The Golden Age" to a sonnet I assume he wrote shortly after his terrible breakdown in the autumn of 1922. This is the sestet:

> O for some force to swing us back there to some
> Natural moving towards life's love, or that glow
> In the word to be glow in the State, that golden age come
> Again, men working freely as nature might show,
> And a people honouring stage-scenes lit with fine sound
> On a free soil, England happy, honoured and joy-crowned.

The penultimate line comes out of Gurney's impassioned love for Shakespeare, Jonson and other Jacobean dramatists, and his belief, as it seems, that England then enjoyed a golden age because art was honoured by all and was for all. Art and politics go together: a healthy state produces great art. Gurney's trust in the polity of the late 16th and early 17th century may be misplaced piety; but his conviction that the finest art comes from, celebrates and is celebrated by, the people is deep indeed.[41a] Hence, his adaptations of song from that period, and the use he makes of flexible five-stress line which is as far from the tame iambics of Georgian poetry as his characteristic use of couplet rhymes to direct and contain the torrent of his rhetoric. The sonnet must have been written very soon after "Sonnet – September 1922". It expresses a similar yearning for a turn-around in the social and political life of the nation.

Such yearning also finds expression in the earlier, "North Woolwich", presumably written soon after his return to England. The poem begins with a starkly ironic contrast: Homer's Aegean versus the Thames:

> Hellene memories taunting of the bright
> Morning of new Time amongst tall derricks
> And floating chimney pots with empty tackle
>
> Drawn by fierce asp-like things slowly out sight.

The analogy of asps with tugs in unnecessarily strained; but the contrast of "new Time" and now is far from facile. The poem turns to consider the poverty-pinched lives of ordinary Londoners. They have no chance to live heroically or well:

> Gaol waits for them would face without a stitch
> Heaven's nakedness, those feet are black as pitch
> Should gleam on gold sands white or in stadium lines.
> Can Aphrodite bless so evil dwelling
> Or Mercury have heed to Canning Town?
> Nay, rather, for that ugly, that evil smelling
> Township, a Christ from Heaven must come down,
> Pitiful and comradely, with tender signs,
> And warm the tea, and shield a chap from fines,
> A foreman carpenter, not yet full-grown.

Gurney's love of tea is repeatedly testified to, in letters and poems alike. "The joyful thought of tea", he remarked in a letter from France, alone disturbed the tranquillity of his mind after listening to some Bach.[42] That it had an almost sacramental meaning for him is clear from the manner in which it is invoked at the end of "Felling a Tree", where he considers that the tree will tomorrow be "fuel for the bright kitchen – for brown tea, against cold night." It is the grace conferred on domestic circumstances by useful toil – the toil of carpenter, of craftsmen, of those whom Gurney met in the trenches and of whom he remarked in a letter of August 1916 that they "are to do the work and to shape England anew."[43] Christ, the foreman carpenter, will warm the tea for such men. This is a political radicalism dressed in the language of Christian socialism we have previously met in Goldring's *The Black Curtain*, and which I assume Gurney came across during student days, when he would have found it focused on missions among London's poor, those whose "feet are black as pitch". Gurney, the soldier-poet, is writing for *them*.

Gurney eagerly desired a radically changed England, a nation which honoured "the dearness of common things", as he called one poem. His vision is, to repeat, intensely democratic, against the exclusivity of the uncommon. No wonder that in the wake of the Kerensky revolution in the spring of 1917 he should tell Marion Scott that "it is the bloomingest nuisance that a thing so well intentioned as the Russian Revolution can so upset things."[44] No wonder that soon afterwards he is complaining about England's "wrong materialistic system," nor that soon after *that* he should be insisting on the need for the Duke of Bilgewater to sympathise with Bill Jones. And no wonder he was suspicious of officers, as "The Silent One" reveals. For there "the politest voice – a finicking accent said:/ 'Do you think you might crawl through there: there's a hole.'" That voice, in its politeness, conceals an order as a question. The line soldier takes full advantage: "I smiled, as politely replied/ 'I'm afraid not, Sir.'" It's a sobering thought that the politest voice might have belonged to Owen or Graves or Sassoon. Class awareness, including an awareness of how "common things" and "lovely chatter" were likely to meet with the derision of those who felt themselves elected to speak for England – this was a potent element in Gurney's political and social make-up. It is why his discovery of Edward Thomas's poems is so crucial to his development.

At first, he is not sure of them. He tells Marion Scott in a letter of November 1917 that "Very curious they are, very interesting; nebulously intangibly beautiful. But he had the same sickness of mind I have – the impossibility of serenity for any but the shortest space. Such a mind produces little."[45] Less than a month later, however, he tells J. W. Haines that "if you think I do not like Thomas's

202

poems you are mistaken." He then writes out a list of the poems he most admires, says that if he had the time "I should study E.T. hard and long," and concludes by remarking that he wishes Thomas would "break out into divine unliterate clearness more often."[46] He wants more by way of common speech. But the qualifications soon go. By February 1918 he has decided that Thomas is a genius. And then in March he tells Marion Scott that his own future writing is likely to be "influenced by E.T. chiefly."[47]

But Gurney doesn't imitate Thomas. Although he perhaps learned something of how to handle run-on lines from Thomas's example, his own use of enjambment tends to be employed less for the carefully weighed qualification of utterance – the brooding hesitancies that are unique to Thomas's mode of spoken verse – than as a way of momentarily halting the onward rush of speech that regularly and impatiently disregards line-endings. Gurney's syntactic elisions seem to be a natural part of his urgency – impatience, even – to get things said, whereas Thomas's syntax feels its way with altogether more care.[48] Moreover, we should note that before he came across Thomas's poems Gurney had already written a number of exquisite lyrics which show how delicate was his ear for rhythm and song-like rhyme. Everybody knows "The Wanderer", fewer perhaps are aware of "Equal Mistress", whose final stanza runs:

> Violets, stars, birds
> Wait on her smile; all
> Too soon must autumn come,
> Sheaves, fruit be carried home,
> And the leaves fall.

The delicate movement along and across the lines, as well as the firm stresses on the stanza's last two words, keep whimsy well at bay. "Equal mistress" belongs to the tradition of English song which Gurney loved, which he traced back to Campion, Shakespeare, and the madrigalists; and which with his friend and mentor Herbert Howells he did much to revitalise.[49]

Thomas influenced Gurney, I am certain, because his example encouraged Gurney in the way he wanted to go. I have earlier alluded to Thomas's indebtedness to William Morris, in particular to his utopian socialism. There is a similarly strong utopian element in Gurney's work, as "North Woolwich" makes clear, and it is further elaborated in "The Golden Age", and "A Wish", a poem which must belong to the same moment of distress, and in which Gurney hopes "for the children of West Ham/Wooden-frame houses square, with some-sort stuff/crammed in to keep the wind away..." These houses, he says, should be

> Not crowded together, but with a plot of land,
> Where one might play and dig, and use spade or the hand
> In managing or shaping earth in such forms
> As please the sunny mind or keep out of harms
> The mind that's always good when let go its way
> (I think) so that there's work enough in a happy day.

The qualification at the beginning of the last line is especially poignant because it signals the repeated efforts Gurney had made during that summer of 1922 to find work. But the Tolstoyan/Morrisian belief in the value of "work enough in a happy day" comes into his poetry earlier, probably from the moment he read "Swedes", "Sowing", and "Digging", three poems of Thomas which he singles out for especial mention. Hence, his own "The Hoe Scrapes Earth":

> The hoe scrapes earth as fine in grain as sand,
> I like the swirl of it and the swing in the hand
> Of the lithe hoe so clever at craft and grace,
> And the friendliness, the clear freedom of the place.
>
> And the green hairs of the wheat on sandy brown.
> The draw of eyes toward the coloured town,
> The lark ascending slow to a roof of cloud
> That cries for the voice of poetry to cry aloud.

The echoes of Thomas ("This corner of the farmyard I like well") and Housman's coloured counties do not detract from this beautifully judged little poem, with its sense of perfect harmony that momentarily exists in a world redeemed by labour, and its instinctive appeal to Vaughan Williams' "lark ascending." (Gurney esteemed Vaughan Williams above all other living composers.)

Like Thomas, perhaps because of Thomas, Gurney evokes a "merry England" which is specifically the England of a field full of folk imaged by Morris in *A Dream of John Ball* ("when Adam delved and Eve span/Who was then the gentleman?"), and which Robert Blatchford had written about in his socialist newspaper, *The Clarion*. The articles, which had been gathered together as *Merrie*

*England* by "Nunquam", and first published in book form in 1893, hard on the heels of the founding of the ILP, were as popular as they were influential in shaping a generation of socialist thought. As A.M. Thompson wrote in his Preface to Blatchford's *Autobiography,* "for every convert made by *Das Kapital*, there were a hundred made by *Merrie England*." One of the key arguments in Blatchford's book is the distinction he insists on making between "work" and "toil". Work implies choice, toil is imposed. Work implies craft and the willing expenditure of labour, toil is dull, repetitious, soul destroying. In "The hoe scrapes earth" Gurney celebrates work, of men "working freely as nature might show," which he had imagined in the "England of the Golden Age". Nature presumably "shows" – bears witness to – free labour in that there is a congruence, a deep natural, or mutual, contract between man and the earth.

The same holds true of "Felling a Tree", – "The surge of spirit that goes with using an axe" that wonderful poem begins – and the celebration of work in "The Valley Farm". Then, in "Hedger", written in the autumn of 1922, Gurney's personal distress is entangled with a sense of his unworthy labour as a musician. He tries to help the hedger, but is "clumsy of muscle", whereas "his quick moving/Was never broken by any danger, his loving/Use of the bill or scythe was most deft, and clear –/Had my piano-playing or counterpoint/Been so without fear/Then indeed fame had been mine of most bright outshining". The poem seems to be sliding towards an introspection close to abased self-pity. But no. It ends: "But never have I known singer or piano-player/So quick and sure in movement as this hedge-layer/This gap-mender, of quiet courage unhastening." "Hedger" refuses to aggrandise one kind of artist/maker over another: the celebration of useful work (to borrow Morris's term) of the gap-mender belongs with a truly radical imagination. There is a similar celebration in "The Mangel-Bury", where Gurney helps a farmer fill his cart with mangels: "We threw them with our bodies swinging; blood in my ears singing;/He was the thick-set sort of farmer, but well-built –/Perhaps, long before, his blood name ruled all,/Watched all things for his own. If my luck had so willed/Many questions of lordship I had heard him tell – old/Names, rumours." The farmer sounds very like Lob. Gurney had tried to learn Thomas's great poem by heart, so he told Haines.[50]

It is then of the utmost significance that "The Mangel-Bury" begins "It was after war; Edward Thomas had fallen at Arras –/I

205

was walking by Gloucester musing on such things/As fill his verse with goodness". I am fairly certain that Gurney saw himself as continuing the work Thomas could no longer do. That is why he writes "The Lock Keeper," which is his own version of "Lob". Not as great a poem, certainly, but a very fine one, and one that rejoices in the lock-keeper as a kind of tutelary countryman, a free spirit, a poacher ("The nights of winter netting birds in hedges;/The stalking wild-duck by down-river sedges"), someone who possesses "A net of craft of eye, heart, kenning and hand" and who, as the word "kenning" implies, belongs within a multi-layered English history, Saxon, Roman, Viking, Norman. Gurney refuses to endorse an "essential" Englishness. He calls the cotswolds his "two thousand years' home," and he knows that country with an intimacy even greater than Thomas's knowledge of the southern counties which the other poet had walked and then written about, first in prose, later in verse.

As Stan Smith has well remarked, Thomas was always haunted by the fear of being the superfluous man; and that could include the fear of belonging nowhere. Gurney, on the other hand, knew Gloucestershire and the adjacent countryside with a deep familiarity which redeems what might otherwise appear to be a snobbishness about "villa" culture. In a comparatively early poem, "The Bargain", he mourns the loss of "Waltheof's Field" to new houses: "Villas will stand there and look polite; with folk polite/Where sedges stood for the wind's play and poet-delight,/But Severn will be sorry and it can never be right." This grieving over the loss of a dear, familiar place recalls Clare's grief at the destruction of Swordy Well and Langley Bush. Moreover, the "polite" villas inhabited by "polite" folk suggests a new subservience or loss of spirit: the invaders represent a world of *petit bourgeois* deference. Gurney's response to this should alert us to the fact that, as Clough Williams-Ellis would argue in *England and the Octopus*, post-war developments were perceived to be doing irreparable damage to an England where loss was felt because of the war to be piled on loss. As I noted in the first chapter, such a feeling easily enough modulates into an unfocussed nostalgia. But not with Gurney. As Thomas's successor he becomes the poet of place. He is its eager celebrant, as in "The Bare Line of the Hill," which ends: "Scabious guards the steeps,/Trefoil the slopes yield." Here, the names of the flowers, in a lovely, witty fancy, re-enact the history of the place. Scabious is the Latin name, trefoil the Anglo-French. (Gurney, it should go without saying, knew much about the names and lore of flowers.)[51] Or there is "Cotswold Ways," in which Gurney, the inveterate walker, like Clare and Thomas before him, reads the evidence of human history in apparently meaningless bits of stone, wall, trough.

> One comes across the strangest things in walks:
> Fragments of Abbey tithe-barns fixed in modern
> And Dutch-sort houses where the water baulks
> Weired up, and brick kilns broken among fern,
> Old troughs, great stone cisterns bishops might have blessed
> Ceremonially, and worthy mounting-stones;
> Black timber in red brick, queerly placed
> Where hill stone was looked for – and a manor's bones
> Spied in the frame of some wisteria'd house ....

This long sentence sequence – there are a further six lines before we get a full-stop – embodies Gurney's desire to incorporate into a poem all he can of a loved place. He is at once its celebrant and memorialist, and his deliberately random, seemingly disordered gathering up of detail is in truth the evidence of his determination to be a wanderer, to be free to go where he pleases, since the land is what we have, or ought to have, in common. "'Nobody can't stop 'ee it's/A footpath right enough", as Lob says. And Lob "was wild and wandered."

There is in "Cotswold Ways" an urgent desire to celebrate and name, name and so celebrate this England before it goes. Elsewhere the desire becomes desperate as Gurney realises that his own time is short. In a bleak little poem called "Moments" he thinks of his death, of the "six-foot-length I must lie in/Sodden with mud, and not to grieve again/Because high autumn goes beyond my pen/And snow lies inexprest in the deep lane."

Not long after he wrote that poem he became so mentally unstable that he had to be institutionalised. Yet in the first years of his madness he was still capable of writing astonishingly good poems. In a sizeable number of these he returns to his war experiences which, it seems perverse to deny, must have done much to accentuate if they did not cause his difficulties. In "Farewell" he laments the deaths of many men of the Gloucesters: "Don Hancocks, shall I no more see your face frore,/Gloucester-good, in the first light? (But you are dead!)/Shall I see no more Monger with india-rubber/Twisted face? (But machine-gun caught him and his grimace)". He has therefore to mourn the loss of their speech, of "west Severn joking at east Severn." The men he grieves for are the "Dear battalion," and the intensity of his identification with them is a bonding of comradeship. It includes those he calls "The Bohemians," among which awkward squad he included himself: "Certain people would not clean their buttons,/Nor polish buckles after latest fashions." Such men are as "bolshie" as he had shown himself to be in "The Silent One." These were the men who by 1918 no longer wanted to fight "the bosses' war." But they "jested in the trench" who now "In Artois or Picardy ... lie – free of useless fashions."

It is therefore significant that Gurney now returns to an early love, to praising Whitman, the poet he had first discovered and delighted in during his early days in the army.[52] In a poem called "The New Poet", he yearns for a coming writer who will take up the example of Whitman and be a spokesman for all: "Greece, Rome, middle England the all-honouring/Provinces of France, and the Indian tradition,/A new poetry of all lights, all times; wherein swords/Are not honoured more than the shares ploughing/The coloured earth to furrows." These lines are scarcely more than notes for a poem that was never to be written, but their import is clear enough. Whitman, the poet of brotherhood, of comradeship, must be the avatar for future poets. Out of war must come the struggle to achieve a lasting peace, and this can only be achieved by the realisation of the just city as yet glimpsed through democratic vistas.[53] Gurney's greatness as a poet is inseparable from his political vision.

## VI

Most of the poems discussed in the previous section were unknown at the time of their writing, and when Gurney was institutionalised in the autumn of 1922 very few people knew or cared. Some months earlier, on 24th January to be exact, the first performance of *Façade* took place. The venue was the drawing room of the house in Chelsea shared by Osbert and Sacherevell Sitwell. William Walton conducted what one commentator has described as "the straggly band of musicians, who had to be sustained by sloe gin, and the rather bewildered audience was gratefully revived with hot rum punch afterwards in the drawing room." A year later the performance was repeated, although some new poems were added, old ones dropped, and now the audience was seated in the Aeolian Hall. This time *Façade* "caused such an immediate reaction of hostility or rage, that the Sitwells knew they had made their mark on the arts in some form or other." Over the next few days newspapers "would create the scandal establishing the Sitwell 'cult' image for the rest of their lives."[54]

The "cult" image was enhanced by Noel Coward's revue sketch of the Swiss Family Whittlebott, for which the Sitwells were in no sense grateful. And F.R. Leavis must have had *Façade* in mind when he famously remarked that the Sitwells belonged to the history of publicity rather than literature. Yet although Pamela Hunter is wrong to say that Edith Sitwell's early volumes of poems had been "unanimously hailed" as the work of a "serious poet of great promise", she is certainly right to imply that those volumes were in no sense treated dismissively.[55] Edgell Rickword, severe as he is on her 1920 volume, *The Wooden Pegasus*, allows that its imagery is "vivid and refreshing." But then the knife slides in. "Miss Sitwell has expressed in her title the limitations of her artifice. A wooden Pegasus cannot be expected to soar, though never so gilded and glossy, but he makes a pleasant figure standing stiffly in the 'fruit-ripe heat of afternoon' that glows continually over her poetic sub-urb, while the circus blares shrilly and insistently from a neigh-bouring meadow."[56] Even Laura Riding and Robert Graves, in their *Survey of Modernist Poetry*, come some way short of writing the Sitwells off. Towards Edith Sitwell in particular they are almost respectful. Describing *Façade* as burlesque, they see it as an example of modern verse, where burlesque follows "the tearless, heart-less tradition of the early Italian comedy." *Façade,* they say, has two aspects, theatrical and poetic, and it is possible "that a sensitive audience which did not catch all her words, so to speak, might by the excellence of Miss Sitwell's pantomime follow with perfect understanding her light-hearted gallop to despair and self-stultifi-cation."[57]

A severe critic might say that Riding and Graves are hedging their bets. So they are. Yet there were good reasons why throughout the 1920s the jury on *Façade* should stay out. For as burlesque the work is great fun and must have felt especially so in 1923. It was one more in the eye for Gibbs, Walpole, club-leather chairs, briar pipes and the cult of monogamy. Besides, Walton's witty, inventive music plays teasingly with the more *outré* musical styles of the period, and manages to be both knowing and in its way celebratory of the daring and the disreputable. And although Edith Sitwell proved unable to sustain a career as a poet, that is no reason to denigrate her ability to handle the light verse of *Façade*.[58] It should also be noted that Sitwell had in 1916 set in motion *Wheels,* an anthology of new verse which ran to six issues, and which gave a first printing to several young women poets, including Nancy Cunard, whose lines provided the anthology with its title. "I sometimes think that all our thoughts are wheels/Rolling forever through the painted world." Rickword chose to quote these lines when the poem from which they come was published in 1921 in Cunard's volume, *Outlaws*. Rickword lets her off lightly. "In spite of her frequent lack of success," he says, "one can feel the pulse of an original mind beating through a rather uncongenial medium. The language, though often striking, lacks that essential rhythm, that dominant note which absorbs and unifies the diverse elements of a poem, drawing them to an awkward conclusion."[59]

Rickword's criticism is both just and generous. Pound was also just when, in response to a poem Cunard sent him in 1921, he wrote to ask her why "the devil do you write in that obsolete dialect and with cadences of the late Alfred Tennyson."[60] Nancy Cunard wasn't really a poet, but it is understandable that she would have wanted to be one. It was a way of breaking into a largely male preserve, of asserting a right to expression which mattered to her because of her radical politics, just as it mattered to other women. For them all, it was one more assault on the world of the club-leather chair. It may be that Cunard's example encouraged a number of women poets who begin to emerge in the 1920s, or whose work becomes more assured, among them H.D., Elizabeth Daryush, Ruth Pitter, Sylvia Townsend Warner, Ida Aflleck Graves. One offshoot of this is the Oxford poetry magazine for women, *Fritillary,* whose editor in 1929 was E.J.Scovell. Moreover, *Time and Tide*, a journal which had started publication in 1920 as a part of the suffrage movement, also provided space for women poets. And against Eliot's dismissal of Cunard in a cancelled passage of *The Waste Land*[61] we can set Riding and Graves' acknowledgement that Cunard's self-aware imitation of Eliot, "Parallax," mocks an "utterly hopeless and unpurposed pessimism."[62] What she wanted to do was to change society.

Riding and Graves wanted to do no such thing. Their *Survey* is a polemic against the modernist rage, as they conceive it, for originality. "The modernist poet has not been able to forsake originality however directly it might contradict the classical idea of discipline."[63] Discipline was what Graves and Riding were after. In their joint *A Pamphlet Against Anthologies*, published in 1928, they argued the need to discard poems that represented different schools or kinds of poetry in favour of a sceptical, cautious concern for what was truly important. The pamphlet powerfully influenced Geoffrey Grigson's taste, as he himself acknowledged; as a result it had an important part to play in his editorial procedures when he set up *New Verse*. By the same token, the *Survey* influenced the young William Empson and his views of criticism, views which were first aired in the Cambridge journal *Experiment* and then in his seminal *Seven Types of Ambiguity*.[64] Riding and Graves's influence is therefore of most concern to poets and critics of the 1930s; and it is not without irony that their "discipline", including the discipline of withdrawal from politics, should recommend itself to writers who were for the most part politically radical. I cannot follow the story here, but that it exists is itself evidence of the folly of trying to define cultural history in terms of decades.

## Notes on Chapter 6

1. Edward Marsh, *Georgian Poetry, 1920-1922,* London, The Poetry Bookshop, 1922. Although Marsh's 21 chosen poets include Graves, Blunden and Nichols, none of them is represented by war poems.
2. Iolo A. Williams, *Poetry Today,* London, Herbert Jenkins, 1927. see pp. 115, 116, and 137. Williams seems to be one of the Squirearchy. At all events Squire put William's poor verse into several of his anthologies.
3. In *Goodbye to All That* Graves recalls his visit to Hardy in August, 1920, and reports conversations during which Hardy is supposed to have made the (in) famous pronouncements. For my doubts as to their authenticity, see my essay "New Polyolbions" in *Critical Dialogues*, eds. Isobel Armstrong and H-W. Ludwig, The British Council/Tubingen, 1995, pp 207-222.
4. Donald Davie, *Thomas Hardy and British Poetry,* London, Routledge and Kegan Paul, 1973, p. 131. Bolt's anthology is, despite some gaps, an interesting one, and as still the only anthology of its kind is of undoubted importance.
5. David Bennett, "Periodical Fragments and Organic Culture: Modernism, the Avante Garde, and the Little Magazine," *Contemporary Literature,* XXX 4, pp. 480-502.
6. See Peter Ackroyd, *T. S. Eliot,* London, Sphere Books, 1985, pp. 123-4. The internationalist stance of *The Criterion* is in the interest of what might be called Arnoldian Europeanism which before the war had been endorsed by Forster in *Howards End*. It is evident in the novel that Forster fears rabid nationalism as the likely cause of conflict, and 1914 was to prove him right, as was the establishing of the 'canon' of English literature which went on during and after the war.
7. Quoted by C. K. Stead in *The New Poetic,* London, Hutchinson, 1964 pp. 114-5.

8. Ted Hughes, *A Dancer to God: Tributes to T. S. Eliot,* London, Faber, 1992, p. 21.

9. Lucy McDiarmid, *Saving Civilisation: Yeats, Eliot and Auden Between the Wars,* Cambridge, C.U.P., 1984, p. 99.

10. T.S. Eliot, "Tradition and the Individual Talent, *Selected Essays,* London, Faber, 1951, p. 15.

11. E. M. Forster, *Aspects of the Novel,* London, Arnold, 1927, pp. 11-12. Forster was famously a "little Englander". But this meant that he disliked the Imperialist enterprise, distrusted patriotism, and anxiously celebrated internationalism. "Only connect," among other things, invited English writers in 1910 to consider the achievements of German culture. The politics of "cultural international-ism," for want of a better phrase, had to do with a refusal to demonologise Germany, and such internationalism is a remarkable feature of writers and artists in England in the 1920s.

12. *A Monthly Chapbook,* no. 9. Quoted by Stead in *The New Poetic,* p. 117.

13. Ezra Pound, "How to read," in *Literary Essays of Ezra Pound,* ed. with intro-duction by T.S. Eliot, London, Faber, 1954, p. 21.

14. He was to claim that *The Waste Land* was merely a piece of private grumbling. Such mock-modesty should not prevent us from acknowledging how ambitious the poem was, both formally and in subject-matter.

15. Alick West, "T.S. Eliot: The Waste Land," in *Crisis and Criticism and Literary Essays,* London, Lawrence and Wishart, 1975. The book was first published in slightly different form in 1937.

16. *Selected Essays* op. cit. p. 21.

17. "The Birth of An Empire," in *Abinger Harvest,* London, Arnold, 1936, 47. and "Notes on the English Character" from the same collection of essays, p. 9. That this essay should have been written in 1920 is of some importance, given its refusal to endorse post-war self-congratulatory smugness passing for patri-otism.

18. See Frank Swinnerton, *Figures in the Foreground* op. cit. pp. 67-9.

19. Douglas Goldring reports that "an eminent poetess [presumably Edith Sitwell] took offence at the modesty of the payment offered by *The New Coterie.* No peri-odical devoted entirely to literature and art could hope to show a profit in 1925," he continues, "and the fact the editors sent token cheques to their contributors was evidence of generosity on their part, since the cheques did not come out of the public's pocket but out of their own." See *The Nineteen Twenties* op. cit. p. 107.

20. For more on both the *Coteries* see Goldring *The Nineteen-Twenties,* p. 107.

21. Chris Baldick, *The Social Mission of English Criticism 1848-1932,* Oxford, Clarendon Press, 1983, esp. pp. 80-9. Although I don't share all of Baldick's emphases – there is more to be said for Newbolt than that he was the author of "Vitae Lampada" – there is no doubting the importance of his study.

22. Quoted by Patrick Parrinder, "Politics, Letters and the National Curriculum," in *Changing English,* Vol. 2. no. 1, Autumn, 1994, p. 27.

23. All this can be found in *The Social Mission of the English Criticism,* p. 96.

24. Ibid, pp. 96-7.

25. Ibid, p. 102.

26. Ibid pp. 102, p. 81. Here, the importance of the Working Men's Colleges needs to be addressed. T. A. Jackson in *Solo Trumpet* writes of the College where he lec-tured, in the North East, in the post-war years; and Harold Heslop recalls the London College's part in his life when he went there in the mid 1920s. See *Out of the Old Earth,* eds. Andy Croft and Graham Rigby, Newcastle, Bloodaxe, 1994, esp. pp. 143-155.

27. T.S. Eliot, *Selected Essays* op. cit. pp. 456-9. Eliot adds a curious footnote to the essay, remarking that the essay was written nine years earlier than its first pub-

lication in 1923. This can hardly be the literal case, given his attack on gramophone music as well as the cinema. More likely he added to an obituary and wanted to bring new evidence to bear on his claim for the incipient death of working-class culture. The evidence is, after all, also adduced in *The Waste Land*, when the typist "smoothes her hair with automatic hand/And puts a record on the gramophone." She is as machine-like as the gramophone she operates.

28. *The Principles of Literary Criticism* 3rd edition, 1928. In this context it is worth remarking that in the opening chapters of *Swan Song*, that novel of *The Forsyte Saga* which covers the time of the general strike, Soames comes across some London labourers and reflects that "People were born gaping nowadays. And a good thing too! Cinemas, fags, football matches – there would be no real revolution while they were on hand...." The cinema as drug against working-class radicalism. See John Galsworthy, *A Modern Comedy*, London, Penguin, 1980, p. 579. The novel was first published in 1928.

29. Baldick deals very well with some of the objections. See pps. 139-156.

30. Charles Hobday, *Edgell Rickword: A Poet at War* Manchester, Carcanet, 1989, pp. 48-9. In the poem "Trench Warfare" the speaker says of his dead chum that "I racked my head/for wholesome lines and quoted *Maud*." This may be less than fair to Tennyson, although his poem does end by seeming to recommend a good military fight as the way out of personal difficulties. Its hero leaves for the Crimea. But Rickword speaks for those who survived the war and for whom high-toned Victorianism was as out of the reach as it had seemed to an earlier generation desirable – witness Herbert Asquith's war poem of 1915, "The Volunteer", with its limp echoes of Tennyson, and its suggestion of how the clerk is bound to prefer a lance "broken in life's tournament" to toiling with his pen in "the city grey."

31. Leavis readily acknowledged that the title for his journal *Scrutiny* came from the essays in *The Calendar of Modern Letters* called "Scrutinies" which put literary establishment figures under the microscope and, usually, the knife. But Rickword would never have shared Leavis's conservative elitist belief that "it must be obvious" that few could benefit from the study of literature. Those few all went to Downing College, Cambridge, of course.

32. For more on this see my essay, "Edgell Rickword: Man of Letters," in *The Sewanee Review*, Winter, 1994, vol C11, pp. 112-121.

33. In his edition of *The Collected Poems* Hobday includes some poems from the manuscript, plus *Twittingpan and Others*, published in 1931, and a handful of other, later poems. These are few in number and not remarkable for their quality.

34. *Edgell Rickword: Poet at War* p. 114.

35. Laura Riding and Robert Graves, *A Survey of Modernist Poetry*, New York, Haskell House Publishers, 1969, pp. 224-6. This is a facsimile of the original American edition of 1928. The book had first been published in London in 1927.

36. *Edgell Rickword*, pp. 96-7.

37. Ibid. p. 99.

38. Ibid. p. 95. When Rickword came to revive his masque in 1947, he added two lines to the Presenter's final speech, which now ends: "with thoughts like pilgrims' staves they picked their way/to a lucid zone, whence fresh horizons blazed." This combines echoes of *The Pilgrim's Progress* and *Paradise Lost* so as to remind its readers of the fact that in 1947 matters did look more hopeful for radicals than they had in 1926. However, the added lines spoil the speech's overall tone.

39. All quotations from Gurney's poems come from *Collected Poems of Ivor Gurney*, ed. P. J. Kavanagh, Oxford. O.U.P., 1982.

40. *Ivor Gurney: Collected Letters* ed. R.K.R. Thornton, Northumberland &

Manchester, MidNAG/Carcanet, 1991, p. 288.

41. His letters from France repeatedly pass on remarks he has heard from his fellow soldiers. How much these meant to him may be gauged from his telling Marion Scott that the soldiers he is with "talk their own native language and sing their own folk songs with sweet natural voices." *Collected Letters*, p. 86. And in an uncollected lyric, "Dawn," he recalls being under fire in the trenches and how that was made endurable by "a companionship of good talk." See *A Second Selection From Modern Poets* by J.C. Squire, London, Martin Secker, 1924, p. 222. As far as I know the poem has been reprinted nowhere else. Nor has the altogether more interesting and much longer "Thoughts on New England". Squire's third choice, "Smudgy Dawn," is in Kavanagh. They must all have been written at about the same time, the late summer/autumn of 1922, when Gurney's mental state was becoming dreadfully precarious. The two short poems are haunted by war, and a desperate attempt to make sense of England prompted "Thoughts on New England". Here New England is both the eastern seaboard of the U.S.A. and writers who mattered to him, above all Whitman, but also I suspect, an England that might be renewed.

41a. The identification of Elizabethan England as the ideal state — post-feudal, pre-capitalist — seems to have been commonly held by early 20th century socialists, R.H. Tawney among them. For more of this see my essay in *The Journal of the Ivor Gurney Society*, no 7, 1998.

42. In another letter he writes "TEA!! that magic word." *Collected Letters*, p. 322. Even his later poems relish the thought of it. See for example "Masterpiece" and "When the Mire."

43. *Collected Letters*, p. 129.

44. Ibid p. 261. It may be relevant to note here that in 1916 Sir Hubert Parry, director of the Royal College of Music, where Gurney had been a student, set Blake's "Jerusalem" to the now famous tune. The resultant song thus become a patriotic song for war as well as a vision of post-war England which could well have been taken as a radical one, even if successive generations of tories have thought otherwise. And it is then also relevant to note that Vaughan Williams had already incorporated some lines of Whitman into his Sea Symphony. Gurney and his fellow students had raved about the symphony and Gurney was an impassioned admirer of Whitman. Whether utopian socialism, or at all events advanced democratic ideas were part of the atmosphere at the Royal College during his time there and indeed later, I don't know; but it would not have been at all improbable.

45. *Collected Letters* p. 375.

46. Ibid, p. 382.

47. Ibid, pp. 403 and 412.

48. There is an excellent brief discussion of Gurney's handling of run-on lines in Donald Davie's review of Kavanagh's edition. See *The London Review of Books,* 3-16 February, 1982.

49. Michael Hurd has something to say about the settings by and of Gurney in his biography, *The Ordeal of Ivor Gurney, Oxford,* O.U.P. 1978. In a sonnet celebrating Hazlitt, written at the time of crisis in 1922, Gurney praises his writings about Shakespeare, and especially Hazlitt's contention that Shakespeare is essentially a writer of and for the people. In himself, Shakespeare contained "companies of men that were lively here/And walked happy in thought in England Merry." Note the political significance of Gurney's use of the phrase "Merry England." He was especially responsive to Shakespeare's love of ideolect, and of his use of song; and his own song-poems, for example "The Wanderer," have the kind of lyric clarity that aligns them with some of the songs in the late plays.

49a. Gurney is undoubtedly here engaged with the issue that concerned many socialists in the 1920s: of arguing for cheap, effective building materials for working-class houses.

50. *Collected Letters* p. 441. The letter was written in August, 1918.
51. The concern with lore and naming can be found, for example, in a number of poems, for example, "Hedger."
52. See a letter dated late September, 1915. "Walt Whitman is my latest discovery and he has taken me like a flood." *Collected Letters* p. 41.
53. In the uncollected "Thoughts on New England" Gurney tries to think through a bewildering tangle of ideas about citizenship, national and cultural history and identity; and he claims that "the mix of Dane thoughts, Roman with Middle-Age/Calls all love out to mark on any page." *Second Selection from Modern Poets* op. cit. Gurney's commitment to a peopled history is unshakeable, despite his conviction that such history is now tragically circumscribed, that common ownership is no more, that the transactional relationship between man and the earth is rapidly becoming a thing of the past and that as it goes so, too, goes the love of common things.
54. *Façade: Edith Sitwell,* with an Introduction by Pamela Hunter, London, Duckworth, 1987, pp. 14-15.
55. Ibid p. 15.
56. Edgell Rickword, *Essays and Opinions 1921-1931* ed. Alan Young, Manchester, Carcanet, 1974, p. 314. The review first appeared in *The Daily Herald.*
57. *A Survey of Modernist Poetry,* op cit. pp. 231-3.
58. Of her 1929 volume, *Gold Coast Customs and Other Poems,* Rickword remarked that Sitwell in the title poem tries to allegorise certain bloody rites of the Gold Coast as customs of "fashionable society," and that although on the whole this is too hysterical to be convincing, nevertheless her "power of expression frequently overcomes this intellectual confusion." *Essays and Opinions,* p. 251.
59. Ibid, p. 39.
60. Quoted by Anne Chisholm, *Nancy Cunard,* op. cit. p. 86.
61. See Chisholm, p. 339. The passage in question is about Fresca, a spoiled city girl with literary pretensions and a hearty sexual appetite.
62. *A Survey of Modernist Poetry* p. 165.
63. Ibid p. 277. For Riding and Graves, imagism belongs to the history of modernism's mistaken trust in originality, rather than discipline. Arguing this way allowed Graves to rationalise his pathological loathing of Pound, and Riding her jealousy – was it? – of H.D., of whom she remarked in the *Survey* that "her immortality came to an end before her bluff could be called." (p. 123). Rickword was far more generous in his review of H.D.'s volume *Red Roses for Bronze,* claiming that "not a few of these poems have a sunlit grace, a stainless clarity, unshackled by the chains of fact." *Essays and Opinions,* p. 261. H.D. has her champions, although the poet Barry Cole thinks her work "boring," an opinion with which I for the most part concur. Anyway, she does not belong within the confines of this study.
64. For Grigson's and Empson's indebtedness to Riding see Deborah Baker, *In Extremis: The Life of Laura Riding,* London, Hamish Hamilton, 1993, p. 350. For *Experiment* see Mark Thompson, "On the Borderland: Empson First and Last," *The Edinburgh Review,* no 85, 1992, esp. pp. 101-109.

## CHAPTER SEVEN

# TAKING SIDES

In this concluding chapter I want to return to the argument that the failure of the General Strike was of crucial importance to the development of radical thought and activity – including writing – and that it, rather than, say, the Wall Street crash was decisive in shaping or conditioning attitudes both at the time and later. For what the strike seemed to require was that people should take sides. As I earlier noted, "Black Friday", April 25th, 1921, had been regarded as a great betrayal, "when not only was the general strike abandoned, the Triple Alliance ruined and the miners sacrificed, but the whole structure of united working-class resistance to an expected attack on wages and living standards was demolished at a blow".[1] Now the chance to make good that earlier defeat had come again and again it had been wasted. On the left and, I suspect, among many who would not have thought of themselves as particularly radical, the anti-climax of May, 1926, became a defining moment: a deep sense of shame worked its way into their consciousness. On the right there was a hardening of conviction as to the dangers to the nation of mass democracy. We need to recall here Churchill's unctuous praise for Mussolini as the man who had provided "an ultimate means of protection against the cancerous growth of Bolshevism". No doubt Churchill felt that by his behaviour at the time of the strike he had performed the same service for England. He had saved it for civilisation.

Churchill's speech was delivered on January 20, 1927. In November of that year Eliot took out British citizenship. "In the end I thought: here I am, making a living, enjoying my friends here. I don't like being a squatter. I might as well take full responsibility."[2] Virginia Woolf noted that Eliot's dress and demeanour were now "of English type" and another woman friend, Mary Colum, recalled how at dinner once he drank sherry before the meal and port after it. "He loved the whole English civilisation", she said.[3] Eliot's self-chosen identity was that of a royalist, anglo-catholic conservative. That he decided to take out British citizenship a year after the general strike is, I think, significant. Looking back to that moment from the vantage point of 1939, he would write in his "last words" for *The Criterion* that, "Only from about the year 1926 did the features of the post-war world begin clearly to emerge". It is also significant that at this time Wyndham Lewis should be working on his atrabilious satire, *The Apes of God*, in the prologue to which he offers a glimpse of "little jumping bolshevists" as tiresome boy scouts, their fists smashing glass – but only of show-cases, and crying out in "idiot-yawp, civilized and whitmanic".[4] And, to repeat a point touched on in Chapter 4, I find further significance in a hardening of authority's attitude to what might be seen as in any way subversive or threatening to "civilisation". Hence, the banning of Lawrence's paintings, of *Lady Chatterley's Lover*, and of *The Well of Loneliness*.

In the years following 1926 many sympathetic to the cause of the strikers sensed a growth in triumphalism among their opponents on the right. Those like Robert Graves who did not wish to take sides responded by going abroad.[5] Those who stayed found themselves increasingly required to commit themselves to furthering the cause of radical politics. This is not to say that all of these people felt the commitment to the same degree or that they were at one in their views as to what radical politics meant. But the failure of the General Strike was a formative moment in the lives of many, if not most, of those who lived through it.

This was certainly Leonard Woolf's view. When he came to that part of his autobiography which covered the inter-war years, he singled out the General Strike as "the most painful, the most horrifying" of political occurences at home to have occurred in his lifetime. Woolf was writing in the 1960s, but the effects of the strike were with him still. (And we shall see that much of the writing about the strike occurs some while after the event: as with all really crucial historical events, the strike's real importance could not at first be understood: time alone would reveal its significance.) The passage deserves to be quoted at length.

> When one comes to the practice of politics, anyone writing about his life in the years 1924-39 must answer the crucial question: 'What did you do in the General Strike ....The treat-

ment of the miners by the government after the Sankey Commission was disgracefully dishonest. If ever there has been right on the side of the workers in an industrial dispute, it was on the side of the miners in the years after the war; if ever a strike and a general strike was justified, it was in 1926. The actions of the mine-owners and of the government seemed to me appalling and when the General Strike came, I was entirely on the side of the workers .... Then when the failure of the strike was inevitable, I was rung up one morning by R. H. Tawney, who asked me to come round to see him in Mecklenburgh Square. When I got there he told me he was going to try and get as many well-known people as possible to sign a statement publicly calling upon the government to see that there was no victimization when the strike was over. He asked me whether I would be responsible for collecting the signatures of as many prominent writers and artists as possible .... We worked hectically, and only one person refused when asked to sign. This was John Galsworthy.[6]

Galsworthy's hostility to the cause of the strikers is more muted in *Swan Song*, the novel in the Forsyte Saga which covers the period during which the strike took place. Yet he plainly sees the strike as a threat to England. Those who oppose it are therefore doing no more than their patriotic duty in combining to defeat it. The point of view we are meant to take as authoritative in the novel is that of Michael, who as a "caring" politician is no extremist, but who knows which side he's on. When his wife, Fleur, says that "I wish we had a Mussolini," he replies, "I don't. You pay for him in the long run."[7] Nevertheless, the strike brings with it a battle for Britain – or at least England. "The multiple evidence of patriotism exhilarated him – undergraduates at the docks, young women driving cars, shopfolk walking cheerfully to their work, the swarms of 'specials', the general carrying-on. Even the strikers were good-humoured". (p. 604). Michael is presented without irony as embodying "England" and "English" values. He is the possessor of what a little later is characterised as "the national outlook". (p. 607) And the nation is, we are to understand, at war. Young Jon, who has returned to England from France to help defeat the strikers, feels "extraordinary pleasure in being up against it ... doing something for England!" (p. 590)

Jon drives a train. Others drive tanks. Soames watches some of these rumble through London's night-time streets as they head for the docks and thinks that there is "a sort of extravagance about them, when he remembered the blank-looking crowd around his car that afternoon, not a weapon among the lot, nor even a revolutionary look in their eyes .... something in Soames revolted slightly. Hang it! This was England, not Russia, or Italy! They might be right, but he didn't like it! Too – too military!" (p. 585) But Soames' doubts are not developed. And perhaps Galsworthy was right to hint that for others militarism equalled patriotism. Undergraduates too young to have fought in the war could now take up arms for England. That the strike was regarded, at least among those who opposed it, as a battle for England seems clear as soon as we notice that not only did Reith give Baldwin and cabinet ministers the freedom of the BBC's airwaves (he even went as far as to help Baldwin with his speeches), but that with the announcement of the strike's collapse he insisted on broadcasting Parry's setting of "Jerusalem". England's green and pleasant land had once again been saved.

The absurdity of this is matched by its nastiness. For it hardly need to be pointed out that the enemy were also English – and Welsh and Scottish. When Michael hears the announcement of the strike's collapse, "For a moment he sat motionless with a choky feeling, such as he had felt when news of Armistice came through. A sword lifted from over the head of England!" Then he sees a "group of men, who had obviously been strikers .... leaning over the parapet. He tried to read their faces. Glad, sorry, ashamed, resentful, relieved? For the life of him he could not tell. Some defensive joke seemed to be going the round of them. 'No wonder we're a puzzle to foreigners!' thought Michael. 'The least understood people in the world'" (pp. 604-5) Never were the failings of literary realism more glaringly exposed. Michael's authority is not to be questioned: he speaks for England. The fact that he cannot "read" the strikers' faces is not to be taken as implying any inadequacy of his authority. His inability to know what the strikers think is deflected into a trivialising joke: "we're a puzzle to foreigners". But in Michael's eyes the strikers are every bit as foreign. They might as well not be English. In fact, they aren't English, because being English means opposing the strike, and its defeat, like the armistice, announces one more triumph over foreign foes. I imagine it was this brutally simplistic identification of class-interest with Englishness, as it developed in succeeding years, which had much to do with helping Forster to shape his famous pronouncement in 1938 that if he had to choose between betraying his country and betraying his friend he hoped he would have the guts to betray his country.

*Swan Song* naturally never allows any of the strikers to speak. They are simply "there": the known enemy. Such misgivings as

Michael and Soames might entertain are dispelled as soon as they are uttered. Galsworthy's "realistic" novel is therefore less adequate to the moment than Bennett's *Accident,* which, as we have seen, does for at least half of its length put realism to the test. Alan Frith-Walter's developing paranoia, although abandoned in the novel's latter half, powerfully suggests the inadequacy he comes to feel about his understanding of England and class relationships: the novel, while concentrating on his point of view, finds a way of unsettling its certainties, its complacencies. By comparison, the complacency of *Swan Song* unintentionally reveals itself to be an insufferable, bullying ignorance. It comes as no surprise that Galsworthy would not sign Leonard Woolf's petition.

Nor is it surprising that in the year of the novel's publication Rickword should have been so keen to carry Lawrence's "Scrutiny" of Galsworthy in the *Calendar.* Although Lawrence does not single out any particular novel for discussion, what he says of the Forsyte Saga as a whole applies perfectly to *Swan Song.* "There is in it all," he remarks, "a vulgar sense of being rich, and therefore we do as we like: an utter incapacity for anything like true feeling".[8] *The Spectator,* speaking for Galsworthy's version of England, found Lawrence's essay "revolting in taste and indecent in expression". But *The New Statesman* praised it. Lawrence's essay was, the reviewer commented, "hard-hitting, well-aimed and well-merited".[9]

## II

Galsworthy's stance was a common enough one among those who claimed for themselves the right to speak for England. It was, for example, the stance adopted by *Britannia,* a journal which Gilbert Frankau edited and which began and ceased publication in 1928. In *Georgian Adventure* Douglas Jerrold presents Frankau as a "Jewish romantic [who] sees the English scene in simple colours .... Frankau finds his escape in the vision of men in khaki and men in hunting pink". He is "really a piece of Kipling's Englishman". Jerrold claims that "the idea behind *Britannia* was a good one – an illustrated news review with intelligent comment and sound anti-Socialist principles. It would have been called today, as Yeats Brown's *Everyman* actually was called, Fascist ... [although] there was .... no sinister political motif behind Frankau's conception". (Jerrold is writing in 1937.)[10] Jerrold suggests that had Frankau possessed more business sense *Britannia* might have succeeded, whereas it collapsed after a mere six issues. Yet it seems symbolically appropriate that Frankau should have no financial acumen, nor even editorial flair. He is a myth of pre-war England made flesh. "It Still Goes On" Graves wrote in exasperation a year later. Yes, but only just.

The same might be said of Patrick Hamilton's father. From Sean French's biography, *Patrick Hamilton: A Life*, Hamilton snr. emerges as a kind of comic monster. Educated at Repton, "a hard-bitten manly school", he called it, and Trinity College, Cambridge, he was a social snob who believed that the poor were beyond help. "We must accept facts as they are. The 'submerged tenth' will always remain submerged". He wrote appallingly bad historical novels and ran through a considerable inheritance on "climbing in Switzerland, sculling, squash, tennis, golf, fishing, shooting, hunting, rose-growing, 'above all, travel in old Europe. All *chateaux* and cathedrals have a perennial interest'". As with all comic monsters who are fun to read about, he was hell to live with. He drank heavily, took mistresses, and bullied his wife and children. Not surprisingly, they hated him.

War came as a relief to Bernard Hamilton. In 1915 he gained a commission in the Territorial Division of the Royal Warwickshire Horse Artillery, and as might be expected "he played the military role with theatrical gusto". [Patrick] Hamilton wrote of how one afternoon, in 1916, his father was having tea and taking it fairly easy while on duty at his office in Leamington, when his orderly brought in an evening newspaper which announced the death of Lord Kitchener. On seeing this he at once rose to his feet, stood at attention, saluted and said, "Carry on". Sometime after the war, having returned home from the Savage Club drunk and not wanting tea, he pushed his cup at his wife, saying as he did so, "You can *take* your tea". Alright, she said, but there was no need to throw the tea in her face. "'I did *not* throw the tea in your face,' he said, and added with obvious pride, 'I am an artilleryman – and I took a low trajectory'".[11]

Patrick Hamilton's novels are, as Arnold Rattenbury has noted, packed with attentive use of the small change of conversational English, those utterances by which people betray themselves. "Speaking to Patrick you would see his eyes glaze over, despite your best efforts, take on a particular stare, and know suddenly that he was listening sideways, ears almost flapping, gathering clichés from the talk of strangers."[12] Rattenbury is here remembering pub talk from the early 1940s; but Hamilton must have begun the practise while he was growing up. From the outset his novels are notable for his mastery of dialogue and speech utterance and to that mastery he also owes much of his success as a dramatist. It is a key device for anatomising (and anathematising) those he dislikes, especially those domestic tyrants who bulk large in his fiction and whose attitudes he so powerfully understands to be dangerous although favoured – dangerous because favoured – versions of Englishness. Militaristic, self-righteously moralistic, unimaginatively complacent, ignorant, often claiming patriotism as both their justification and their defence, the tyrants, men who no doubt owe much to Hamilton's observations of his father's behaviour, are a lingering parody of all those certainties which the events of 1914-18 called into question, and whose survival was therefore bitterly resented by the younger generation. In *Lions and Shadows* Christopher Isherwood notes that while serving his apprenticeship to the art of writing on the Isle of Wight he would jot down the inanities of contemporary bar-room slang and sporting talk; and it seems that Henry Green regularly made a habit of drifting between pub groups to overhear their conversations.[13] Behind all of these young novelists is perhaps the example of E.M. Forster, whose pre-war novels had made use of small talk in order to reveal or betray the inner feelings and qualities of his characters. But Hamilton's second novel, *Craven House*, develops the possibilities inherent in the Forsterian method in a manner especially appropriate to the post-war period.

The novel, written while Hamilton was still only twenty-one, at first seems to owe more to H.G. Wells than to Forster. The lodging-house setting and inmates, who include a retired major, the inevitable spinster, a young married couple, and a mother and daughter, appear to offer the opportunity for a relaxed, none-too serious account of aspects of middle-class English life, with an occasional glimpse of below stairs and a pair of comic servants thrown in for good measure. And in the First Book, set in pre-war England, the smooth-running comic orderliness is maintained, although with one or two corrugations: the recently married Mr Spicer, who takes on himself the role of lodging-house arbiter of values, creeps off to a drunken encounter with a prostitute; and young Elsie is thrashed by her mother for daring to enjoy herself contrary to parental permission. Then "The Great War Falls on Craven House". So the Second Book is called. Yet the war seems hardly to affect the house. The major dies, but of a heart attack, and Mr Spicer returns unharmed from inglorious army service. But in Chapter two of the Second Book we are alerted to the fact that the war years were ones "in which the Servant Problem first arose in stark uncompromise, and an alarming bent in the Lower Order towards Answering Back became acute".[14]

Throughout the novel Hamilton uses capital letters as a means of indicating how various inhabitants of Craven House see issues as emphasised in ways they can hardly bring themselves to discuss. That he should do so is part of his radical comic procedure, and throughout his career he will continue to use typographic means as just one of the many ways by which he unsettles and finally capsizes the calm certainties on which the daily lives and happenings of his novels appear to float. It is therefore especially galling that, with the honourable exceptions of Peter Widdowson and Arnold Rattenbury, those who have commented on his novels regard him as formally uninventive, even reactionary. They don't even notice the implication of the novel's title. *Craven House* may not be an allegory of England, but it is certainly about kinds of Englishness, including that craven acceptance of the class system in which the lower orders are not meant to Answer Back.

But then one of the servants, Audrey, *does* answer back. She tells Miss Hatt, who owns Craven House, to keep her hair on. A discussion follows between Miss Hatt and some of her paying guests about what action Miss Hatt shall take. Mrs Spicer suggests waiting until her husband returns from work. Men know what to do. Mr Spicer is duly told that Audrey has Answered Back and his opinion sought as to Miss Hatt's best way of dealing with so unforgivable an incident. "Whereupon Mr Spicer hums, and Mr Spicer haws, and Mr Spicer says it's very ticklish, and at last decides that the point is, What's to be done?" (Bk 2, ch IV.v.) And, no thanks to him, Audrey is dismissed. The mode is comic but the tone deepens, and with the going of Audrey Craven House begins to fall apart. There is a brilliant scene in which the now grown-up Elsie, wanting to go to a dance with the now grown-up son of the major, Master Wildman, is told by her mother she can't. She can't because she has dared to oppose her mother by having her hair bobbed. To ensure her order is obeyed the mother then cuts up the dress Elsie intended wearing to the dance. Whereupon young Mr Wildman takes Elsie into London, buys her another dress, and when on their return her mother threatens Elsie with the stick with which she has previously thrashed her, Elsie snaps it in two. She then goes to the dance.

It is difficult to communicate just how powerful this episode is, because in the re-telling it can seem both trivial and lightly comic. In fact, it is a moment of huge release, an important freedom gained, and the real nastiness of Mrs Nixon in her bullying opposition to her daughter, her authoritarian, joyless hatred, emerges when she summons her son to take Elsie away from Craven House. We have already heard about this son. Sometime before Elsie's act of defiance Mrs Nixon has greatly enjoyed herself by reading out at dinner a letter from him in which he recounts how he "had taken an insult from, but had subsequently thrashed, a Coal Heaver". (Bk2, ch.V.i) Now he appears, a bragging Scotsman. Or so it seems, but it turns out that he isn't Scottish after all, he merely pretends to be of Baronial descent. He joins the rest at dinner and makes clear that he knows Mr Wildman is his enemy. Again the dialogue is on the surface comic. He boasts about good Scottish food, tells Mr Wildman he should travel a bit so as to avoid thinking that all Scotsmen carry haggis with them all day

> And the silence that follows is the silence of distant thunders gathering.
> "I don't like Scotch food, very much, myself," says Elsie, by way of conversation.
> "Ay, and that's because ye don't like what's good for ye, Miss Elsie," says Mr Nixon, smiling. "If you refuse good Scotch food, meleddy, what you want is a good dose of that castor oil." .....
> "Like the Fascists give the Bolshevists," says Mr Nixon.
> "Good Punishment, that," says Mr Spicer. "Does no harm, and just Teaches them. Always think that a very good punishment."
> "Ay, that it is," says Mr Nixon. "Did I ever tell ye, mother, what we did to the Bolshie up our way?"
> "No. What's that Jock?"
> "There was one of they Socialists, ye see," says Mr Nixon, looking round at every one except Master Wildman to whom he is obviously addressing this story. "Holdin' meetings with a few associates in his rooms of a night."
> "Oh, yes?" says Miss Hatt.
> "So we watched him a few nights, ye see, and then we got a few boys together and went round there one night. And we waited till the others went out, and then we broke in at the door, and went up to his rooms, where he was standin' looking wild."
> "Oh!" exclaimes Miss Hatt.
> "So we got his books first, all that low Socialist stuff, ye know, and we burnt them over the fire, an' he was screeching out

the Red Flag in defiance all the while, and we just let him do it. But he up and hit one of our chaps at last, and then we started in. An' we gave it him where he wasn't looking for it."

"Where was that?" asks Master Wildman, and there is a pause, in which both young gentlemen's eyes meet across the table.

"And when we'd finished wi' that," continues Mr Nixon, "we set in wi' the Castor Oil, and we got near half a pint down him before we'd done. And then we told him we weren't having any of that Remsey *MacDonald* (Mr Nixon brings forth the word Remsey as thought it is the very worst epithet to apply to the very vilest substantive) Ramsay MacDonald stuff in our parts, and then we left him to look after himself. Bit in the papers about it, and all ...."

"Expect he Deserved it," says Mr Spicer.

"Ay, he did that. But there was another trouble with *that* young man. He'd been interferin' with one our chap's sisters up there. Carryin' on with her against her people's wishes ...."

Mr Nixon again meets Master Wildman's eyes across the table ....

"Oh, that's bad," says Mr Spicer.

"Ay, it was," says Mr Nixon laughing, and the others laugh. For him," says Mr Nixon.

Mrs Hoare wants to know if wasn't a little cruel.

"Oh, I don't know. They Deserve it, these chaps," says Mr Spicer.

"Yes," says Mrs Spicer to the Universe.

"Scottish way," says Mrs Nixon, "we take care of our bairns up there."

"Ay, Scottish way," says Mr Nixon, again looking over at Master Wildman. "An' we're always ready with it."

"Scotch way," says Master Wildman contemplatively. He looks at the table cloth, and the air shudders in the first spasm of the thunders long gathering. *(Bk 2. ch X. i.)*

Mr Spicer's ready identification with Jock Nixon is as revealing as Nixon's not always certain control of Scottish pronunciation and his mother's use of the Scottish "bairns". They are all shams, and Spicer's own hypocrisy is underlined by his wife's agreement with his observation that "They Deserve it, these chaps". She has recently discovered about his meetings with prostitutes. Against their thuggish nastiness are ranged the hesitancies of Miss Hatt and Mrs Hoare, and Elsie's timorous but courageous determination to resist her brother and mother's coercion. Her remark, "I don't like Scotch food, very much, myself," is beautifully done not merely because it suggests there are certain things she won't swallow but because the nervous qualification, "very much", is followed by the insistence of "myself", where she makes it clear that she is on Master Wildman's side.

And taking sides is what we as readers are compelled to do here. We can hardly be other than for Elsie and Master Wildman and against Jock Nixon. His bully-boy fascism and his moral stupidity, his assumption that he is called on to defend his family's and more particularly his sister's honour, may be presented in comic mode, but the threat they carry feels disturbingly real and would surely have done so to the novel's first readers in 1926. Being forced to take sides is part of a political strategy by means of which Hamilton requires those readers to consider the deep divisions of the society they live in, with tanks sent out against strikers, and thousands of "specials" mobilised to put down "low stuff". To repeat, Craven House isn't England but *Craven House* requires its readers to consider what living in England entails. It should be noted that three years later, in his play, *Rope,* Hamilton similarly confronts his audience with two murderers whose guilt is known only to themselves and the audience. The audience is therefore necessarily implicated in guilty knowledge. And as in *Craven House* Hamilton took over the seemingly safe form of the domestic novel and exploited its comic possibilities so as to subvert its reassuring and known qualities, so in *Rope* he confines the action to a box-set and a single room and subverts the "safe" conventions he inherits from numerous English playwrights of the pre-war period. These conventions were of course still being unadventurously adhered to in the post-war years, as endless west-end comedies and whodunnits showed. Having an actress sister, and having himself worked as an adolescent in theatre[15], Hamilton was in a good position to criticise its inanities, and he did so in his third novel, *Twopence Coloured* (1928)[16], in which he has an actress reflect that the plays she acts in comprise "a world in which Comedy was either the pat utterance of humorous quips, or a series of creaking Situations in which somebody discovered somebody else doing something he shouldn't and watched him toying ineffectually to hide it up".

It might be thought that Mrs Spicer's discovery of Mr Spicer's visits to prostitutes is nothing if not a "creaking Situation". Going through his pockets one day she comes upon a letter in which the writer requests Mr Spicer to provide her with a regular income, "as a lady cannot manage to subcist on a little preasent now and again when she is a lady and not like others". (Bk 2. Ch 8. ii.) But in

*Craven House* this isn't milked for easy laughs. Certainly, Mr Spicer is ridiculous. He's terrified of nudity. When he undresses for bed in his wife's presence he "removes his shirt and vest, lays his night-shirt carefully over the bed, dives, and emerges with a swimmer's action, and having shaken the thing well down, performs the ensuing phrases of disrobement quietly under its flowing and voluminous cover – the trousers and socks thus shed not appearing until he steps away". To guard against the chills of the night he wears on his head "a certain blue Cricket Cap". But then this self-righteous, prudish to the point of prurient, overgrown schoolboy is, we have to recognise, the natural ally of Jock Nixon: he is with the Fascists. As was remarked in Chapter 4, radicals identified sexual freedom and uninhibited enjoyment of sexuality, as an expression of radical energy. Hamilton always uses comedy for serious purposes.

Peter Widdowson is undoubtedly right in remarking that "*Craven House* is in no sense a descriptive novel, and in the end it is not really concerned with the *mores* of the middle class in themselves. It is what they mean, rather than what they are, which interests [Hamilton], and they are .... perceived as symptomatic, as metaphors of social dissolution".[17] This is very well said, although Widdowson might have added that in the novel social dissolution is tracked from pre-war to post-war England. Like *Lolly Willowes*, *Craven House* is about key aspects of English society altered through time, even if there are those like Mr Spicer (or Galsworthy), who might not wish to acknowledge the actuality of such alteration.

As for the novel's ending, we may feel that Master Wildman and Elsie's meeting at the empty house and their mutual declaration of love comes rather too pat. And we may also reflect that the walk-on parts for the working-class removal men are there simply to make a point about the men's kindness and warm-hearted generosity towards the young lovers. But it has at least to be said that Hamilton's refusal to treat the men as opportunity for reductive humour – the working class as comic turn – is a welcome alternative to Galsworthy's treatment of them in *Swan Song*, where they are either demonologised as the enemy within or dismissed as of absolutely no importance. They simply aren't "England". Lawrence apart, *Craven House* is one of the first post-war novels, if not the first, to direct the focus of its concern away from an exclusive concentration on aristocratic or middle-class characters and issues.

In this sense Isherwood's first novel, *All The Conspirators*, may seem a more reactionary work. Its protagonist, Philip Lindsay, doesn't at all like involvement with other people. He resents having to work in an office. "He disliked the aroma of the girls' increased sexual vitality, their whispered holiday schemes, giggled anecdotes and the snapshots which they passed around for their friends' inspection .... He made stupid mistakes in his work and was rude to other young men. They were accustomed to his petulance and tolerant of it. He had been discussed and dismissed long ago as a queer chap."[18] This is perhaps best read as a coded declaration of Philip's homosexuality, although it isn't at all clear how far Philip can have known about the men's discussions. Nor does Isherwood always resolve the question of whether we are supposed to trust Philip's account or that of some narrator standing at guard. The problem arises in the very next paragraph. After a day at the office, Philip climbs on to a homeward bound 'bus.

> It was nearly full. He had to sit next to a woman with a dirty baby. The woman had been shopping. Her parcels had dark stains of oozing greasy substances. The baby had a sore on the corner of its mouth. His fellow passengers were greasy and tired. Philip withdrew his leg as far as possible and sighed. The Thames gull, poised in serene evening, regarded swarming thoroughfares, the scarlet crashing piece of mechanism on which he rode. Along. Penny tumbling through his worn grooves; an automatic slot machine. In silver wrappings, the chocolate, familiar day-dream, with a portrait in four colours: Percy Philip Bysshe. *(Ch. 9)*

Philip's withdrawal of his leg is accompanied by his withdrawal into his imagination. The Joycean stream-of-consciousness becomes the sign not only of this but of Philip's essentially aesthetic point of view, one presumably half-mocked in his self-identification with the beautiful ineffectual angel, Shelley. In a "Foreword" to the republished edition of the novel in 1957 Isherwood said that "the echoes of James Joyce annoy me, because they are merely echoes. I find this repeated use of the Joycean thought-stream technique jarringly out of style. Its self-consciously grim, sardonically detached tone doesn't suit any of these characters".[19] This is odd, because Isherwood is here describing Philip in terms which for all their severity are entirely accurate. It may be that he was unaware of the degree to which his would-be writer appears detached from the social world he inhabits; in which case the confusion can be traced to the narrator's readiness to take his protagonist's part.

For what is throughout consistent is the dislike, amounting to detestation, of family circumstance, and how that can be linked to the war. At one point Philip's mother, wanting to keep him away from Alan Chalmers, whom she regards as a bad influence because Chalmers plainly scorns the values by which she lives, says to her daughter that she hopes Joan will be able to lead Philip's thoughts "'away from all this discontent and misery. I suppose it's the effect War's had. Your father was such an exceptionally happy man ..'" To which Joan replies, "'But, Mummie, you talk all the time as though Phil hadn't anything definite to complain of, or anything that he wants to do'". Philip in fact wants to be a writer and/or artist. But he also wants independence of his family, above all of his mother and her domineering ways. This is Forster territory, the territory, too, of Ivy Compton-Burnett. But Isherwood's novel is given a keener cutting edge because of the inference we draw that Philip's family clings to values associated with those that carried England into war and that they see no reason to suspect their own culpability. "Your father was such an exceptionally happy man."

In *Lions and Shadows* Isherwood recalls the horror with which he had to listen to an ex-soldier recount his wartime experiences. "Lester's world had exploded, thirteen years ago. And now Lester had no world. With his puzzled air of arrested boyishness, he belonged for ever, like an unhappy Peter Pan, to the nightmare Never-Never-Land of the War. He had no business to be here, alive, in post-war England. His place was elsewhere, with the dead."[20] Just how deeply Isherwood disliked the ethos to which "Lester" clings emerges in his story, "The World War", which he apparently wrote in the spring of 1927, after he had finished his novel. This hilarious send-up of military heroism was never published in Isherwood's lifetime, in all probability because of its explicit, often bawdy homosexuality. There is, for example, the tale, told by a chaplain, of how his young lover gave his life for country: acts of "heroic venery" saw off the enemy's Admiral of the Fleet, the War Minister, the Air Marshal, the Chief of Intelligence, the Minister of Munitions, the Imperial Commissar. "All [lay] upon their stomachs. All dead."

The story also includes a character called Reynard Moxon, who assumes control of the country when war is declared. Moxon tells the assembled troops:

'I have been appointed supreme generalissimo of all forces – land, sea, and air. I am vested with all rights: civil, military and religious. I am Prime Minister, Surgeon-in-Chief, Viceregent, President of the Academy of all arts and sciences, Supervisor of Customs and Sanitation, Censor, Surveyor-in-Extraordinary and Grand Patriarch. It is my intention to wage this war to the last drop of your blood. There will be no retreat, no capitulation, no surrender. There will be no prisoners or wounded. There will be no relaxation of any kind. You may go.

Moxon himself advances onto the battle-field in a tank which "contained two arm-chairs, a sofa, a dumb-waiter, a gramophone and a library of the hundred best authors". But he later turns out to be commanding enemy troops from an airship, and at the story's end he sails above the rectory lawn from where the narrator looks up at him and realises that he himself is about to die.[21]

In her introduction to *The Mortmere Stories*, which includes "The World War", Katherine Bucknell remarks that as a schoolboy at Repton Isherwood was deeply influenced by Edward Upward, whom he fictionalised as "Chalmers", and that "he played the Mortmere game to its extreme, [acting] himself into a real rebellion, and [wresting] his future away from conventional institutional life". This is very much the rebellion of Philip Lindsay. It is also, of course, the rebellion implied by the anarchic comedy of Isherwood's Mortmere Stories, which Bucknell sees as unleashing the "boyish hysteria described by Auden in his Berlin journal as the 'Prep School Atmosphere' – which was later put to use by Auden in *The Orators* and by Auden and Isherwood in *The Dog Beneath the Skin*".[22] But the especial quality of Isherwood's early fiction is surely most apparent in Auden's charade, *Paid on Both Sides*? To see why, you have only to compare Moxon's speech with the following, from Auden's charade:

> Yes. I know we have and are making terrific sacrifices, but we cannot give in. We can not betray the dead. As we pass their graves can we be deaf to the simple eloquence of their inscriptions, those who in the glory of their early manhood gave up their lives for us? No, we must fight to the finish.[23]

The words are uttered by John Nower, whose mill-owning family is at war with a rival family, the Shaws. The two "sides" are, John Fuller suggests, not merely two families but a "society" which

231

becomes "an allegory also of an individual psyche, sick and irrevocably divided".[24] Both Isherwood and Auden delight in parodying the language of stiff-upper-lip militarism, whether delivered on the parade ground or from the headmaster's dais or church or chapel pulpit. Here, then, it will help to refer to a passage from *Lions and Shadows* in which "Weston" [ie Auden] and Isherwood discuss Norse literature, its warriors and their dark threats, "conveyed in puns and riddles and deliberate understatements". Why did they seem familiar? "They were the boys at our preparatory school." Isherwood "actually tried the experiment of writing a school story in what was a kind of hybrid language composed of saga phraseology and schoolboy slang. And soon after this, Weston produced a short verse play in which the two are so confused that it is almost impossible to say whether the characters are epic heroes or members of a school O.T.C."[25]

Auden's adroit and resourceful pastiche of the language, atmosphere and landscapes of Norse saga has an added resonance, however. In the early years of the war Herbert Asquith and others had appealed to dim memories of saga stories in their patriotic war poetry. Asquith's frequently reprinted *The Volunteer and Other Poems*, first published in 1915, has at its heart a poem called "The Western Line", which includes the following near refrain: "the floods of battle ebb and flow,/The soldiers to Valhalla go!", and which imagines dead soldiers as "Winged with the wings of Victory,/And helmeted by Thor". Auden does not try to imitate Asquith's Tennysonian cadences, although in his dystopic "Get There If You Can" he takes over trochaic octameters of "Locksley Hall", that hymn to militarism and a golden world future; instead, he sardonically mimes the terse cadences of the sagas: "There he died Nor any came/Fighters home Nor wives shall go/Smiling to bed They boast no more". But as Fuller notes, "the public school is a special kind of microcosm of the society anatomised in the play", and from his own experience Auden knew that the public school ethos, in which the inculcation of warrior-like resistance to soft pleasures – of "swimmers into cleanness leaping" in Brooke's formulation – deeply affected, even conditioned, those many thousands who in August 1914 eagerly went to war.

*Paid on Both Sides* can be read as an anti-war text. Yet to say this does not get us very far. It is also about ways of being English. The charade was written in Berlin in 1928. As all biographers note, while he was in Berlin Auden met John Layard and through him

became interested in Homer Lane's theory of the psychosomatic nature of illness. We suffer when we act in disobedience to our own inner nature. Isherwood had gone to Berlin for boys. Auden, too, was homosexual. In England homosexuality was a criminal offence. And England, as Auden would have his headmaster say in *The Orators*, is "this country of ours where nobody is well". *The Orators* was written in 1931. Two years earlier, not long after completing *Paid on Both Sides*, Auden wrote a poem to which he subsequently gave the title, "A Free One", although when it appeared in *Poems, 1930*, it simply bore a number. Auden here characterises a typical English hero, apparently in control of his insouciant manner, his calm, poised, untroubled certainty, "His dextrous handling of a wrap as he/Steps after into cars, the beggars envy".
And yet this hero is

> not that returning conqueror,
> Nor ever the poles' circumnavigator.
>
> But poised between shocking falls, on razor-edge
> Has taught himself this balancing subterfuge
> Of the accosting profile, the erect carriage.

"The shocking falls" must refer to fears that the "free one's" inner self will be exposed. Far from being free, he is a prisoner of the image he has created: of the acceptable hero, much as T.E. Lawrence for instance was. I have no reason to suppose that Auden had Lawrence in mind here; but Lawrence is a good example of the English hero required to keep out of sight his sexual preferences. Like others, he cannot allow himself to travel "by daylight on from house to house/The longest way to the intrinsic peace,/With love's fidelity and with love's weakness". The poem's closing lines evoke an aching desire for sexual candour: for a "daylight" acceptance of promiscuity and rejection of the steely, puritanical norm of sexual monogamy. "The song, the varied action of the blood/Would drown the warning from the iron wood,/Would cancel the inertia of the buried." These lines, which form the poem's penultimate stanza, testify to the same imaginative desire for the release of anarchic energy as motivate Auden to introduce the Spy in *Paid on Both Sides*. The Spy features as the Accused in a Trial Scene at the end of which he is shot. During his Trial he repeatedly groans, and Auden directs that his cries should be "produced by jazz instruments at the back of the stage". The spy is to be identified with the forces of sexual pleasure, of abandonment of moral propriety, with which we have seen jazz was so regularly identified at the time, and because of which it was as regularly accused of being "uncivilized", of the "jungle".

The Spy can, then, be interpreted as John's Id or pleasure principle, whom John shoots in order to keep faith with his self-imposed desire to "fight to the finish". For in the Trial Scene another character appears. A stage direction reads *"The Man-Woman appears as a prisoner of war behind barbed wire, in the snow"*. And at the end of the Man-Woman's speech the Spy groans, because the speech reveals truths about the repression of sexual love which John finds unbearable. "I lay with you; you made that an excuse/For playing with yourself, but homesick because/Your mother told you that's what flowers did,/And thought you lived since you were bored, not dead,/And could not stop." The Man-Woman articulates varieties of sexual failure or frustration, and crucially hints at the role of the mother in warping and preventing the development of guilt-free sexuality. At the end of the speech John cries out "I can't bear it", and shoots the Spy. The shooting dramatises a kind of psychic suicide. Fuller is surely right to suggest that the Man-Woman's final words, that "you, if you come,/Will not enjoy yourself, for where I am/All talking is forbidden" look towards D.H. Lawrence's loathing of "sex in the head". Where the Man-Woman is, talking is forbidden.[26]

John Nower is, then, an English hero. He is self-denying, emotionally under-developed (Forster's influence here should be noted), and sexually repressed. And although he tries to break out of this mould, this frozen poise, by proposing marriage to Anne Shaw, he is denied the chance to heal the feud between the two sides. Anne's mother instructs her son to kill John. The Chorus comments "His mother and her mother won". John's mother is, indeed, as determined to continue the feud as is Mrs Shaw. At the charade's opening she sings an anti-lullaby over the infant John's cradle. Its last stanza runs:

> Unforgetting is not today's forgetting
> For yesterday, not bedrid scorning,
> But a new begetting
> An unforgiving morning.

This is speech from the iron wood. Joan voices an adamant resolve to maintain the feud, to keep things as they have been.

This, too, is about England. But at this point the psychological blends into the social. Joan Nower's rigid stance has to be read both as a form of matriarchal tyranny and as a political resolve to maintain the status quo. Lawrence had had much to say about this tyranny, both in *Sons and Lovers* and his *Fantasia of the Unconscious*, and my own reading of the literature of the period 1914-1930 convinces me that there is within it a discoverable streak of male paranoia about the role of women in forcing men to war and self-destruction. Men were required to act out the part of heroes that as good as guaranteed their deaths. Even more than fathers, mothers carried the blame for urging their sons to become warriors. It is to be expected that fathers should wish to produce warrior sons. For those too young to have fought, mothers were despised or detested as class warriors: upholders of the system which was irredeemably tainted by war guilt. Katherine Bucknall notes that from childhood Edward Upward "hated his mother's social snobbery, and his impulse to rebel was perhaps born out of and certainly intensified by his wish to defy her." As for Isherwood's mother, although "handsome, dignified, and capable of great charm ... her son felt she was obsessed by class distinctions and propriety; moreover, her intellectual aspirations were narrow and traditional, despite her genuine intelligence. As the surviving figure of authority in his family, she represented everything against which, like Upward, he wished to rebel".[27]

It is significant that at the beginning of *Paid on Both Sides* we should be told that John's father was ambushed and killed while he had gone out to Colefangs, "would speak with Layard". The father was in league with the Spy, or at all events with forces that stand for Love as opposed to Hate. The mother, by contrast, is a hate figure, as she is in *All the Conspirators*. (And as she is in *Blindness*.) This may seem deeply anti-woman, but I think it is less that than bitterly hostile to those who uphold social propriety and class distinctions and who in the post-war years often were women. As war widows, women had to – or chose to – take on the roles previously played by their husbands. The feuding families of Auden's charade are plainly middle-class. As Monroe K. Spears suggests, Auden at this period tends to present conflict both as an internal psychomachia and as class conflict. "The middle-class .... is doomed, not only by the Marxist wave of the future but also by its own subconscious death-wish (in conflict with its conscious resistance) and evolutionary urge towards its own extinction."[28]

By the Marxist wave of the future I assume Spears to mean a coming revolution. That Auden believed in the redemptive possibilities of "new styles of architecture, a change of heart", is plain; it is also clear that he regarded social change as inseparable from a change in consciousness. If commentators have tended to emphasise the latter rather more than the former this is no doubt because they feel the need to guard Auden against accusations of rash optimism and because they themselves write as troubled liberals, or as Cold War warriors. Hence, Spears' remark that "the terms of the conflict are much too nebulous to fit the Marxist analysis", and hence Fuller's assertion that the revolution Auden desired is "that according to Blake, Baudelaire or Homer Lane, not according to Marx, whose insistence on its proletarian character is effectively denied both by Auden's messianic mythologising and (in the third ode [of *The Orators*]) by his direct Skiltonic sneers at the working class".[29] But this is to forget the moment in *Paid on Both Sides* where John says

> Sometime sharers of the same house
> We know not the builder nor the name of his son.
> Now cannot mean to them; boy's voice among dishonoured
> portraits
> To dockside barmaid speaking
> Sorry through wires, pretended speech.

He is here talking to the spy and I assume by "the same house" he means either the womb or society at large. But class makes for divisions that deny the possibility of real communion and community. The middle-class boy has no way of speaking naturally to the dockside barmaid. His words are a pretence at communication, as distant and liable to distortion as speech heard over telephone wires. Even to try to speak to the barmaid is to "dishonour" his class and its traditions.

Yet Auden had chosen such dishonour when, unlike the vast majority of his class and his generation, he had chosen to work for the strikers in May, 1926. And *Paid on Both Sides* has to be understood as at least as much concerned with the social as with the psychological. I would even suggest that part of the inspiration for this dense, difficult work of genius comes from Rickword's "The Happy New Year". This is admittedly suppositious, but it is worth noting that Auden's description of his Free One as "stepping after into cars", is stikingly anticipated in Rickword's "Theme for the Pseudo-Faustus", the last poem of *Invocations to Angels*. There, Rickword speaks of women "wrapped against winter stepping into cars". It is very likely that Auden had read Rickword's volume. If so, Rickword's decision to use the traditional device of a masque with chorus may well have prompted Auden's decision to mingle charade and mummer's play as well as to use a chorus for his own work. This is not to suggest that Auden is in any way dependent on Rickword, still less that "The Happy New Year" is at the level of achievement of *Paid on Both Sides*. It is, however, to suggest that we do Auden less than justice if we fail to recognise that his work is partly prompted by a deep disquiet about English society in the years following the general strike. It is also to suggest that his charade's insistent modernism, its fragmented narratives, abrupt switches of style, sometimes obscure allusiveness, is in diametric opposition to those for whom art's "traditional" virtues were at one with the virtues of the social status quo. But then *Paid on Both Sides* is recognisably the work of a writer who a year earlier had said that "no universalised system – political, religious, or metaphysical – has been bequeathed to us".[30] In which case it becomes necessary to oppose those who try to foist such a system onto "us", to choose, in other words, to take the other side. And although I agree with Samuel Hynes that the charade's end "is a dark reminder of the power of the enemy, of the past", I cannot then agree that *Paid on Both Sides* "is not itself a political work".[31] That Auden's charade should so definitely and I would say defiantly identify the enemy in terms of certain kinds of Englishness – class snobbishness, sexual repression, public-school ethos, militarism, the tall, unwounded heroes – is nothing if not political.

### III

Auden's dockside barmaid is rather like Hamilton's removal men: a not very convincing gesture toward's working-class "vitality" or "warmth" or "uninhibited sexuality" – or whatever uninspected phrase is used to paper over the clichés on which previous generations of middle-class writers had typically relied. But inadequate though such gestures are, they hint at something which becomes increasingly noticeable in the later years of the 1920s, and that is a desire to write about working-class circumstance or to unearth working-class writers themselves. Hence, as we have seen, the new radical theatre groups. Hence, too, the interest that begins to show and be shown in writers such as Harold Heslop, whose first novel had been completed in 1924, when it was first turned down by

Herbert Jenkins Ltd and then published in Russia the following year. There, it sold half a million copies, and news of its success filtered slowly back England. Heslop's next novel, *The Gate of a Strange Field*, was not published until 1932, although it was written in the aftermath of the General Strike and took its title, so Heslop recalled, from H.G. Wells's novel, *Meanwhile*. Heslop was reading *Meanwhile* at the time he was working on his own novel and "came across the sentence in which [Wells] catechised the General Council of the Trades Union Congress, as being 'like sheep at the gate of a strange field".[32] Andy Croft deals sympathetically with Heslop's "semi-autobiographical story of adolescence and politics in the Durham coalfield, culminating in the 1926 lock-out" in his *Red Letter Days: British fiction in the 1930s,* and as the novel was not published until 1932 I do not propose to discuss it here.[33] I will however note that it is one of the first of what became called "proletarian" novels. It is entirely concerned with a working-class community. Proletarian novels, which are usually as formally unadventurous as their politics are drably defeatist, become a notable feature of writing in the 1930s and this has led unwary commentators to imagine that as the calendar flipped over for the start of a new decade so fiction, or the material for fiction, took an entirely new turn. But Heslop wrote *The Gate of a Strange Field* in the 1920s. More particularly, he wrote it as a way of trying to understand and account for the strike's disastrous outcome.

A similar motive prompted Ellen Wilkinson to produce *Clash*. This first novel, published in 1929, covers the days immediately before the calling of the strike, then the days of the strike; and it ends with the strike's collapse and aftermath. *Clash* is far more interesting than Heslop's novel. In the first place it is very astute about the politics of the moment – which effectively means about taking sides. Heslop's focus on his coalfield community happens to produce a fatalistic reading which engenders a feeling that nothing is to be done. He doesn't exploit the possibilities that lie within his novel's good title. *Clash,* on the other hand, does. There is an especially telling moment near the novel's end, after the strike has collapsed, when Gerry Blain, a middle-class socialist, is talking to the novel's protagonist, Joan Craig. He tells her that he thinks she's in danger of being seduced into liking the wrong people. He has in mind a group of London "arty" folk, by whose attention Joan is clearly flattered. She is, after all, a working-class girl who has "made good" at university, and Wilkinson ably sketches in the real attractions of the group Blain has in his sights: they are witty, bohemian, outrageously indifferent to prudential taste. They are, if not the Bright Young Things, at all events among those who might be thought to have kicked over the traces and who live by a more generous openness to the possibilities of life than their elders. Stung by his criticism, Joan tells Blain that "they were some of the nicest people I've ever met. They were awfully decent about the miners, and were as pleased as anything when I showed up that nonsense .... about the fifteen-pounds-a-week miner". (She is referring to a right-wing character in the novel who maintains that miners are secretly milking the owners.) Blain replies:

> They don't care enough about miners – at least, when they are not dangerous – not to be perfectly charming to anyone who cares enough to defend them. But you think what that crowd did during the General Strike .... We saw them with bared teeth all right when their class-privileges were in danger. It's not people like that uncouth fool of a mine manager ... who are dangerous to the workers. They carry their own antidote. Decent people like that vicar's wife will help the workers to do 'em in. But it's these kindly wealthy people who play the devil with people like you, Joan. They are so reasonable and they can be so kind. It seems a shame to fight them, and after a while you'd find yourself not wanting to put things so strongly – it might hurt your new friends' feelings.[34]

This is a crucial speech, not because Blain is necessarily right in all he says, but because he focuses Joan's need to choose between commitment to politics and the life of alluring, cultured friendship – which also means in her case choosing between a life of public activity and a life of domesticity. Blain is one of the two men in her life. The other is a man to whom she is sexually attracted, who plays at radical politics, and who belongs to the London set Blain has anathematised. (So, yes, jealousy plays its part in Blain's denunciation.) Tony Dacre wants Joan to be his wife. He also wants her to give up politics.

Those politics are very close to Ellen Wilkinson's own. Not that Joan is an MP, as Wilkinson was, and had been since 1923. But she is an organizer at "the Yorkshire offices of the National Industrial Union of Labour" (p 7) and this requires her both to travel widely about the north as well as down to London, and to speak on public platforms. Moreover, novelist and heroine share a working-class background and a university education, and Joan's attraction to the London set feels plausibly to emerge out of the inevitable social tensions that arise when a working-class person moves out from the containments of birth and upbringing – containments which press with particular force when the person in question is a woman. The novel's use of London is therefore astutely deployed to give a sense of the alluring freedoms the city offers.

*Clash* is about North and South. It is also about middle-class freedoms and working-class constraints, about an England which contains but perhaps cannot reconcile such differences. The attractions of London seem real enough, but what can be said for the drab ugliness of the industrial north? At one point, when Joan is with her London friends, "Through the chatter of the crowded restaurant she seemed to see England – the great steel towns of the north, the mining villages she knew so well, the little homes in which she had stayed during her organizing tours. Decent men and women working far too hard, crowded together in uncomfortable homes. Lack of obvious things like baths and hot water, lack of comforts, and, for at least five years, lack of food and warm clothes". (pp. 50-1)

In its demonstrative, affectionately intimate mode of address, this is a moment of the utmost importance. Quite suddenly England is NOT London, nor middle-class affluence; nor is it the big men of commerce and politics whose enemies are – well, are all those who between them had threatened the England of *Swan Song* and against whom war, it will be recalled, had necessarily to be waged. It now appears that Galsworthy's enemies of England *are* England. The moment has an especial eloquence because it comes just after the announcement of the strike when Joan hears a union leader say "'Those who want war must take the responsibility'". To which another man replies "'We are in for it now. It's worth having come through that war for. I've often wondered lately why I did. We'll show the beggars .... fighting their war, and then our men getting treated like dogs'". (pp. 47-8) The enemies of England from this perspective are those for whom "we" fought "their war". This catches up the identical anger at betrayal of class by class which I have already noted as a property of some of Gurney's post-war poetry.

But Wilkinson does not sentimentalise the England with which Joan identifies. True, Gerry enthuses about the efficiency of the strike committees across the nation. "'It just shows,'" he says, "'what a lot of organizing ability is running to waste among the workers of this one-eyed country, where a man is called a 'hand' and not allowed to think. Crewe and Coventry, and scores of the towns I've visited, are being run by sheer soviets. The permit business is marvellous. Just to see the big employers of the town coming cap in hand for permits to move cargo does one's heart good."' These are not the words of uplifting fiction. As I mentioned in Chapter 5, across the country the strike was in fact extraordinarily well organized. The problem was at the centre, with the general council of the T.U.C. And both Joan and Gerry fear for what will happen to the strikers should the strike fail.

It is then important to note that Wilkinson confronts her 1929 readers with the consequences of the strike's failure. Or rather, she shows them what the mining villages are like, the poverty, unemployment, the terrible hardships. *Clash* inevitably asks those readers not merely Leonard Woolf's question "whose side were you on", but "whose side *are* you on". Hence the significance of the following scene. The strike is now over and Joan is in the north where she is asked to help out on a Woman's Committee begun by the Labour Party.

> Joan's services were welcomed by the efficient secretary of the Relief Committee and she was sent to take charge of their relief work in a small neglected mining area some miles south of Shireport. Joan was accustomed to poverty, but she had never seen such sheer ugliness as in these little mining towns. Coal dust and the mud of the mines saturated the whole place. The coal-pit was the only thing in each village that mattered, the only part of life on which capital and care and brains were expended. Human beings were usually fed into its mouth at eight-hourly intervals, and just as regularly coughed up again. Now the wheels of the winding cage were silent, but the domination of the pit remained. On the refuse-heaps men, women, and children grubbed like maggots trying to find precious bits of coal to sell for bread ....
>
> The local authority was dominated by the colliery manager. He was a powerful man, strongly built, stern of temper. He would hear nothing of feeding the children in the schools. The pit was open, he said, work was waiting for their fathers. If they refused work then they were not destitute and the law gave the Guardians no power to relieve them. *(pp. 235-6)*.

The manager is not demonologised. Wilkinson refuses to turn him into a caricature. These are real human beings being locked into a war – and which side are *you* on?

There is a further point. The "sheer ugliness" which Joan encounters in these small mining towns had also very recently attracted Lawrence's attention. In a famous passage of *Lady Chatterley's Lover* Connie is chauffeur-driven through a colliery village.

> The car ploughed uphill through the long squalid straggle of Tevershall, the blackened brick dwellings, the black slate roofs, glistening their sharp edges, the mud black with coal-dust, the pavements wet and black. It was as if dismalness had soaked through everything. The utter negation of natural beauty, the utter negation of the gladness of life, the utter absence of the instinct for shapely beauty which every beast and bird has, the utter death of the intuitive human faculty was appalling. The stacks of soap in the grocers' shops, the rhubarb and lemons in the greengrocers! The awful hats in the milliners' all went by ugly, ugly, ugly ..... Standard Five girls were having a singing lesson .... It was like nothing on earth and it was called singing. Connie sat and listened with her heart in her boots ..... What could possibly become of such a people, a people in whom the living intuitive faculty was dead as nails .....

Leavis used to quote this as an example of Lawrence's supreme genius. It provided, so he said, conclusive evidence of Lawrence's ability to understand what was wrong with England, its spiritual, living degradation. Leavis either did not know or conveniently forgot to mention that in the first, greatly superior version of the novel, Connie has no sooner entertained these thoughts than she is obliged to recall that Tevershall is where her lover – Parkin in that version – comes from. In other words, her reaction to the undoubted ugliness of the place is that of the outsider; and her perhaps understandable leap to the conclusion that anyone who lives among such ugliness is as good as dead is also that of the outsider.[35] In *Clash,* Joan has no sooner registered the ugliness of the places where she has chosen to work than she is taking part in discussions with their inhabitants about the future of the unions. No evidence of death here and especially not among the "responsible women" with whom she discusses the "harassing difficulties of men and women ... without a penny of margin for lunches, fares and postage stamps". (p. 239)

Joan is inevitably on the side of these women. She chooses to identify with their England, their class and, of course, their gender. This last and most significant choice is well discussed by Maroula Joannou in her essay "Reclaiming the Romance: Ellen Wilkinson's *Clash* and the Cultural Legacy of Socialist-Feminism". Joannou quotes the moment where Joan, deep in discussion with her new women friends, suddenly thinks she "badly wanted to bring Anthony Dacre into some of the villages and say to him, 'You say I can't be your wife and lover and do my job. Look at the work these women have to do'". (p. 239) Joannou comments:

> Seeking to end the private world of feeling and the public world of work, [Joan] chooses independence within marriage instead of romantic love. Her marriage to Gerry will be one of equals, with an understanding that her work must come first: "The universe wouldn't be expected to stand still, as at some miracle, to allow Gerry Blain's baby to be born. It's mother would probably be correcting proofs or planning speeches to the minute of its arrival." *(p. 300)*[36]

## IV

Joan's choice is not available to Lily, the main woman protagonist of Henry Green's *Living,* which like *Clash* was first published in 1929. But in many other respects Green's novel is also about taking and choosing sides. Although it has nothing to say about the strike, I believe that it could only have been written after it. I must not however give the impression that *Living* is in any sense diagrammatic or dependent on obvious manoeuvrings of opposites into position. It is a dramatic novel in the sense that it makes extraordinary use of dialogue, although not of "big" scenes. Like Hamilton, Green loved listening in on other people's talk. Talk was what prompted his imagination. So much so, that it seems his deafness in late-middle age brought an end to his career as a novelist. I have a very great regard for Green and for *Living* in particular. Even the novel's failings are part of its ambitious attempt to find ways of writing that will justify Green's choice of subject matter. *Living* is for the most part concerned with the lives of factory workers in Birmingham and Green chooses to present these lives very largely through dialogue. This can of course leave him dangerously open to the charge of mere ventriloquism. Still worse, ventriloquism can easily modulate into parody or caricature, as it does in the pub scene in *The Waste Land.* Worst of all, it may betray a deadly combination of sentimentality and ignorance on the part of its middle-class author.

Green on the whole avoids these dangers. One reason for this is his obvious relish for other people's conversations. After Oxford he began working life in the Birmingham factory – H. Pontifex and Sons it was called – of which he was eventually to become a managing director. He had, then, plenty of opportunity to overhear the men talking, and he made good use of it. As here, for example, where two factory workers discuss why one of them had refused to come to the aid of a foreman who had slipped over:

> 'Elp 'im, I'd be dead before. Look what 'e's done to others, what 'e's said along 'o their private lives. Give 'im a hand, might as well 'elp the devil to shovel coals.'
> 'Ah. Well so long, Joe.'
> 'Elp that carcase. It was as much as I could do not to wipe me boots on 'is lying mouth. I'll be ..... before I 'elp 'is kind.'[37]

Green's ability to transcribe the speech of the factory workers is remarkable for its phonic accuracy as much as for their actual words. In the moment just quoted, for example, he hears among all the fallen aspirates the one that's retained on "hand", and you know it's right. "'Give 'im a 'and,'" might look convincing, but it couldn't be said.

The novel is threaded through with this kind of attentiveness, and were that to be its chief claim on our attention it would be much. But Green's Joycean delight in the day-to-day eloquence of working-class speech serves a further purpose, one that is also Joycean. It takes away authority from those who profess to speak with and for authority. In *Living* there are people – especially those who own the factory – who believe authority to be on their side. For them, authority is power. But the novel undermines their belief, not only by showing how little they understand of the men and women whose lives they wish to control, but by giving those same men and women their own voices, as a result of which we are allowed access to very different versions of their lives, *their* versions. To be sure, there is always the likelihood, perhaps even certainty, that in any novel dialogue frees its users from an author's intentions, his authority. But that authority can be re-imposed through narrative structure. Joyce's novel had taken away such authority, not only by its implied circularity, but by its use of Dublin in order both to de-centre the narrative, to allow different, seemingly random views of people together, meeting, parting, re-joining in different configurations, and also to make possible the many voices of its citizens. The radicalism of *Ulysses* is a world away from *Swan Song* where, it will be remembered, strikers are not allowed to speak.

244

*Living* owes a very considerable debt to *Ulysses,* although not one that puts Green in hock to Joyce. There are some superficial borrowings – as for example, the run of mock-epic similes brought into play when the novel deals with Hannah Glossop, the bored, pitiable London socialite who has been marked out for marriage to the factory-owner's son, young Mr Dupret (see pp. 303 and 316); and Molly Bloom's soliloquy is unmissably echoed in Lily Gates' recall of how when Jim had looked at her "dafty with his eyes yes, she had said, yes". (p. 233) More important are the endless crossings and interweavings of dialogue in the factory itself and, perhaps most importantly of all, Green's recognition of the "Wandering Rocks" as a truly radical break-through for fiction, and his readiness to adapt it to the purpose of his own novel. Green is in no sense helplessly dependent on Joyce's device of using the afternoon streets to show how the lives of city people casually intersect as well as being carried on in frequent and inevitable ignorance of each other (and who then dare claim the authority to "know" or place these lives); but there can be no doubt that Joyce's example gave him what he needed.

I shall return to this, but before doing so I would like to tip in the name of Forster to this discussion. I do so, not to suggest that Green's novel owes anything to Forster's fictional methods, though it may, but to note that in *A Passage to India* Forster's decision to follow Indians into their own houses and to set scenes where they talk among themselves valuably unsettles the authority of his white spokesmen and women. The whites pronounce on the Indians. They *know.* And then we see and hear the Indians on whom they have pronounced and the knowledge of Ronnie Heaslop and of Mr and Mrs Burton becomes suspect, is exposed as prejudice, ignorance, stupidity. In recent years Forster has been taken to task for allowing too much authority to rest on the words of Fielding, his white liberal, and on his own interpolated narrative voice. Even the novel's narrative procedure has been held to account as in some ways intended to authenticate or privilege Forster's liberalism. No doubt these adverse criticisms carry weight. But they should not be allowed to obscure Forster's achievement. In 1924 *A Passage to India* was a liberating, radical novel; and its anti-imperialism is inseparable from Forster's ability to provide Indian voices which undercut the authority of white India.[38]

The famous "bridge-party" of Forster's novel is a cynical pretence by the white governors that through it they will be enabled to meet the Indians over whose lives they have dominion. In fact, at the party they choose to talk only to themselves. Why, after all, should they wish to meet people whose lives and characters they so confidently know? I suggest that the Indians in Forster's anti-imperialist novel are analogous to the troubling working-class men and women of Green's anti-capitalist work. There is a moment in *Living* where young Mr Dupret, up from London for the day, walks along the same Birmingham street as Lily Gates, who works in his factory.

> He thought it was not poverty you saw in this quarter, the artisan class lived here, but a kind of terrible respectability on too little money. And what was in all this, he said as he was feeling now, or in any walk of life – you were born, you went to school, you worked, you married, you worked harder, you had children, you went on working, with a good deal of trouble your children grew up, then they married. What had you before you died? Grandchildren? The satisfaction of breeding the glorious Anglo Saxon breed.
>
> He thought of how he would sit in office chairs for another forty years, gradually taking to golf at the week-ends or the cultivation of gardenias. All because of Miss Glossop.
>
> But these people, how much worse it was, he at least, he thought, had money. These people had music, of course, but second-hand music. Still they had really only marriage and growing old. Every day in the year, every year, it they were lucky they went to work all through daylight. That is, the men did. Time passed quickly for them, in a rhythm. But it was the monotony, as one had said to him.
>
> Coming to the recreation ground he went into it and made to go across. At the gate he passed Lily and did not notice her, she was so like the others. Here, because it was mid-morning, some mothers had brought out their children too young still to walk ... he shuddered, a sense of foreboding gathered in him. What will they grow up to he thought in mind – they'll work, they'll marry, they'll work harder, have children and go on working, they'll die. He shuddered. Then he forgot all about them and thought about himself.
>
> But Lily coming though the gate saw children running and those mothers and she stood watching them feeling out of it. 'I must have babies,' she said then, looking at baby in mother's arms. She was not excited when she said it. Just now she was being very practical. *(pp. 328-9)*

Lily is being practical because, like Ellen at the end of *The Fox*, she is expecting her young man, Jim, to emigrate with her to Canada. As it happens, their plans are thwarted. But the ending of Green's novel, though sombre, is not defeatist. The future must be made here, not elsewhere. And Lily's "practical" wish to have children must be read as an instinctive desire to help make the future. For all the hardships she has to endure, she has a far more positive outlook than Dupret, whose "authoritative" reflections on the working-class – his workers – is shown to be a reflection of his own ennui. He doesn't even recognise Lily, she is simply "like the others". The Joycean device of having the two pass each other in the city is made good here: Dupret's "knowledge" is thrown back on himself. Even his belief that "these people had music, of course, but second-hand music" – shades of those denunciations of popular culture, of jazz in particular – even this we know to be false. Green has deftly prepared for the moment. For earlier in the novel "one morning in iron foundry, Arthur Jones began singing". (In passing, I should note that Green, like early Auden, often does without the definite article, a gimmick that may have come to both of them from their Oxford days and the discovery – could it be in Green's case also? – of the sagas.) Jones is Welsh. "When he came to end of a song or something in his work kept him from singing, men would call out to him with names of English songs but he would not sing these." Now though, he continues to sing. "Still Arthur sang and it might be months before he sang again. And no one else sang that day, but all listened to his singing. That night son had been born to him." (pp 265-6)

From this welcoming of new life we switch immediately to old Mr Dupret, who "had fallen into a greater apathy, nor was there anything which pleased him now". (p. 266) To borrow Auden's phrase, old Mr Dupret has lapsed into a classic fatigue. He is without inner resource, energy, purpose. Like Arnold Bennett's Lord Raingo he is hollow at the core. Bought riches and love cannot help him.

> Electrical equipment was given him, many other remedies were tried, even the most strikingly beautiful nurses were found to tend him, once a well-known courtesan was hired for the night, but the old man still showed no interest and little irritation ... *(p. 266)*

Galsworthy's "Old English" is intended to be an image of noble pathos. Old Dupret is a crumbling wreck, and those with whom he is associated are as purposeless as he is. Green's radical awareness of the inanition of those gathered round Dupret extends to Hannah Glossop. She too is dying of boredom.

247

She cried all weekend, and she got quite weak. Doctor became quite worried about her. At last he told her mother was nothing physical the matter with her he was sure. What really was wanted he said was for something to do to be found for her, some work for her to do he said.

Her mother said work? What work could she do? It was true, she said, she had enjoyed enormously General Strike when she had carried plates from one hut to another all day, that was true enough, but what work could she do? Doctor said of course to be married would be the best thing for her but 'in the interim' he thought some kind of work was what she wanted, and he went away with hired chauffeur. *(p. 283)*

A little later Hannah herself reflects that her mother never lets her do anything, "when she enjoyed washing up – which she had never done but three times at picnics and the General Strike". (p. 286) Hannah is like Fleur in *Swan Song,* for whom canteen work on behalf of the strike breakers brings some much needed life into her "life". But Green's sharp irony is, it hardly needs saying, at the opposite extreme from Galsworthy's complacent underwriting of Fleur's "work".

Richard Dupret is himself nauseated by the vacuous existence of the London society in which he has been reared. Shortly before he goes to Birmingham for that day visit already alluded to – in fact what drives him there – a house party to which he had been invited takes place. The party is stuffed with the kind of people familiar to 1920s readers of Huxley's novels, of Waugh's *Decline and Fall* and, of course, Coward's *The Vortex.* "He arrived in the middle of fish course at dinner. He had warned hostess was only train he could come by, having to work late that day in London; but yet, as he passed by open door of dining room to go and dress and saw brilliance of lights there and clash and glitter of women's dresses, and heard their laughter, he had a sickening in stomach." (p. 295)

Green, however, does not allow for a simple taking of sides in *Living.* True, his largely symbolic presentation of London society is deftly and ruthlessly dismissive; but although he uses Richard Dupret as the narrative link between the dying and what might look to be the new-born, he does not indulge a sentimental view of working-class life. That life is hard, often mean-spirited, gripped by financial anxieties; Lily's "practical" desire for children lapses when she encounters the strange ugliness of Liverpool and its poverty. (She and Jim go there prior to the planned move to Canada.) "Ugly clothes, people, houses. They went along through

248

these, strangers to it, she did not recognise her own form of ugliness in it." (p. 355) Green's final comment is a mistake, although he presumably feels the need to remind his readers that we are all likely to be strangers to each other and that Lily's response to Liverpool, like Connie Chatterley's to Tevershall, is that of the outsider. But after all Lily does recognise her own form of ugliness. Afraid of this strange place, "Kids, I don't want 'm she cried in mind". (p. 354)

Yet for all its refusal to endorse a simple reading of the future as inevitably belonging to the working-class and its discoverable energies, *Living* shows where the choices lie. It is both an intervention in a specific moment and a radical account of that moment. I think it both right and natural that the novel should end with an incident in which Lily runs to shield a baby from a marauding pigeon, not because the moment releases any great charge of symbolism but because such very ordinary activity, its dailiness, suggests that living happens in the unemphatic occurrences by means of which one person takes instinctive regard for another. Such regard cannot however thrive in a society where one class claims the authority of knowledge for all: where "England" is supposed to belong to those for whom a general strike is not a strike of the generality. In such circumstances regard is therefore inevitably radical, and taking the radical side is, or ought to be, unavoidable.

******

A year after the publication of *Living*, Jonathan Cape brought out *A Brass Hat in No Man's Land*. Its author, Brigadier-General F.P. Crozier, who had fought throughout the war, provides an at times harrowing, often moving, account of the war years. He ends with the warning that "The great war was the SOS danger signal to civilisation. If we ignore that SOS and the lesson of the war, civilisation is doomed."[39] In an epilogue, set in the year 2119, Crozier imagines a ceremony held in London to celebrate the work of the League of Nations in its successful campaign to achieve world disarmament and co-operation. People had said that such a lasting peace could not be achieved because they believed "Human nature never changes." But people had changed. "They woke up to the appalling price they had to pay in blood, morality, and treasure for their victory."

1930 was also the year of *Vile Bodies*. At the end of Evelyn Waugh's novel, set in the sometime near future, its anti-hero,

249

Adam, sits "On a splintered stump in the biggest battlefield in the history of the world".[40] Waugh's novel is much concerned with a society literally speeding towards destruction. The frontispiece shows a racing car, numbered 13, tilted on two wheels, about to go smash; behind it sharp-edged flames shoot up and outward.[41] It is usual for commentators to suggest that the novel's misogynistic bitterness must be ascribed to the collapse of Waugh's marriage, which occurred with – to him – devastating suddenness while he was working on the novel. Perhaps. Yet *Vile Bodies* belongs perfectly to its moment. And this is not merely because of the Wall Street Crash, nor of the election of another minority and inept Labour Government, both of which events belong to 1929, and which find their echoes in the novel. No, Waugh senses that the society of the bright young things to which he had belonged is not so much a protest against the rottenness of post-war England as part of it. His loathing for the world of socialites, those butterflies of a day, is extremely powerful. They really *are* vile bodies. And after all, several of those who belonged to Waugh's coterie would rejoice at the coming to power of Hitler, as they had rejoiced to defeat the General Strike. After 1926, Waugh's own position, in spite of his choosing to defend Franco at the time of the Spanish War, was always more ambiguous.[42] But he and Crozier make a good stopping point for my book because they testify to concerns which had grown rather than diminished as the 1920s ran its course. The war to end wars had come to be an ever-present spectre. It not only made future war seem inescapable, as Lord Halsbury had suggested, it created or let loose a kind of mentality, a paranoia, where the enemy within had to be identified and then rooted out. "England" had to be defended at all costs, and the "England" which required defending was, of course, the place of apparent (pre-war) settled values. Hence, the General Strike as a kind of civil war. Hence, too, the need to take sides.

But those sides had been preparing to do battle, metaphorically at least, as soon as returning soldiers found that they had not been fighting for a better world but for the same old, discredited civilisation from which they had left for France. They had fought "the bosses' war". In this sense the 1920s did not end in 1929, nor even in 1930. The period which began with the armistice might more appropriately be said to have reached some sort of conclusion with the general election of 1945. But to argue this out would require another and very much longer book.

# Notes on Chapter 7

1. C. L. Mowat, *Britain Between the Wars* op. cit. p. 123.
2. These remarks appeared in *Time,* Nov 28, 1927, and are quoted by Peter Ackroyd, T.S. Eliot, op. cit. p. 167.
3. Quoted by Ackroyd, p. 166.
4. *The Apes of God*, Harmondsworth, Penguin, 1965, pp. 24-5. The novel was first published in 1930. To be fair to Lewis, I must note that he also treats Mussolini with genial contempt. Musso is "the Italianate potentate in the political Dime Novel of Modern Rome – that boy scout Caesar", p. 491.
5. There were, of course, other reasons for Graves's departure. But I do not think you can read *Goodbye To All That* and *But It Still Goes On* without recognising that between them they articulate a rasping contempt for the state of the nation and a desire to escape from its entanglements in the interest of furthering that disciplined art which Graves saw as bound up with or predicated on "essential" or archetypal myths and the pursuit of a "pure" language rinsed clean of the dirt of politics and social history. That his private need to leave England is then justified by putting the blame on England is also obvious.
6. Leonard Woolf, *An Autobiography 2: 1911-1969* Oxford, O.U.P. pp 348-9. The passage comes from the middle volume, *Downhill All The Way,* which covers the inter-war years.
7. John Galsworthy, *A Modern Comedy,* London, Penguin, 1980.
8. D.H. Lawrence, *Selected Literary Criticism*, ed. Anthony Beal, London, Mercury Books, 1956, p. 130.
9. Hobday, *Edgell Rickword,* op. cit. p. 109.
10. Douglas Jerrold, *Georgian Adventure,* The "Right" Book Club Edn. 1938. (First published by Collins, 1937) see pp. 293-298.
11. See Sean French, *Patrick Hamilton: A Life,* London, Faber, 1993 pp. 3-43 passim.
12. Arnold Rattenbury, "Literature, Lying and Sober Truth: Attitudes to the Work of Patrick Hamilton and Sylvia Townsend Warner", in *Writing and Radicalism,* ed. John Lucas, London, Longman, 1996.
13. In a TV profile of his life, the landlady of the pub he frequented near his London home recalled that he would go in every evening, early, order a gin and tonic, and leave it on the bar while he wandered about the room. She obviously thought this behaviour eccentric and didn't like to mention that he must have been eavesdropping on other people's conversations.
14. *Craven House* Book 2, Chapter 2. My text is the revised edn. first published in London by Constable, 1943, and reprinted in 1948. Future quotations will be followed by identification of Book, chapter and section.
15. For Hamilton's theatrical experiences see Sean French's biography, pp. 48-52. Hamilton's sister, Lalla, married the actor Sutton Vane, whose tacky play *Outward Bound* enjoyed a huge if temporary success in the early 20s when it was transferred to the West End from the Everyman Theatre, Hampstead (where *The Vortex* had also started life).
16. *Twopence Coloured*, London, Constable, 1928, p. 345.
17. Peter Widdowson: "The Saloon Bar Society: Patrick Hamilton's Fiction in the 1930s", in *The 1930s: A Challenge to Orthodoxy*, ed. John Lucas, Hassocks, The Harvester Press, 1978, p. 122.
18. Christopher Isherwood, *All The Conspirators*, London, Minerva, 1990. Ch 9, p. 97. Future quotations will indicate the chapter reference.
19. Minerva edn. p. 7.
20. Isherwood, *Lions and Shadows*, London, Four Square, 1963, p. 158. The book was first published in 1938.

21. "The World War" appears in Christopher Isherwood and Edward Upward, *The Mortmere Stories*, with an introduction by Katherine Bucknell, London, Enitharmon Press, 1994, pp. 111-124.

22. *The Mortmere Stories*, pp. 17 and 21.

23. *The English Auden*, ed. Edward Mendelson, London, Faber, 1977, p. 8.

24. John Fuller, *A Reader's Guide to W. H. Auden*, London, Thames and Hudson, 1970, pp. 14-15. Although I do not share Fuller's emphases, his reading of the Charade is as indispensable as is the rest of his *Guide*.

25. *Lions and Shadows*, p. 119.

26. *A Reader's Guide to W. H. Auden*. Fuller points out that Auden greatly admired Lawrence's *Fantasia of the Unconscious*, and that in this work Lawrence directs his fire, *inter-alia*, against "the compulsive verbaliser".

27. *The Mortmere Stories*, pp. 10-11.

28. Monroe K Spears, *The Poetry of W. H. Auden: The Disenchanted Island*, O.U.P., paperback, 1968, p. 34. The work was first published in 1963.

29. *The Poetry of W. H. Auden*, p. 34, and *A Reader's Guide*, p. 52.

30. From the preface to *Oxford Poetry*, 1927, Oxford, Basil Blackwell, 1927, p. viii.

31. Samuel Hynes, *The Auden Generation: Literature and Politics in England in the 1930s*, London, Faber, 1976, p. 54.

32. Harold Heslop, *Out of the Old Earth* eds. Andy Croft and Graeme Rigby, Newcastle, Bloodaxe, 1994, p. 192.

33. Andy Croft, *Red Letter Days: British Fiction in the 30s*, London, Lawrence and Wishart, 1990, esp. pp. 62-4. Idris Davies' book-length sequence of poems about the General Strike, especially its affect on the South Wales miners, *The Angry Summer*, was written in 1941 and first published by Faber in 1943. According to Dafydd Johnston, Davies' participation in the strike itself was less than whole-hearted, and he sees the poem as "inspired by the need to make good his personal failure at that time". See *The New Welsh Review* no 21, Summer 1993, pp. 16-18. But the poem can also be understood as Davies' acknowledgment, however long delayed, of the need to take sides; and writing in 1941 makes sense as the act of someone recognising that now, too, is a time of ineluctable choice. After this war there can be no going back. It is then relevant to note the massive victory of Labour in 1945 and the programme of nationalising large industry which followed.

34. Ellen Wilkinson, *Clash*, London, Virago, 1989, p. 293. All future quotations will be from this edition and will be followed by page references. The novel was first published in 1929. *In Britain Between the Wars*, Mowat remarks that after the strike was over the government claimed that it had been "defeated by the community; by the ordinary people rallying to the support of the government. In such a context, 'ordinary people' means the middle classes. As one writer put it, the strike only showed what was known already, that people who dress like gentlemen will instinctively take sides against people who commonly work with their coats off; if such people, and the armed forces, had beaten the working class, it was not much to boast about." pp. 329-330. The writer in question was that great and good man, G. K. Chesterton.

35. For a fuller analysis of Lawrence's passage and Leavis's championing of it see my essay on "Mrs Gaskell and Brotherhood" in: Goode, Howard and Lucas, *Tradition and Tolerance in Nineteenth Century Fiction*, London, Routledge and Kegan Paul, 1966. I have not been able to discuss the interest shown by 20s writers in environmental issues, although I hinted at it in my section on Gurney. However, it should be noted that Clough Williams-Ellis's *England and the Octopus* was published in London in 1928, by Geoffrey Bles, and that this very radical book argues for the need to recognise and halt the hastening despoliation of England. On p. 15 of his book, Williams-Ellis writes: "Everyone who reads this book – indeed, everyone who reads at all or has eyes in his head –

knows that England has changed violently and enormously within the last few decades. Since the War, indeed, it has been changing with an acceleration that is catastrophic, thoroughly frightening the thoughtful amongst us, and making them sadly wonder whether anything recognisable of our lovely England will be left for our children's children". Lawrence reviewed the book enthusiastically. "Mr Williams-Ellis makes us conscious," he says. "He wakes up our age to our own immediate surroundings." And then, in language very close to the passage in *Lady Chatterley's Lover* from which I have quoted, he says that "as a nation, it is our intuitive faculty for seeing beauty and ugliness which is lying dead in us. As a nation we are dying of ugliness." For this see *Selected Literary Criticism*. op. cit. p. 143. Lawrence's essay on "Nottingham and the Mining Villages" takes the argument much further.

36. M. Joannou's essay appears in *Heart of the Heartless World: Essays in Cultural Resistance* for *Margot Heinemann*, eds. D. Margolies and M. Joannou, London, Pluto Press, 1995. pp. 148-166. My quotation is from p. 155.

37. Henry Green, *Loving, Living, Party Going*, London, Picador, 1978, p. 210. All future quotations will be from this edition and will be followed by page reference.

38. In a fuller account I would want to draw attention to other anti-imperial writing of the decade, for example Edward Thompson's four-act play, *Atonement,* which like Forster's novel was published in 1924. Here, I will say only that recent accounts of Forster's novel, which have tended to rap him over the knuckles for a betraying "eurocentricity" and a corresponding "orientalism" seem to me as mean spirited as they are, usually, derived from crude, (mis) readings of that subtle, discomposing and — yes — radical novel.

39. F. P. Crozier, *A Brass Hat in No Man's Land*, London, Cape, 1930, p. 243.

40. Evelyn Waugh, *Vile Bodies,* London, Chapman and Hall, 1930, p. 247.

41. The artist, who owes something to McKnight Kauffer, is not identified, but deserves to be. Whoever it is has thoroughly understood the meaning and spirit of Waugh's satire.

42. In response to the invitation to contribute to the *Left Review* pamphlet, *Authors Take Sides on the Spanish War*, Waugh wrote: "If I were a Spaniard I should be fighting for General Franco. As an Englishman I am not in the predicament of choosing between two evils. I am not a fascist nor shall I become one unless it were the only alternative to Marxism. It is mischievous to suggest that such a choice is imminent."

# INDEX

259